I'm excited to endorse this book . . . example of how God communicates with . . .

Anyone who reads and "doeth" these words will surely be blessed and will find themselves entering into the most exciting and fulfilling time of their lives. They will see God leading them in amazing ways and with Him in control, truly, "All things are possible." Matthew 19:26.

**Mike Adkins, Mike Adkins Ministries, West Frankfort, IL**

Obedience must be a constant as a Christ follower. The author reminds us of the value of answering "Yes," no matter the call. The blessing is in the act of obedience.

**Rev. Nathan Sheridan, Lead Pastor, First Assembly,
Garden City, KS.**

The author presents various life situations and shows how a person of faith can emerge victorious through prayer and application of God's Word. It is a valuable aid, to include scripture references in the text. The reader can see the application of the scripture without interruption. I recommend this book to everyone who desires to have a stronger prayer life and yearns to live the victorious Christian life.

**Rev. John Hubbard, Senior Adult Pastor,
First Assembly, Garden City, KS.**

In "Sensitive to Listen and Willing to Obey," the author guides us on a journey. She uses scripture, life experiences, and God's faithfulness to respond to our pursuit of Him. After reading it, I am encouraged to listen more in prayer, to hear and understand God's Truth as revealed by the Holy Spirit.

**Lois Hubbard, pastor's wife.**

# SENSITIVE TO LISTEN
## —————— *and* ——————
# WILLING TO OBEY

"And your ears will hear a word behind you,
'This is the way, walk in it,
Whenever you turn to the right or to the left" (Isaiah 30:21).

## DORIS M. ARWINE

WESTBOW·
PRESS
A DIVISION OF THOMAS NELSON
& ZONDERVAN

WestBow Press books may be ordered through booksellers or by contacting:

WestBow Press
A Division of Thomas Nelson & Zondervan
1663 Liberty Drive
Bloomington, IN 47403
www.westbowpress.com
1 (866) 928-1240

ISBN: 978-1-4908-3080-3 (sc)
ISBN: 978-1-4908-3081-0 (hc)
ISBN: 978-1-4908-3079-7 (e)

Library of Congress Control Number: 2014905418

Printed in the United States of America.

WestBow Press rev. date: 05/14/2014

# *Dedication*

To God our father, Jesus Christ our Lord, and the Holy Spirit our teacher.

And to all family, friends, children and adults who have enriched and blessed my life.

To all who read this book, may you, be drawn closer to the Lord and be "Sensitive to listen and willing to obey," His voice.

Carlene,
Your faith in God blesses me.
"Trust in the Lord with all your Heart."
Prov 3:5-6

Doris Gruwire, August 2014

# Contents

# *Acknowledgments*

It has been a great privilege to walk the journey of life with numerous wonderful, and creative, men, women and children. I am very thankful to my parents for the godly molding they instilled in my sisters and me.

I am grateful for the encouragement and influence of my husband and sons that helped me move beyond my comfort zone and accomplish new things. I am deeply appreciative for my husband James Arwine, and Lois Hubbard who edited the manuscript. I am especially thankful to my son Alan Arwine, whose computer expertise and patience was extremely valuable.

My special thanks to the Illustrator, Jim Fehlauer, for so aptly portraying my thoughts in picture. I am also thankful for many men and women who humbly shared their written works and songs with me to enhance this book and show how Our God can use different mediums to express His message to us. My extreme gratitude to Mike Adkins, Deanna Edwards, William and Gloria Gaither, David Kauffman, Chris and Diane Machen, Paul Marino, the Willow Creek Singers and Greg Ferguson for their beautiful songs that instructed my soul.

I express deep gratitude to Bob Gass, Discovery House Publishers, RBC Ministries and Oral Roberts Ministries, numerous pastors and other writers for their written work. It helped show the significance of the Word of God and produced sensitivity for me to listen more closely to the Lord's voice.

I am grateful to WestBow Press for the opportunity afforded me to publish this book. Your, dedication and sharpening skills helped me refine this book and get the Lord's message across in a more succinct manner.

You have all sharpened me, "Like Iron sharpens Iron." "I always thank God for you because of His grace given you in Christ Jesus." (1 Corinthians 1:4, NIV).

Doris M. Arwine

# *Preface*

I can't remember when God instructed me to write this book. It has been a long process. At first I felt this was an impossible dream. So I tucked it into the back of my mind. There it stayed untouched for a long time.

Eventually, in my journey, I encountered situations that made me begin to seek the Lord and rely on His provisions more earnestly. It was during this season, I began to keep notes on what God was speaking to me through everyday occurrences.

The learning, growing and recording process continued until one day I asked, "Lord, why would you want me to write a book?" I'm not a learned theologian, a pastor, lecturer, or a writer. I have no claim to fame, great achievements or talents. I'm weak, sometimes afraid and I often miss the mark. I'm just an average person, and a counselor.

God answered me, "That's precisely why I want you to write the book." He then reminded me of His Word, "But God hath chosen the foolish things of the world to confound the wise; and God hath chosen the weak things of the world to confound the things which are mighty." (1 Corinthians 1:27).

This book is to help all of us to realize that God does speak to His children through everyday experiences. No one is too ordinary or insignificant for His service. As, 1968 Olympic Gold Medalist, Madeline Manning Mimms stated, "God is not looking for ability, but for availability." It's not so important to God that we be talented but that we are willing to be used by Him and obedient to His will.

Doris M. Arwine

# *Introduction*

". . . Speak, for thy servant heareth." I Samuel 3:10.

Samuel heard an audible voice speak to him three times as he lay on his bed. Each time he answered, "Here am I," and ran to Eli. After the third time, Eli a priest, in the temple, realized the Lord was speaking to Samuel. Eli then instructed young Samuel, his helper, to go lie down and wait for the Lord to speak again. If the Lord speaks to you again just say, "Speak Lord, for thy servant heareth . . ." I Samuel 3:9. Samuel did as he was told and the Lord gave him, a message for Eli.

I've always been fascinated with this passage of scripture and how God spoke to young Samuel. We may not experience God speaking to us in an audible voice like Samuel did. However, God still speaks to us today in numerous ways if we will just be sensitive enough to listen.

We can prepare ourselves to hear God's voice if we will develop a relationship with him. As we get to know God better through His Word, and communicating with him in prayer, we will know when we are hearing His voice.

God can and does use most of His creations as vehicles through which He speaks. He especially uses His Word, our prayers and quiet times to manifest Himself to us. God uses nature as a metaphor to reveal His truths to us. It is a way He communicates how important we are to Him.

During His earthly ministry Jesus used parables to teach His disciples and all who came to hear him. These stories Jesus told were built around ordinary situations and events.

Today we aren't much different from the men and women in biblical times. They raised families and worked hard. They listened to music, learned from spoken and written messages.

Many of them received inner nudges and dreams. However, they sometimes failed to hear God through these modes.

As a result, some of the great men and women from the Bible fell into deceit. They were no more immune to deception than we are today. This is the reason we need to be able to discern our Father's voice so we don't fall into Satan's traps. If we hear and recognize God's voice, we can follow His leading.

In this book, we will take a journey and learn how to listen to God in many different ways. We will be able to spot deception quicker and stay out of its grip. As we grow stronger and more in love with the Lord, we will be constrained to a life of obedience. I want to be a faithful servant like Samuel and say, "Speak Lord, for thy servant heareth" (1 Samuel 3:9).

## CHAPTER 1

# God's Word

"Thy Word is a lamp unto my feet, and a light unto my path."
Psalm 119:105

As we journey with God, listen and you will hear him speak in numerous ways. The most reliable method God uses to communicate is His Word. "For thou, hast magnified Thy Word above, Thy Name." (Psalm 138:2). God's Word is above His name. It's our ultimate guide. We are to check all other messages we receive, regardless of the source, against the Holy Scriptures. We are to say, "Does the message I'm hearing agree with the Word of God?" If it does, you can depend on it.

This is like using the Word as a lamp that sheds light so we know which path to take. "He who carries a lantern on a dark road at night sees only one step ahead. When he takes that step, the lamp moves forward and another step is made plain. This is the method of God's guidance."[1] We reach our destination safely without walking in darkness. God illuminates one step at a time through the application of His Word.

## Description of God's Word

Man often seeks to explore and apply the Word of God to his life. He depends on his own intellect to discover what sets it apart from other books. No matter how hard we try to describe the Bible, we cannot do it justice. Here are some of the comments by notable leaders in history. Ulysses S. Grant: "Hold fast to the Bible as the anchor of your liberties." Abraham Lincoln: "I have only to say that it is the best gift God has given to man." Daniel Webster: "There is no solid basis for civilization, but in the Word of God." George Washington: "It is impossible to rightly govern the world without God and the Bible." Thomas Jefferson: "The Bible is the cornerstone of liberty." Patrick Henry: "This is a book worth more than all other books which were ever printed."[2] Man's descriptions are but a mere reflection of God's Holy Word.

The Bible is divided into two parts. The Old Testament is (the blueprint) and the New Testament is (a building, Jesus).

God's Word is arranged in a divine plan. "From Genesis to Deuteronomy we see the revelation of man - who he is and his need of a Savior. Then from Joshua to Esther we see God preparing man to receive that Savior. From Job to the Song of Solomon we have inspiration in the beautiful books of poetry. They stir us to know who God is and what He can do in our lives.

From Isaiah to Malachi the Bible shows expectation. They make us anticipate Jesus. The Four Gospels show us the perfect picture of Jesus Christ. Matthew shows Him as a king. Mark presents Him as a servant. Luke shows him as the Son of man. He understands everything we'll ever go through. And John shows Him as the Son of God. From Acts through Jude we see the realization of Christ in us. And Revelation is the culmination of it all."[3]

God's Word represents most categories of literature and comprises the best library for daily instruction known to man. The Word is laced with promises, instructions and revelations.

An anonymous writer describes the Bible as a unique book. It consists of 66 books and was written over a period of fifteen to sixteen hundred years by 40 different authors, on three separate continents, in three languages.

This book is remarkable because it speaks with ease and authority of the known and unknown, of the pleasant and unpleasant, of man's accomplishments and failures, of the past and the future. Few books ever covered such a scope.

God's Holy book has often been referred to as a guide, road map, blueprint, recipe, lamp and sword. These things all have something in common. We utilize each of them to help us find a specific location, create an object or protect us. Without a source of light (the Word of God) none of these items would be of assistance to us. Explore with me what the Bible has to say about itself.

## Book of Law

The Word is called the Book of the Law. Rules are designed to guide and protect us. "The statutes of the Lord are right, rejoicing the heart: the commandment of the Lord is pure, enlightening the eyes" (Psalms 19:8). The Lord's Book uplifts our hearts and opens our eyes. We can depend on it to guide us.

When we use the Word of God as a lamp unto our feet and a light unto our paths, it can create powerful changes in our lives. The Holy Scriptures are powerful and sharper than any sword. It knows the intent of our heart. (Hebrews 4:12). There is no evil thing in our hearts that the Word of the Lord can't heal.

Jesus (the Word) came down from heaven to live among us. He came to fulfill the plan of God by dying on the cross. (John 1:14). This bought eternal life for us. "I am come that they might have life and have it more abundantly" (John 10:10 b).

When we let the Lord use His Scripture in our lives, it can cut out the evil nature without damaging our precious spirit, made in the image of God. Spiritual surgery performed by our maker can produce healing. (Psalm 107: 20). As we experience restoration, we will be set free. "And ye shall know the truth, and the truth shall make you free" (John 8:32). Knowing what God's report says, removes the shackles that keep us bound. We can move, walk out in faith and be changed. Faith comes by repeatedly hearing the Word of God. (Romans 10:17).

As we hear the Lord's message, it will make us wise. All scripture has been inspired by God, and can instruct us in righteousness. (2 Timothy 3:16-17). We have God's promise that He can make a powerful change in our lives with the Bible.

The Word becoming flesh (Jesus) is what sets this document apart from any other book ever written. It our most important guide.

Jesus showed us how to use God's manuscript, to guide us through temptations and testing. He prayed and fasted for forty days. The tempter was very sly and asked the Son of God, to command the stones be made bread. But The Lord answered and said, "It is written, man shall not live by bread alone . . ." (Matthew 4:3-4). Here Jesus was quoting Deuteronomy 8:3 to Satan. Jesus used the scripture against Satan many times. We must do the same and run the enemy off.

## The Word a Lamp

God's Book is a lamp that gives light to our pathway when it is rugged, somewhat obscure and laced with detours. When faced with these types of obstacles, we need a guide to show us the best and safest way to continue our journey.

The Bible tells us that we are to "Trust in the Lord with all your heart, and lean not on your own understanding. In all thy ways acknowledge Him and he shall make your paths straight" (Proverbs 3:5-6 NIV). Seek the Lord. Don't try to understand the situation from our limited perspective but rely on His resources. He will guide in the direction that is best for us.

Often I have struggled with difficult decisions, unsure of which path to take. Here, I acknowledge that God is able to direct my paths much better than I can. When I seek the Lord's direction, He sends me back to His Holy utterance and asks, "What does My Word say about your problem?" I appreciate God's approach because it makes me dig deep and learn. The Scriptures are more meaningful when I am forced to prove it.

## Live On His Promises

While living in England, the Lord spoke to me through scripture and asked me to trust Him. My family and I lived on a military installation. We had moved from Germany, where all our furniture had been provided by the United States Army. At this base furniture wasn't provided. This put us in a dilemma. The military would lend us some basic furniture for ninety days, while we acquired our own.

After the move, we had little extra cash. I usually landed a job quickly upon arriving at a new military base, but this time was different. I was unemployed. I sought the Lord and asked, "What are we going to do?" He steered me right back to the Bible. "But my God shall supply all your need according to his riches in glory by Christ Jesus" (Philippians 4:19). I still didn't understand how this promise could be mine. Then the Lord asked me, "Is this a want or a need?" I responded with, "It's a need, Lord." "Then stand on My Word," He said. From that dialogue I realized I had to claim His promise. I repeated the scripture over and over. As I sent out this promise, He reminded me, "It shall not return unto me void, but it shall accomplish that which I please..." (Isaiah 55:11). His promise was to meet our need but we had to be sensitive to listen to His leading.

One day a friend told us about a little antique shop in a neighboring village. Even though we didn't think we could afford to purchase antiques; we made a quick trip to the shop. Much to our surprise, the prices were extremely good. We told the sole proprietor what we needed. He assured us there was a ready supply of antiques, which he purchased on a daily basis.

Each week we made a visit to his small shop and collected one or two pieces of furniture. By the end of ninety days we had a house full of British antiques.

We had some unique furniture which we used in unusual ways. We acquired two local doctor's office day bed cots, which both our sons used as beds. Another sleep surface had a horse hair mattress which was very firm, and made a sleeper itch.

An antique wash basin became a desk. A dining room buffet became a dresser for undergarments. We became owners of a solid oak dining table, which comfortably seated four people or would extend to accommodate eight.

Acquiring each piece of furniture was a walk of faith. It required listening to the Lord speak through His promises. I began to see that God has a sense of humor in all He does. Truly, our needs were met. God had been faithful to His Word.

Each time we prove God trustworthy, it strengthens our relationship with him. It's through His message that we know Him and His agreements. Each promise fulfilled gives us holy boldness. We then go to God's throne with His Word in hand. It's the answer to our problem.

## Life Solutions

One evening, a problem confronted me. I didn't have a clue how to solve it. My mom called from the United States and said my dad had suffered another stroke. She was concerned that he might have recurring strokes while alone and operating farm machinery. He could be seriously hurt or killed. She was vigilant for dad's safety as well as his health. Mom was afraid he might not survive the next attack, and frankly, so was I.

I felt helpless across the ocean in England. I hadn't seen my folks for three and a half years. It almost wiped me out to think that I might not get to see my dad alive again. I sought the Lord and poured out the desires of my heart to Him. I told Him, "I want to see my dad at least one more time before he goes home to be with you." Then the Lord again reminded me of His promises. "Delight thyself also in the Lord; and he shall give thee the desires of thine heart" (Psalm 37:4). Then I asked myself, "Have I been delighting myself in the Lord?" The Lord assured me that I had been delighting Him and could trust His Word.

God then spoke to me, "Give the situation into My hands." "Commit thy way unto the Lord; trust also in him; and he shall bring it to pass" Psalms 37:5. I committed my dad and his life into God's keeping. I was assured that the Lord heard me and was telling me not to worry. It was as clear as if someone had spoken out loud to me, "You will get to have a visit with your dad again." Because my earthly father loved the Lord, He would deliver him and protect dad because he knows My Name. (Psalm 91:14). God was telling me through His Word, that He would protect my father from harm I carried this promise deep in my heart for several months.

Finally, we got military orders to return to the United States. We checking in at our new assignment, and went home to Kansas for a visit. It was a good visit, but the last one I was privileged to have with my dad.

Several weeks later, he had a massive stroke, while harvesting garden produce. This attack was the most severe yet. He died sixteen days later in a hospital. He left this world being serenaded with praise music by my mom and sister.

God was true to His word. I got the desire of my heart, one more visit with dad. He was protected from harm even when he had the final stroke. He had the best home going possibly.

After several times of seeing God work mightily in my life, you'd think I'd never doubt again. However, I'm just like the Israelites, often questioning and complaining, as many people do. Our natural tendency is to believe only what we can see. The Scripture tells us, "We live by faith and not by sight" (2 Corinthians 5:7). I'm so thankful that God is patient with us. This helps us grow, on our journey of learning to listen to Him through His word.

## Steps of Growth

A leap of growth was taken, when I entered a new job. I wasn't receiving instruction to accomplish the task at hand. Again, I cried out to my Savior. He answered me with His promise. "So do not fear, for I am with you . . . I am your God. I will strengthen you and help you; I will uphold you with my righteous right hand" (Isaiah 41:10 NIV). The Lord would equip me to meet the challenges. I was to fix my eyes on His power and not the situation. As I sought the Lord, He would show me what to do. "The Lord himself goes before you . . . He will never leave you nor forsake you . . ." (Deuteronomy 31:8 NIV). Since He had gone before me and knew all about the situation, assuredly, I could trust Him.

My maker instructed me again, "Cast your cares on the Lord and he will sustain you; He will never let the righteous fall" (Psalm 55:22 NIV). Yes, He had heard my cry. He would be my helper.

The way God chose to resolve this lack of "on the job training," was marvelous. Two of my co-workers felt a deep sense of empathy for me. They went to the supervisor and explained, I hadn't received enough training. They also reminded her, I had preformed another job in the organization well. I had the abilities and dedication to be a good addition to the team. From that point on, I received all the training I needed with patience and understanding.

Truly God had been my helper through this experience. He was preparing me for an even greater challenge.

After another move I found myself in a similar job. This time I needed little training. However, the work was six months behind schedule. This created a real dilemma because people hadn't received scheduled pay raises.

My partner and I were to work together on this back log. Suddenly, she began to miss work. She was physically ill and suffering marital problems. The backlog was too much for me alone.

How was the mission to be accomplished? Supervisors were alerted to the need for help. They informed me, no additional help was available. I would have to do the best I could. This created a real burden and fear. How would I cope with the ever increasing backlog on both desks?

Then, I cried out to the Lord, "Please help me!" He answered by sending me back to His word. "God did not give us the spirit of fear, but a spirit of power, of love and a sound mind" (2 Timothy 1:7). When fear is in control of our minds, they are tied up in knots. God was telling me that fear had to go, so He could work on my behalf.

How could I get rid of the fear in my life? God said, "Trust Me, and My Word, not how the situation looks." Then I said, "Okay Lord, what do you want me to do?" He instructed me, "This is the day the Lord has made; let us rejoice and be glad in it" (Psalm 118:24 NIV). I said, "Lord you want me to rejoice today with all this mess of work facing me?" "Yes," He emphatically showed me through the next verse. "A cheerful heart is good medicine, but a crushed spirit dries up the bones" (Proverbs 17:22). God was saying to me that a bad attitude would dry and shrivel me up. It would close me off from His help and others. No one wants to be around a person who is weighted down with cares. It's mighty depressing. However, when we are around someone who is cheerful and has a good attitude, it perks us up. We feel better about everything.

Now I was beginning to understand that I had a part to play in receiving God's help. First I had to confront fear and to head off the possibility of a bad attitude. These things were like weapons coming against me. Then I discovered what the Lord's Word had to say about that. Nothing that came against me would get worse. I was to put down every tongue that rose against me. This was my promise. (Isaiah 54:17).

God spoke to me through this verse, no bad circumstance, force or weapon that came against me had to continue to get worse. "Why," because I was His child and my victory came from Him. Wow! Now I knew God was fighting my battles and I would be victorious.

With these thoughts in mind, I listened for God's guidance. He instructed, "Take two co-workers with you and approach the head of the department." This is something an employee fears doing. But, because God instructed me to do it, there was nothing to lose. We went to the boss and presented the dilemma. He assured us that the situation would be corrected.

He authorized overtime for the whole department and insisted that every desk be put in order to assure no more delays in any employee's pay. Once again God proved His Word is our guide, through difficult situations.

## Application of God's Word

Applying the Bible persistently brought results in my life. I had been out of high school for more than twenty-five years. My first university algebra course created panic in me. Math had always been difficult. However, God began to review the many times He had helped me achieve victory by standing on His Word. Again I went to the Lord for help with this formidable task. His utterance said, "I can do all things through Christ which strengtheneth me" (Philippians 4:13).

God's Word further encouraged me. "If thou cans't believe, all things are possible to him that believeth" (Mark 9:23). My job was to believe God could help me through this math endeavor.

Often it is very difficult to keep fear at bay and believe. God was patient with me and gave me more of His word. The Lord had made the heavens and earth by His power and there was nothing too hard for Him. (Jeremiah 32:17). That was my answer! Not even this algebra course would be too difficult for the Lord to help me surmount.

The Lord then began to show me that I had to rely on His word. ". . . The Joy of the Lord is your strength" (Nehemiah 8:10). I must try to enjoy the course and trust Him. Joy could be mine daily, if I praised Him. I would have the strength to complete this task.

I plodded through the semester, understanding most of what I was learning and carrying a "B" average in the math course. However, the final test had me concerned. If I flunked it, the entire course was voided, regardless of the grade average. I took this concern back to the Lord and he assured me to remain steadfast in His Word. "But he knoweth the way that I take: when he hath tried me, I shall come forth as gold" (Job 23:10).

That was my assurance. I would do well on the test. However, in route to take the final exam, I had an automobile accident, during a near blizzard. The car was destroyed. I was terribly shaken, but physically unharmed.

Two days later, I summoned the courage, to drive again by relying on my Maker. I took the test. Later I discovered, I missed only one point on the exam. The score vaulted me to a new level. I was awarded an "A" for the course. God had brought me through as gold during this difficult time of spiritual and academic testing. Truly God had a plan for my life.

Often we can only see a small part of the Lord's plan for our lives. When we've committed our way to Him and the arrangements suddenly go awry; we begin to question. I found myself in this situation my senior year in college. It appeared, I might not get credit for an internship. My agency instructor felt Jesus Christ had no place in my life or her agency. She was judging me on my belief, not my work. She wanted me gone. If that happened, the hope of graduating in the spring might be dashed. What was I to do? Would the agency instructor or the college permit me to stay? Would I be let go and forfeit the academic credits needed to graduate? Neither appeared feasible.

## The Battle Is the Lord's

I sought God as I had done so many times in the past. He gave me a message through a Christian sister. "Stand firm, the battle isn't yours, but it's the Lord's." Now I'd heard that before. So I went to the Bible to confirm it. "For the battle is not yours, but God's" (2 Chronicles 20:15 NIV). "You will not have to fight this battle. Take up your positions, stand firm and see the deliverance the Lord will give you" (2 Chronicles 20:17 NIV)

I was to stand tall, and have faith in the Lord My God and deliverance would be mine. After standing fast, I was to thank God for victory and sing His praises. This attitude of honor would carry me through, and ambush my enemy.

Part of standing firm was to find out what needed to be done. I consulted my school liaison and was told to stay put. Later, I was let go by my internship instructor without the colleges' permission. The director of the program instructed me to prepare my own evaluation of the course work I had completed. It was reviewed by a board and full credit for the course was granted. Not only did I finish that spring, but I graduated with honors. When the Lord fights the battles, He doesn't bring a person through by a narrow escape but with unbelievable victory. He brings us forth with gold.

I never really understood what makes something the Lord's battle until I read an article. The author used the story of David and Goliath to show a truth. When Goliath defied the living God, he changed the nature of the battle. It went from the natural to the spiritual. He asked us to check our battles by determining who our enemy is. Then ask, "Has that person defied God? Is that person coming against you because of your faith in God or because of your stand for God?"[4] Then the battle is no longer a flesh and blood battle. It is a spiritual battle.

What does it mean to say the battle is the Lord's? It means the Lord is in the battle and He is on your side! You can't lose! This is an excellent way to judge whether the battle is ours or God's. If the battle is the Lord's, we need to let Him fight it so we can be victorious. "He has redeemed my soul in peace from the battle that was against me . . ." (Psalm 55:18 NKJV). Now that's triumph!

Victory is found in clinging to God's Word. I had to prove this again when bad news was received. The collision insurance, on our automobiles was due to be canceled. But why, I couldn't understand. It was to be erased because of an auto accident I had almost two years earlier. So why should they rescind it now?

This question plagued me while sitting in church. Suddenly I heard this verse being read, "He will have no fear of bad news; his heart is steadfast, trusting in the Lord"

(Psalm 112: 7 NIV). This was just what I needed to hear. Immediately, I knew the Lord had this under control.

Later, My God instructed me to write a letter to the insurance company and ask for an explanation. This I did. It wasn't long before the insurance company called to say they would be reinstating our insurance. Once again God fought the battle with His Word.

## Answers for Life's Problems

The Word of God literally has an answer for every dilemma. One day while contemplating whether I should confront a peer about a situation, a verse jumped off the page of my Bible. "A gossip betrays a confidence, but a trustworthy man keeps a secret. For lack of guidance a nation falls, but many advisers make victory sure" (Proverbs 11:13-14 NIV).

According to the first verse it sounded like I shouldn't talk to the person. However, the second verse indicated that I needed to seek the counsel of an uninvolved person to see if the matter needed to be discussed. So I sought wise counsel. God's Word was confirmed by my advisor saying, "Let the matter rest." Wisdom from family or friends is always important.

From time to time relationship problems crop up for most of us. Often it is difficult to convey thoughts without hurting or putting another person on the defensive. On one of those occasions,' the Lord reminded me of His answer to this dilemma. "For the Holy Ghost, shall teach you, in the same hour, what ye ought to say" (Luke 12:12). The Lord showed me that (in the same hour) means 'now.' I didn't have to wait until later to learn what I should have said. This verse definitely took much of the stress and fear out of putting my "Foot in my mouth." Now I can trust God's ability in me to problem-solve and communicate better with others.

There are many times I need a word of encouragement for others who are experiencing physical, emotional and financial problems. While reading my Bible, this verse stood out on the page. "Although the Lord has given you . . . water of oppression, He, your Teacher will no longer hide Himself, but your eyes will behold your Teacher. And your ears will hear a word behind you, 'This is the way, walk in it,' whenever you turn to the right or to the left." (Isaiah 30:20-21, NAS).

The Lord spoke through this passage, "You've had trials and many problems. Look to me, I'm your teacher. You will hear my voice behind you. Walk in the way I tell you.

It is comforting to know that God's Word has answers for all problems we may confront in life. I was beginning to feel the weight of the world on my shoulders and to feel burned out dealing with others' needs and problems in my Hospice work. I sought the Lord and He showed me what He said to His people who became discouraged while rebuilding the temple. "Take courage, declares the Lord, and work for I am with you, says the Lord of Hosts. . . . My spirit is abiding in your midst; do not fear" (Haggai 2:4-5 NAS). The Lord was saying to me, "Continue on with your work, I'm right there in your midst. So don't be afraid, I'll sustain you."

After that I realized that I had been trying to take care of too many things myself. Again the Lord took me to His Word. "The things that you carry are burdensome, a load for the weary beast. . . . They could not rescue the burden, but have themselves gone into captivity" (Isaiah 46:1-2, NAS). What the Lord spoke through His utterance, was that if I continued to carry those burdens, captivity would snare me. I could easily burn out if I didn't let Him lighten my load.

## He Carries Us

God was telling me, I could always trust Him to carry me and my burdens. I didn't need to feel discouraged and burned out.

About that time, I read a story that explained how God carries us. Henry Moorhouse, a 19th - century evangelist was loaded with burdens of his ministry. The Lord gave him an object lesson through his child. The daughter was crippled and in a wheelchair. She wanted to carry a package upstairs to her mother. Moorhouse said to his daughter, "Minnie dear, you can't carry the package? You can't even walk yourself." Smiling Minnie said, "I know, Papa. But if you will give me the package, I will hold it while you carry me."[5]

Oh, what a picture of how our Heavenly Father carries us. I had to say, "Yes Lord, just hold me. Bear me up like you said you would.

## Applying the Word

The Bible (our lamp) has, "The one sure means to getting the right answers to complicated questions of our origin, purpose, behavior, and our ultimate destination."[6] The importance of hearing God's Word and applying it, can't be stressed enough.

I began to get a better understanding of what it means to ask, seek and knock and how to apply it to life. (Luke 11:9). If I ask from life instead of from God, I am asking from the wrong source. If I search for self realization, I'm not seeking God. He is all I am to run after. I must seek God with my whole heart. What does it mean to knock? It means I must draw close to God. I must cleanse my hands and heart. It's humbling to rap at the Father's door. "When we knock at God's door like the crucified thief did on the cross, the door will be opened by God Himself."[7]

The Word of God is powerful and has the answers for life's problems. "Is not My Word like fire, declares the Lord, and like a hammer which shatters a rock? . . . Thus shall each of you say to his neighbor and to his brother, 'What, has the Lord answered?'" (Jeremiah 23: 29 & 35 NAS). When others ask me for a word of advice, I am to use scripture. I'm to ask them, "What has the Lord spoken to you through His Word?" I can encourage them with His truth.

One day when I was feeling blue, God spoke powerfully to me. He told me not to fear because I was His child. "Can a woman forget her nursing child, and have no compassion on the son of her womb? Even these may forget, but I will not forget you. Behold, I have inscribed you on the palms of My hands" (Isaiah 49:15-16, NAS).

God reminded me that when we want to remember something and have no paper to write on, we jot it on our hand. He has written our name on both of His hands, not just one. I'm so thankful God has used this analogy in scripture to show how very important we are to Him.

While reading a devotional, the Lord instructed me. Jesus' household was divided by the issue of belief in Him. Jesus experienced the heartache, misunderstanding, and conflict that result when families are divided over matters of faith.

Later we are told Jesus brothers believed in Him. "And when they had entered, they went up to the upper room, where they were staying . . . These all with one mind were continually devoting themselves to prayer, along with the women, and Mary the mother of Jesus, and with His brothers" (Acts 1:13-14, NAS). The Lord instructed me, He truly understood how it felt to have His family divided on belief in Him. Jesus encouraged with the truth that His prayers made a difference in His household and would in all ours, where there is division of belief. He loves our family even more than we do. God desires to answer our prayers and bring our loved ones home to Him.

God has answers for every problem, in life. Author O.T. Gifford makes this comment to encourage Christians. "If you're getting lazy, read James. If your faith is below par, read Paul's letters. If you're impatient, consider the book of Job. If you're a little strong headed, go and see Moses. If you're weak-kneed, have a look at Elijah. If there is no song in your heart, listen to David. If you feel spiritually chilly, get the beloved disciple John to put his arms around you. And if you're losing sight of the future, climb to Revelation and get a glimpse of heaven, through God's Word."[8]

## Scripture Our Guide

Scripture should be our guide in everything we do. An anonymous author instructs us to, "Go to your Bible regularly; open it prayerfully; read it expectantly; live it joyfully. Let the Bible fill your memory, rule your heart, and guide your feet."

As we carry the lamp of God's Word on a dark road, we see only one step ahead. As we take that step forward, the lamp moves with us and we see the next step clearly. All the way is light, but only a single step at a time. This is the Lord's way of guidance. If we are sensitive to listen to God speak through His Word, it will truly become "A lamp unto our feet and a light unto our path" (Psalm 119:105).

## CHAPTER 2

# *Prayer*

*"The effectual fervent prayer of a righteous man availeth much."*
*James 5:16*

Prayer is the most important two-way communication between God and us. We have the privilege of talking and listening, as Our Heavenly Father instructs us on our journey. Jesus modeled this process for us. He was our best example of a righteous man who prayed fervently. "But Jesus often withdrew to lonely places and prayed . . . And the power of the Lord was present for him to heal the sick" (Luke 5:16 & 17b, NIV).

If Jesus, the son of God, had to get alone and talk with God, then shouldn't we? Prayer was the enabling force in Jesus' life. The Lord instructs the righteous through effectual and fervent prayers which produces results.

Effectual is an effort that produces an intended effect. Fervency means to show great warmth, or earnestness of spirit. If we expect to hear His voice, we must have a relationship with Him. We must be righteous, to be effective in communication with God.

## Right Standing

Evangelist Jerry Savelle wrestled with the meaning of righteousness. He concluded that, "Righteousness is right standing with God. To be righteous in Christ means we have just as much right to stand before the throne of God as Jesus has."[1]

This blows me away! How can I have the same standing with God as Jesus does? It's only because of what He did on the cross. In one of Jesus' prayers he verifies this: "I have given them the glory that you gave me, that they may be one as we are one . . ." (John 17: 22 NIV).

God loves us very much and desires we have a good relationship with him. This requires we be cleansed from our sins and please Him with word and deed. "And without faith it is impossible to please God . . ." (Hebrews 11:6, NIV).

The Bible tells us of Abraham's faith. God promised Abraham a son. He believed His Creator, even though he and his wife Sarah were both nearing a hundred years old. Abraham did not waiver, but grew stronger in his faith. He was assured that what God promised He would perform (Romans 4:20-22). Faith in God justified Abraham.

Trust in the Lord, helps us develop a closer relationship with Him. This confidence is pleasing to our Heavenly Father and constructs effective communication with Him.

## What Is Prayer?

This utterance with Our Maker has been defined in many ways. It is an earnest, humble request addressed to God. "Prayer is an admission that we believe there is a God. It is talking to Him and letting him talk to you. It is listening to God to find out His will for your life. It is a two-way street between just you and God. Prayer is a heavenly communication system."[2] It is praising God for what He does for us. It is asking Him to show us His will. Prayer is how we reach God, and how He touches us. It is the remover of guilt. This communication is a great source of power and strength. "Prayer is the exercise of drawing on the grace of God."[3]

Talking to the Lord was succinctly summarized, in the book, *"The Kneeling Christian."* The author relates an incident with an evangelist, Reverend Moody, in a meeting in Edinburg, Scotland. Moody asked "What is prayer?" He didn't expect to get an answer. However, a young lad responded with: "Prayer is an offering up of our desires unto God for things agreeable to His will, in the name of Christ, with confession of our sins and thankful acknowledgment of His mercies."[4]

The fore mentioned description alerts us to various kinds of communication with our Father. The four most common types of prayers are: petitions, confessions, intercessions and thanksgiving. The utterance of petition is most often offered up on our own behalf. Often our requests can resemble a grocery list of what we desire from the Lord. When we pray, we shouldn't give God orders. We should report for duty.

Confession must be entered into by each individual. It cannot be done by others. Here, we admit our mistakes and ask forgiveness of our sins. This kind of utterance humbles us before the Lord and opens the lines of communication between us.

A prayer of confession was humbly offered by, Reverend Billy Graham for our nation. "Heavenly Father, we come before you today to ask your forgiveness and to seek your direction and guidance. We know Your Word says, 'Woe to those who call evil good, 'but that is exactly what we have done. We have lost our spiritual equilibrium and reversed our values. We have exploited the poor and called it the lottery. We have rewarded laziness, and called it welfare. . . . We have killed our unborn; and called it choice. We have shot abortionists and called it justifiable. We have neglected to discipline our children and called it building self esteem. We have abused power and called it politics. . . . We have coveted our neighbor's possessions, and called it ambition. . . . We have polluted the air with profanity and pornography, and called it freedom of expression. We have ridiculed the time-honored values of our forefathers and called it enlightenment. Search us, Oh God, and know our hearts today; cleanse us from every sin and set us free. Amen!"

Commentator Paul Harvey aired this prayer on his radio program, "The Rest of the Story," and received a larger response to this program than any other he had ever aired. With the Lord's help, may this prayer sweep over our nation and become our desire for the whole world.

The prayer of intercession is a petition offered up on someone else's behalf. It is the highest form of prayer. "Intercession means we arouse our self to get the mind of Christ about the one we are praying for."[5] These kinds of prayers can have great results if motivated by Christ like love and concern for someone else's well being. A minister stated, "It takes three things to make intercession work: the power of the Holy Spirit, authority of the believer and the dominion of love. When we are interceding, we are speaking the Words of God. We make a hedge around someone, hold up a shield, wield the sword and release the power of life and Our Creator. Intercession can accomplish soul winning, release power for gifts to operate and place demands on the operation of gifts."[6]

The prayer of thanksgiving is an effective way to show Our Father gratitude for hearing and answering our prayers. It is pleasing to the Lord and establishes a closer relationship. Many utterances of gratitude are quickly and desperately offered, when we don't know what to do. We breathe them out like a breath. They often sound like this: Oh Lord, please help me! Bless you Lord, for your protection. I'm so grateful, no one was hurt. Or just, "Thank You Lord."

## The Five Finger Prayer

Other prayers help us remember who to pray for.

1. Your **thumb** is nearest you. So begin your requests for those closest to you. They are the easiest to remember. "To pray for our loved ones is, as C.S. Lewis once said, a "sweet duty."

2. The **index finger** is the pointing finger. Pray for those who teach, instruct and heal. This includes teachers, doctors, ministers and counselors. They need support and wisdom to steer us in the right direction.

3. The **next finger** is the tallest finger. It reminds us of our leaders. Pray for the President of the United States, leaders in business and industry, and administrators. These people shape our nation and guide public opinion. They need God's guidance.

4. The **fourth finger** is our ring finger. Surprisingly, this is our weakest finger. It should remind us to pray for those who are ill, in trouble or in pain. They need our petitions day and night.

5. And lastly, is our **little finger**. It is the smallest finger of all. This is where we should place ourselves in relation to God, and others. As the Bible says, "The least shall be the greatest among you." Your pinkie should remind you to seek the Lord for yourself. By the

time you have prayed for the other four groups, your own needs will be in proper perspective. You will be able to pray for yourself more effectively.

## Purpose of Prayer

Prayers of praise and adoration delight the heart of the Lord. These utterances address God the Father, Jesus the son, and the Holy Spirit with an attitude of worship. It is a thank offering to the Lord God for whom and what He is. It doesn't ask anything. This adoration is very pleasing to the Father.

Why does God desire that we talk with Him? "My Utmost for His Highest," answers this question. "Prayer is getting into perfect communion with God. The meaning of prayer is that we get hold of God, not of the answer. Seek to have no other motive than to know your Father in heaven. Prayer doesn't fit us for the greater works: prayer is the greater work . . . Prayer is the battle; it is a matter of indifference where you are. Whichever way God engineer's circumstances, the duty is to pray . . . You labor at prayer and results happen all the time from God's standpoint."7

Another purpose of prayer is to help us grasp God's promises. "Cast thy burdens upon the Lord, and he shall sustain thee: he shall never suffer the righteous to be moved" (Psalms 55:22). Communication gives us an opportunity to present our requests to the Father. "Be careful for nothing; but in everything by prayer and supplication with thanksgiving let your requests be made known unto God" (Philippians 4: 6).

## Benefits of Prayer

Prayer has many rewards. It is a mighty weapon for spiritual victory. It drives worry away. It helps us withstand temptation and be on the offensive with our enemy. Satan is always looking for the sleeping believer. "Watch ye and pray, lest ye enter into temptation. The spirit truly is ready, but the flesh is weak" (Mark 14:38).

When I feel vulnerable spiritually, it helps to share concerns with a prayer partner. This poem expresses it well.

> "Because you prayed with me today,
> My fear began to melt away;

I knew that Jesus heard our prayer,
And I was really in His care."[8]

Bring all concerns to God in prayer. He will calm our fears and renew our courage. This is essential for good spiritual, mental and physical health.

A prominent physician addressing the British Medical Association said, "The best medicine I've discovered is prayer. As one whose whole life has been concerned with the sufferings of the mind, I would state that of all hygienic measures to counteract disturbed sleep, depression of spirit, and a distressed mind, I would undoubtedly give first place to the simple habit of prayer. It does more to quiet the spirit and strengthen the soul than any other therapeutic agency known to man."[9]

Prayer can help us have a more abundant life. It also assists us to recognize and acknowledge the authority of the Lord in our lives. "And Jesus came and spake unto them, saying, 'All power is given unto me in heaven and on earth'" (Matthew 28:18).

Utterances to The Lord are powerful forces. A little plaque says, "Prayer changes things." But it should also change me. As I listened to a sermon one Sunday, I was challenged by this statement: "My prayers will change little until they have changed me."[10] God is more interested in changing me than, He is in changing my circumstances. Will I let God change me? My request is, "Change me O God!"

Prayer that brings results must be based on God's Word. "For the Word of God is quick, and powerful, and sharper than any two-edged sword . . ." (Hebrews 4:12).

## Praying the Word

Praying the Word of God is powerful. "Father, I come to you, in Jesus names, using your Word. It tells me that, "No weapon formed against me will prosper; and every tongue that shall rise against me in judgment, you will condemn . . ." (Isaiah 54:17). I'm standing firm on Your Truth, Lord. It is my sword in all circumstances Satan has surrounded me with. I will not believe his lies. Your Word says, the thief cometh not, but for to steal, and to kill and to destroy; I am come that they might have life . . . more abundantly." (John 10:10).

Lord I'm thankful for the abundant life you have given me. I receive it now. Your Word says, "You have given me power to tread on serpents and scorpions, and over all power of the enemy; nothing shall by any means hurt me." (Luke 10:19).

Lord, I take Your Word (my sword), and I cut through this problem. Lord I thank you that, "It will come to pass, that before I call, you will answer; and while I am yet speaking, you hear me." (Isaiah 65:24). Jesus, I'm grateful you teach me and my family to live in peace no matter what Satan hurls at us. "All my children will be taught of the Lord: and great shall be the peace of my children." (Isaiah 54:13).

Lord, I thank you that, "Greater are you within me than he (Satan) that is in the world." (1 John 4:4). For Lord, you have said, "You will never leave me, nor forsake me. Therefore, I can boldly say, you are my helper, and I will not fear." (Hebrews 13:5-6).

Thank You Lord, You and I together can wield the Sword of Your Word against my enemy Satan. For I know that victory against my enemy is, "Not by my might, nor by my power, but by your spirit, Lord of hosts." (Zechariah 4:6). I praise You Lord, for the victory. Amen.

This type of prayer is much more effective in combating fear, sickness or despair. When we use the Word of God, we are putting faith into action.

## Wear the Armor

Here is another prayer that implements the Scripture." The Lord instructed me to use His Word and positive statements, to dress myself for battle with the enemy.

### Wearing the Armor of God

I gird myself with the "Truth" of your word, Lord.
I will not believe the lies of the enemy.
I put on the "Breastplate of righteousness."
Because of what you did on the cross, I can stand righteous before God.
Thank you for protecting my heart and emotions, Lord.
I put on the "Shoes of the gospel of peace."
I will walk in peace this day and every day.
I take up the "Shield of faith," which protects me from all the fiery darts of doubt and fear.

"I do not have the spirit of fear but of power, love and a sound mind."
I put on the "Helmet of salvation," which keeps me steadfastly focused on you, Lord. It helps me "Take captive my thoughts to make them obedience to you, Christ."
I take up the "Sword of the spirit," which is the word of God.
"It is sharper than any double edged sword." I will use it at all times.
"No weapon formed against me shall prosper.
And every tongue that rises against me shall be put down.
This is my heritage as a servant of the most High God."
And I "Pray in the spirit," at all times for all people.
(Ephesians 6:13-18, 2 Timothy 1:7, 2 Corinthians 10:5, Hebrews 4:12 and Isaiah 54:17)

It is essential we come to God in prayer, have faith and believe He will do what His Word says. The book of James, instructs us, we must have faith and not doubt. Or we will be like a wave on the sea that is tossed by the wind. We won't receive anything from the Lord. (James 1:6-7).

This passage of scripture doesn't mean that if we have doubt we shouldn't pray. Rather, we can do as a father did when he brought his son to Jesus. The man said, "Lord, I believe, help thou mine unbelief" Mark (9:24). Author Os Guinness states, "Even the most devastating doubt remains faith and does not become unbelief when we pray." We are also instructed to pray about everything. "Do not be anxious about anything, but in everything, by prayer and petition, with thanksgiving, present your requests to God" (Philippians 4:6 NIV). If we are praying about everything, it will include both the big and the small issues of our daily lives.

When we learn to beseech The Lord about everything and immediately seek His help, we will pray constantly and be sensitive to listen to what God speaks to us. Scripture tells us to, "Pray without ceasing" (1 Thessalonians 5:17). Jesus again tells us to pray: "And he spake a parable unto them to this end, that men ought always to pray, and not to faint" (Luke 18:1)

In a story, Jesus told his listeners about a widow coming before a wicked judge who wouldn't avenge her of her enemies. However, because of her constant appearance, he tired of her requests and eventually granted it.

God, unlike the judge, cares about our concerns and wants us to constantly bring them before him in prayer.

## Be Specific

Our Father also wants us to be specific about our needs when we pray. God knows our needs. He wants us to state our concern. It helps us get a firm grasp on what we desire from God. Praying in generalities is like going to a restaurant and not being selective about what we want to eat. If we did that, the server might bring us something that wouldn't satisfy our taste.

While studying about prayer and the urgency to ask on target, the Lord spoke to me through blind Bartimaeus. He started out praying in generalities rather than in specifics. God instructed me to read the story again. As Jesus and his disciple were leaving the city, the blind man began to shout Jesus, have mercy on me.

"Jesus stopped and said, 'Call him.' So they called to the blind man, 'Cheer up! On your feet! 'He's calling you.' Throwing his cloak aside, he jumped to his feet and came to Jesus. 'What do you want me to do for you?' Jesus asked him. The blind man said, 'Rabbi, I want to see.' 'Go,' said Jesus, 'Your faith has healed you . . ."' (Mark 10:46-52 NIV).

Many people are crying out to Jesus to relieve them of their physical sufferings and are being rebuffed and quieted by others who say Jesus isn't listening. Some say, He doesn't perform miracles today like He did when He walked the earth. Jesus still performs wonders. "Jesus Christ the same yesterday, and today, and forever." (Hebrews 13:8). All people who have been told to be quiet and not expect healing, need to continue to cry out like the blind man did.

Jesus heard Bartimaeus' cry and asked others to call him. Jesus hears everyone's cry and is asking Christian brothers and sisters who believe in the resurrection power of the Lord, to call that one who needs healing to the Lord. We are to tell them "Cheer up! On your feet! He's calling you." What does it mean to tell someone to be cheerful and stand up? We are to spiritually encourage them with the Word of God. Help them accept Jesus and His promises. We are to assist them as they use their own initiative to stand on The Lord's utterance. When a person arrives at this point, they will hear Jesus' call and respond.

## Cloaks Off

Bartimaeus threw off his cloak. I believe this symbolizes throwing off our doubt, pride, past unbelief and things that hinders the Lord's power in our lives. At this point, Jesus can finally ask us, "What do you want me to do for you?" We need to be specific and say, "I want to see, walk, and be free from my disease."

After we tell Jesus what we need, and believe, then we can receive our miracle. Our action doesn't stop here; we are to follow Jesus as the healed man did.

Jesus heard the blind man's general prayer, but commanded him to be specific. After he pin pointed his need, Jesus responded and healed him. A specific request gets God's definite response. In praying, if you aim at nothing, you're bound to hit it.

God's Word specifically instructs us to pray for wisdom. "If any of you lacks wisdom, he should ask God, who gives generously to all without finding fault, and it will be given to him" (James 1:5 NIV). Often, I have found myself in urgent situations not knowing what to do. Then I quietly whispered, "Lord, what do I do now." Other times, I intuitively know what to do and praise Him for the results. This is one of the simplest ways of praying for wisdom.

Occasionally, it feels as though all wisdom has left us and we have no idea how to pray. It is then we need a prayer partner. The Holy Spirit is our best companion. He prays for us. (Romans 8:26). Author, Charles Spurgeon states, "Groanings, which cannot be uttered are often prayers which cannot be refused."

## The Holy Spirit Prays for Us

God understands our human helplessness and that's why He has given us another way to pray. "For he that speaketh in an unknown tongue speaketh not unto men but unto God" (1 Corinthians 14:2a) When we pray in the spirit, it is effective because the Holy Spirit is interceding for us. He helps us touch the heart of Our Father and builds up our spirit man. In so doing, it releases our faith to touch the very core of the situation. In my own life, I have found these prayers to be very effective.

No matter how well we know a person and their situation, we don't always know the most effective way to intervene for them. We can't always be with our children. Hence, we really don't know what their needs are, but the Holy Spirit does.

One morning a mother felt the overpowering urge to drop to her knees and pray in the spirit for one of her sons who had gone to school. She had no idea what she was praying or why. She only knew she had to pray. Later she was notified that her son had been hit by a car and severely injured. Because she heeded the call to pray, her son's needs were met. Intercessory prayer, in the spirit, is an effective spiritual tool.

We can pray in the spirit as a weapon against Satan. He is our accuser and will stop at nothing to destroy us. He surveys our prayer life and comes before God daily to accuse us. We must find a way to get past Satan's surveillance. "When you pray in the spirit, you go before the throne of God undetected by Satan because you speak mysteries to Him. Your prayers are like stealth bombers that bypass Satan's detection. Praying in the spirit is a frequency Satan can't pick up. It's an emergency channel that enables us to pray devil stomping prayers without being shot at."[11]

These prayers can often be intercessory. This is the most unselfish form of prayer. It touches the heart of God in a special way. Jesus interceded for us. "I pray for them . . . for they are thine. I pray not that thou shouldest take them out of the world, but that thou shouldest keep them from the evil" (John 17:9 & 15).

Jesus also prayed for Simon (Peter). The Lord told Simon that Satan wanted to destroy him. ". . . But I have prayed for thee, that thy faith fail not . . ." (Luke 22:31-32).

## The Lord's Prayer

Jesus' Prayer's teach us about communicating with the Father. The Lord's Prayer is the best model and captures the essence of heartfelt requests.

"Our Father which art in heaven, Hallowed be thy name. Thy kingdom come, Thy will be done on earth, as it is in heaven. Give us this day our daily bread. And forgive us our debts, as we forgive our debtors. And lead us not into temptation, but deliver us from evil: For thine is the kingdom, and the power, and the glory, forever. Amen" (Matthew 6:9-13)

Larry Lea explains The Lords' Prayer in, "Your Guide to Successful Prayer."

"Our Father which art in heaven, Hallowed be thy name."

The prayer begins with promises and praise. We need to honor the name of God by agreeing that God is our father and we are His children. We thank Him for being our Father and for what He has already done in Jesus Christ. Then apply His promises to our lives.

"Thy Kingdom come, Thy will be done."

This portion of the prayer deals with priorities. God reigns over us when we obey Him and accept His will for our lives. We need to pray that God's will and priorities are established in our lives.

"Give us this day our daily bread."

This sentence deals with provisions. There are four basic requirements for appropriating God's resources for our needs. First, we must be in the will of God. Next, we must believe it is God's will to prosper us. Third, we must be specific and lastly, be tenacious.

"Forgive us our debts as we forgive our debtors"

This addresses people and relationships. We must ask God to forgive us our wrong attitudes, relationships etc. Then we must release others, if we want God to forgive us and remove our sin.

"And lead us not into temptation, but deliver us from evil."

The cry from this passage is one that speaks of power. When we begin the day, we pray a hedge of protection about ourselves, our loved ones and our possessions. My hedge of protection is to plead the blood of Jesus over family and friends. When we do this, we are drawing the blood line and telling Satan he can't come any closer to us.

According to Psalm 91, there are three reasons we can claim God's protection. First, "Because thou hast made the Lord . . . thy habitation" vs. 9. Second, "He he has set his love upon me" vs. 14. And third, "Because he hath known my name" vs. 14. We need to make certain we are walking in God's protection daily. We also need to put on the armor of God. "For thine is the kingdom, and the power, and the glory forever. Amen."

As the author guides us to the last prayer topic, we find it speaks of praise. We need to praise God because He has invited us to be participants in His kingdom, His power and His glory.

We should never enter or leave God's presence without humbly bowing before Him and offering a sacrifice of praise."[12]

In giving '*The Lord's Prayer,*' I believe Jesus was trying to teach His disciples (that includes us) how to become effectual and fervent in prayer. First we are to come before Him with praise. "Whoso offereth praise glorifieth me . . ." (Psalms 50:23). Then we are to claim the promises of His Word. We can determine His priorities for our lives, acknowledge His provisions, effectively deal with people, and receive God's power in our lives. Praise the Lord for who He is and what He has done.

## Hindrances to Prayer

Prayer is work and requires discipline if it is to be effective. Three of the biggest enemies of prayer are interruptions, drowsiness and wandering thoughts. Here are tips on how we can come against these enemies of communion with The Lord. Choose a quiet time and place to combat interruptions. Stand or walk while praying, it chases drowsiness away. Pray out loud and those wandering thoughts will flee. Strive to root these enemies out of your prayer life.

These frustrations are not the only roadblocks to prayer. There are other subtle ones, which we fail to recognize. The Word tells us to live in peace with one another. It also states we aren't to repay evil with evil or insult with insult, but with blessing. It's important to speak the truth and not be deceptive in our speech. "For the eyes of the Lord are on the righteous and His ears are attentive to their prayer, but the face of the Lord is against those who do evil" (1 Peter 3: 12 NIV).

God is telling us that if we do evil or sin, He turns His face from us. Just as in the natural when someone's face is turned from us, they don't hear us as well. "If I had cherished sin in my heart, the Lord would not have listened" (Psalm 66:18 NIV).

Other hindrances to prayer are: guilt, worldliness, resentment, unbelief and excuses. Guilt leaves us with a sense that God doesn't want to hear from us. "My iniquities have overtaken me, so that I am not able to see" (Psalm 40:12, NAS). We believe the lies of the enemy and come under condemnation. God only wants us to feel conviction. When God convicts, He reveals our sin and draws us to Himself.

When we turn away from others in resentment, it will also hinder our prayers. "And whenever you stand praying, forgive, if you have anything against anyone; so that your Father . . . may forgive you your transgressions. But if you do not forgive, neither will your Father . . . forgive your transgressions" (Mark 11:25-26, NAS). We are pardoned in the same measure that we pardon others. The highest form of spiritual pride is the inability to forgive. If we don't acquit others, we put a blockage between us and God.

Unbelief also walls us off from God. If we don't believe, we won't pray. "And all things you ask in prayer, believing, you shall receive" (Matthew 21:22, NAS). Unbelief causes us to make excuses not to pray.

Often our defense, hinder our prayers. One that we've all used from time to time is "I'm too tired." The Lord's answer is, "Awake, sleeper, and arise from the dead, and Christ will shine on you" (Ephesians 5:14, NAS). Another excuse is, "I'm too busy." God's word tells us to, "Be careful how you walk, not as unwise men, but as wise, making the most of your time . . ." (Ephesians 5:15-16, NAS). If we are wise, we will redeem the time by praying. Another excuse that feels valid is "I'm too dry." We can't wait till we feel like praying or we will become more dry.

Yet another excuse that hinders our prayers is "I'm too preoccupied." If we've got too many problems facing us, then we can remember, "The righteous cry and the Lord hears, and delivers them out of all their troubles" (Psalm 34:17, NAS). It is precisely when we're overwhelmed that we need to take time to quiet ourselves and know God is there ready to help us.

One minister summarized the hindrances to prayer this way. Often we don't ask the Lord until it's almost too late. Sometimes we pray with wrong motives. We may have un-forgiveness in our lives. We don't always pray in line with God's will; nor are we submissive to His authority.

If any of these hindrances are present in our lives, sin can subtly enter into our hearts and hinder our prayers. Then the lines of communication close. To be fervent and effectual in prayer, we need to keep the language paths open.

## Driven to Pray

Developing a prayer habit requires work and discipline but keeps communication ongoing. We must have a plan and goals. Our plan can be focused on worshiping God, then praying for others and lastly for ourselves. We can begin by establishing a minimum time goal. Without goals we usually don't accomplish much. Prayer needs to drive us. We must be motivated to pray. Usually if we can have a set time and place to pray it helps establish a habit of prayer. But we also want to be flexible enough to be able to follow the Lord's leading. We can do that if we establish a priority to pray. If we don't have the urgency to pray about everything first, we will not have discernment. We will rob God and ourselves.

The priority of prayer was Jesus' concern, when He cast the money changers out of the temple. "And said unto them, 'It is written, My house shall be called the house of prayer" (Matthew 21: 13). Jesus wanted the temple to be used first and foremost for prayer not business transactions. Communion with His Father was the most important priority in Jesus life.

Prayer was also important in Solomon's life. After He petitioned God the fire came down from heaven. The glory of the Lord was so thick that the priests couldn't enter God's holy house. (2 Chronicles 7:1).

Wouldn't it be great if our prayers brought down the glory of God and filled us like it did the temple? It can happen if communion with Our Father is our priority and we humble ourselves. "If my people, which are called by my name, shall humble themselves, and pray, and seek my face, and turn from their wicked ways; then will I hear from heaven, and will forgive their sin, and will heal their land" (2 Chronicles 7:14). God is calling us to prayer, humility and repentance. Prayer must be a priority.

No matter how busy we are, prayer can have top billing in our lives. Communication with The Lord was a priority, for John Wesley's mother. She had fifteen children. It was often difficult for her to find time or a place to pray. But she had a prayer habit and made it a priority in her life. All her little ones knew to be quiet, when she put her apron over her head and prayed.

When we establish a quiet time with God like Jesus, Solomon and Mrs. Wesley, we will begin to release bold prayers and receive answers. We have many examples of brave communication in the Bible. "And Jabez called on the God of Israel saying, 'Oh, that You would bless me indeed, and enlarge my territory, that Your hand would be with me, and that You would keep me from evil, that I may not cause pain!' So God granted him what he requested." (1 Chronicles 4:10 NKJV).

Another courageous prayer was offered up by King Jehoshaphat. "O Our God, wilt thou not judge them? For we have no might against this great company that cometh against us; neither know we what to do: but our eyes are upon thee." (2 Chronicles 20: 12). God heard and answered Jehoshaphat's prayer by instructing him to send the praising troops out first. Their praise ambushed their enemies.

A minister instructed us on praying bold prayers. He relates that courage is a behavior, born out of belief. What we pray reflects what we believe about God. We pray with great boldness by praying for courage and wisdom. The apostles prayed "Now, Lord, consider their threats and enable your servants to speak your Word with great boldness." (Acts 4:29 NIV). "After they prayed, the place where they were meeting was shaken. And they were all filled with the Holy Spirit and spoke the Word of God boldly." (Acts 4:31NIV).

"Great things happen when we bravely come to God. We should boldly pray for miracles. The Lord wants us to rely on Him and pray big, bold prayers for salvation, marriages, family relationships and many other issues."[13] Praying courageously gives us power in our lives.

One of the boldest prayers is to pray God's Word and then the answers to your prayers. When we thank God for answering our petitions before anything happen, it is a bold use of faith. "Now faith is the substance of things hoped for and the evidence of things not seen." (Hebrews 11:1). Another verse that helps us voice the answer to our prayers is "Even God, who quickeneth the dead, and calleth those things which be not as though they were." (Romans 4:17). "Were" means it is already done, finished. I have prayed these prayers many times and God moves on our behalf. One prayer I sent up was, thank You Lord for giving me favor, justice, and Your will. Thank you for bringing me through as gold, from this investigation. God answered that courageous prayer in a marvelous way and I saw the glory of the Lord abound in that situation.

## Recipe for Answered Prayers

After bold prayers God often gives us instructions and guidance. Once we've received counsel it is important to be obedient, if we are to see results.

Betty Miller in her "Cake Recipe" gives us an excellent formula for answered prayers from God's word. She states, "If a cake fails we don't usually blame the recipe, but we go back and find out what we did wrong. So if a prayer isn't answered, we need to go back to the Word of God and check our actions against it."

Betty's recipe has all the normal ingredients of a cake.

## Flour - Claiming Scripture

Stating scripture alone won't get a prayer answered any more than flour alone will make a cake. But it is essential to apply the Word of God to our situation. "But my God will supply all your need according to his riches in glory by Christ Jesus" (Philippians 4:19).

## Milk - Confession

We say we have all that we need. We confess our goal. It is God's will that we have all we need and that we see our loved ones saved. The admission of the heart and mouth must agree. If we stopped here, we would have flour and milk, a paste or an unanswered prayer.

## Baking Powder - Faith

Baking powder makes a cake rise. But faith alone won't move our mountain. We must sow seed to see our belief grow. We must develop the attitude of "I desire to do the will of God." An act of our will, overcomes the flesh. The Holy Spirit can't control us unless we choose to let Him. We must choose to do God's will.

## Eggs - Works and Obedience

We must be willing to be a vessel that can bring an answer to every prayer we utter. We must be obedient and choose The Lord's will and not give an inch to Satan. If we don't agree with our adversary, and we are totally committed to Christ, then the enemy can't touch us. "What I have belongs to My Maker. Satan you're tampering with God's property." When we commit ourselves to God, He will empower us to do the job.

## Shortening - Motives

Why do we want our need's meet? Why do we want our loved ones saved? Would that make our life more peaceful or do we really care about their souls and where they spend eternity? God's Word says "If ye shall ask any thing in my name, I will do it" (John 14:14). We don't have what we want because we don't ask or we asked with the wrong motive. It's imperative to pray in line with God's will.

Salt - Wisdom

We don't need much salt in a cake. However, if we didn't have some, it would be flat and tasteless. So, without wisdom, our prayers would be ineffective, and we might make fools of ourselves. "If any of you lack wisdom, let him ask of God . . ." (James 1:5).

Sugar - Praise

"I will bless the Lord at all times: his praise shall continually be in my mouth" (Psalm 34:1). We are to praise God for bringing us through our circumstances not because of them. Evil or tragedy isn't from God. But, if God allows tragedy after we are committed to him, then it helps us grow in Him and be victorious. If we are one hundred percent committed to God, then we can't be defeated.

Adversity will come our way. We must be wise to Satan's attacks. If we are having difficulties, we can remember we're on the right track. Satan wouldn't be causing us trouble, if we weren't tearing down strongholds in his kingdom. We also need to be aware that nothing touches our life, except what God permits for our best.

Spice - Fasting

Not every cake requires spice. But when used, only a small amount is necessary. The same is true with fasting, and a little goes a long way. It should be used only as the Holy Spirit quickens you.

Blending Cake - Balance

Mix the cake batter. Then put it in the pan and it's ready for the oven. The oven must be hot. When the cake goes into the heat, it has all the ingredients necessary to make it a cake. So it is with prayer.

Oven Baking and Timing - Fiery Furnace

This is a time of waiting. It is often a time of trial, a test of patience and endurance. But God is with you in that fiery furnace. When Jesus is with me, that is where I want to be.

It takes time to bake a cake. We have to wait until it is done. As with prayer we have to endure until the answer comes. There is a growing process for all our seeds and prayers. So set the timer. God has a time and season for everything. "To everything there is a season, and a time to every purpose under the heaven" (Ecclesiastes 3:1).

Don't stand at the oven waiting. Go do other things, sow other seeds. When the cake is baked, take it out of the oven.

Icing - Answered Prayer

Answered prayer is like icing; it's the finishing touch. Often it overflows."[14]

God's word is our recipe book. If we follow the instructions and wait or abide in Him we will see the answers to our prayers.

## Make the Devil Pay

A praying lady lived next door to an atheist. Every day, when the lady petitioned The Lord, the atheist could hear her. He thought to himself, "She sure is crazy, praying all the time like that. Doesn't she know there isn't a God?" Many times while she was praying, he would go to her house and harass her, saying, "Lady, why do you pray all the time? Don't you know there is no God?" But she kept on praying.

One day, she ran out of groceries. As usual, she was praying to the Lord, explaining her situation and thanking Him for what He was going to do. The atheist heard her petition and thought to himself. "Humph . . . I'll fix her." He went to the grocery store, bought a whole bunch of groceries. He took them to her house and dropped them off on the front porch. Then, he rang the door bell and hid in the bushes to see what she would do. When she opened the door and saw the groceries, she began to praise the Lord with all her heart, jumping, singing and shouting everywhere!

The atheist jumped out of the bushes and told her, "You ole' crazy lady, God didn't buy you those groceries, I bought those groceries!" Well, she started running down the street, shouting and praising the Lord. He chased after her, questioning, what's your problem? She said, "I knew The Lord would provide me with some groceries. But I didn't know He was going to make the Devil pay for them!"

This woman had faith and a sense of humor. She was able to wait on the Lord to answer her prayer.

Abiding or waiting, in the spirit of prayer is difficult for most of us. But it is very important. It is the second part of the two-way communication that prayer produces. Speaking is the easiest communication task, while listening is the hardest. It is the same way with prayer. It is much easier for us to talk to God and list our needs than it is for us to listen for God's instructions to us. This is why God's Word says, ". . . Be quick to listen, slow to speak . . . (James 1:19 NIV). We have two ears and one mouth to learn the art of listening more than we speak. An embroidered craft item I purchase said it well, "Talking is sharing, but listening is caring."

The act of prayer isn't complete if we don't listen to our Father, God and show Him our desire to know Him better. We can't receive much from God when we talk. We learn more when we listen. "Be still, and know that I am God . . ." (Psalm 46:10 NIV).

"And when He had sent the multitudes away, He went up into a mountain apart to pray . . . He was there alone" (Matthew 14:23). Jesus took time alone to be quiet and listen to His Father's instructions. We need to do the same.

## Quiet Time with God

It's often difficult to find quiet time with The Lord. He wants us to be still and wait before Him.

Often I feel weak because I haven't waited upon the Lord. God had such a hard time getting me quiet. He began to speak to me upon awakening, or sometimes as I went to sleep. I thought this was strange. But the Word of God shows how people have always had a hard time hearing from the Lord. "Indeed God speaks once or twice . . . then He opens the ears of men, and seals their instruction." (Job 33:14-16 NAS).

I began to realize that God wants to communicate with me all day long. He desires to keep me out of trouble. I don't want to miss any of His important instructions. So at different times through the day I still my mind and ask "Lord what would you have me do about this situation?" As I began to make a conscious effort to be silent and listen, I realized God was speaking to me.

As God instructs us in the quiet times of waiting on Him, He often gives us the means and answers to our prayer. I sought The Lord about an urgent need.

We were new to a military base and city. Several people on the base had advised us to enroll our son in a certain high school. It was reported to be in the safest district with the best curriculum. This meant we needed a place to live within that school district. As I began to listen for God's answer, He instructed me to call a specific housing agency. I explained the situation to them and they gave us one house to look at. The minute my husband and I saw the house, we knew it was right for us. And it was in the best school district.

When we listen to God, we find He has our best interest at heart. Again, I came to the Lord with a housing need. We were living in Southwestern Kansas. My husband had recently started a new job in Eastern Kansas. He was looking for a house we could rent. He found a nice house in the country and made a deposit to secure it.

Suddenly the landlord decided he wanted to sell his house instead of renting to us. The landlord was a kind gentleman and refunded our deposit. But that left us with a dilemma. We would load our household goods and start the trek across the state in a few days. So, I went to the Lord and reminded Him of His Word. "But my God will supply all your needs . . ." (Philippians 4:19). Then the Lord reminded me, "No weapon that is formed against thee shall prosper . . ." (Isaiah 54:17). God instructed me to stand on His Word and thank Him for meeting our need. A couple days later my husband secured a place for us to live and we successfully completed the household move.

This relocation put us close to a university. I felt the Lord leading me to return to college to pursue a bachelor's degree. Our youngest son was a senior at the university and helped me enroll.

After receiving a copy of my Associates Degree transcripts, the University of Kansas evaluated it and decided they wouldn't give me credit for six hours of Western Civilization. They had a policy that the courses had to be taken from their university. I didn't understand their reasoning and sought the Lord's counsel. He instructed me to review the requirements, prepare a letter to the dean of the school, bring all books I had utilized in the courses and have the dean examine them. I followed these instructions and obtained an interview with the dean of the school. After he reviewed my course work and books, he granted me complete credit for the courses. This totally amazed everyone.

Yes, God is able to work abundantly in our lives to the extent we let His power guide us. (Ephesians 3:20). Many times we saw God's mighty power at work in our lives.

One day after graduation from college, our son announced the Lord wanted him to move to Japan. He purchased an airline ticket without a job in hand. The thoughts and fears started to tumble in my mind. It's expensive to live in Japan. How will he make it in a foreign country without a job, without knowing the language, and without knowing the culture? Where would he live? It is nearly impossible in that country to get an apartment without help from one's employer. Frankly, I was worried. So I packed up my concerns and poured them out to the Lord in prayer. I ask the Lord to guide, protect and supply our son with a job. Then I left it in God's hands.

A few weeks before leaving the United States, our son received a call telling him he had a job teaching English as a Second Language. God heard our cries and met the needs. It was a real growth experience for us and our son. We depended on the Lord to keep our son in His care and guide him daily.

## Seek God's Guidance

Often the Lord gives us guidance as we seek Him. The Lord gave me a glimpse of a Christian Family Life Center he wanted to be established. This agency was to provide assistance to homeless people and others that needed help. It would give them a place to live, and learn two occupations. They would become self-sufficient and begin to asist others.

I didn't have a clue how to prepare or begin this task. So I sought the Lord for His direction. While listening to the Lord, I heard Him say, "You will have to enlarge your tent." "Enlarge the place of your tent; stretch out the curtains of your dwellings, spare not; lengthen your cords, and strengthen your pegs" (Isaiah 54:2, NAS). And I responded with, "Which way do we stretch our tent." The Lord simply responded with a question, "Which directions do you usually extend a tent? I replied, "Every direction, to the north, west, south and east." And that was God's instruction to me. We were to start small with the land we already owned.

Being sensitive to listen and receive insight from the Lord is essential. We need to depend on God's wisdom. This will be accomplished when we have a right relationship with Him in prayer and are ready to listen for His instructions.

## God's Silences

Listening, and the quiet it sometimes produces, has been difficult for me. Silence has its purpose in the communication process. It often allows us to get an answer from the other person. God's silences, or seemingly unanswered prayers, are intended to draw us closer to Him. If God responded right away, we might never learn to trust. Or, we might quit talking to Him after our needs were met.

There have been many difficult silences in my prayer life. One time was when our son's job ended. His apartment lease also expired. This necessitated moving with little idea of where to go. I trusted the Lord to supply a job for our son. A job didn't come before he had to move out of his apartment.

Weeks, then a couple months went by before our son got any job interviews. We were all discouraged. But I continued to pray that the Lord would give him the right job. I prayed the new employment would blow our son's mind, and that he would know it came from the Lord and not himself. Our son got a very good job. Many people marveled and told him that someone was watching out for him. God gives us His best when we wait upon Him.

Yes, the times of silence after praying are difficult. But God is teaching me to never give up. In His timing, we will see the answers to prayers for salvation, physical, emotional healing and restorations within our homes, families and world.

Oswald Chambers tell us in "My Utmost for His Highest," that silence is God's answer. There are many silences recorded in God's word. "Now, Jesus loved Martha, her sister, and Lazarus. When therefore He heard that Lazarus was sick, He stayed then two days longer in the place where He was" (John 11:6, NAS).

Why didn't Jesus start out for Bethany immediately upon hearing about Lazarus' illness? That must have been an extremely difficult time for Martha and Mary when they didn't hear anything from The Lord.

God's silence is the sign that He is bringing us into an understanding of Himself. Are we mourning before God because we haven't had an audible response? The silence is God's way of trusting us in the most intimate way. He knows we can stand a bigger revelation. His lack of an answer is the proof that He has heard us. His silence is contagious. It gets into us and we become perfectly confident that God has heard us. When Jesus brings us into the understanding that prayer is for the glorifying of His Father, then He will give us the first sign of His intimacy -- silence.

"If we think of prayer as the breath in our lungs and the blood from our hearts, we think rightly. Prayer is our daily lifeline of communication to the Father. It is the way we get to know God himself. Prayer is the way the life of God is nourished in us. Prayer doesn't fit us for the greater work, it is the greater work. Prayer is the battle."[15]

Since prayer is the battle, we need to be persistent in talking with God. We need to stand on the Word of God and remember our prayers do make a big difference in ours and other lives. "The effectual fervent prayer of a righteous man availeth much" (James 5:16).

# CHAPTER 3

# *Nature*

"But ask now the beasts, and they shall teach thee; and the fowls of the air, and
they shall tell thee: or speak to the earth, and it shall teach thee:
and the fishes of the sea shall declare unto thee"
(Job 12:7-8).

God created the heavens and the earth. He made man in His own image.
Humans were to rule over the fish of the sea, the fowl of the air, over the
cattle and all living creatures. (Genesis 1:1, 26-28). God created all things
and gave man dominion over them. The Almighty speaks powerfully to
us through all of nature if we are sensitive enough to listen.

Our Lord used nature as a backdrop for teaching the Word of His
Father. He utilized hills, fields, mountains, lakes, seas, market places, and
synagogues as He traveled the countryside. Jesus taught in this manner
because it was common and understandable to His followers. Nature
helped the people relax, and learn of God.

## Jesus Taught With Parables

Jesus often reflected on nature when He used parables as a way to teach and fulfill prophecies. "Therefore speak I to them in parables . . . And in them is fulfilled the prophecy of Esaias . . ." (Matthew 13:13-14).

A parable is a short, simple story from which a moral lesson may be drawn. Jesus' word pictures used nature to teach truths about human relationships and God's kingdom.

The parable of the man, who planted, and the soil speaks to us about the Lord's domain. A man scattered some seeds. Some of the grains fell on the side of the road and the birds devoured it. Some seeds landed on stony places. When the sun came up it got scorched because it didn't have any roots and it died. The other grains fell in the thorns. As the thorns began to grow, it choked out the seeds. But other grain fell into good ground and produced a bountiful harvest of a hundred times, some sixty times and some thirty times. (Matthew 13:3-8).

Jesus explained this word picture to His disciples. The people who hear and don't understand the Word, are like those seeds that fell by the way side, and the enemy comes and snatches it a way. The stony places are like people who receive the Word with joy but have no roots or faith and when persecution comes they wither. The thorny places are those that hear the Word and let the cares of this world choke it out. The good ground is like people who hear the Word, understand it and bear fruit. Some people bear a hundred, some sixty and some thirty times. (Matthew 13:18-23).

Another parable, The Prodigal Son, tells us more about the Kingdom of God. In this story, Jesus speaks of an earthly father and two sons. The younger son wanted his share of the property. His father obliged him and the younger son set off for a distant country and squandered his wealth in wild living. After he had spent everything, there was a famine in the whole country and the son was in need. He hired himself out and was sent to feed pigs. The son was so hungry. He longed to fill his stomach with the pig's food, but no one gave him anything to eat. The son came to his senses, and realized that his father's hired hands had food to spare. He decided he would go back to his father and tell him he had sinned against heaven and against him. The son no longer felt he was worthy to be called a son. He wanted to be a hired man. The younger son began the journey back to his father.

While the son was still a distance away, but visible; his father had compassion and ran to him. He threw his arms around and kissed him. The son confessed his sins to his father. The father said to his servants, bring the best robe. Put a ring on his finger and sandals on his feet. He ordered that a fattened calf be killed. He said, let's have a feast and celebrate for the son of mine that was dead is alive again.

The older brother who had faithfully served his father came in from working in the fields. He heard the merriment. He was angry and jealous. He began to talk to his father about his feelings. The father reminded him that he was always with him and all that the father had was his. The father also reminded the older son that they needed to celebrate because the younger brother was "dead" and is alive again. He was lost but now is found. (Luke 15:11-31 NIV).

This parable is so beautiful because it shows that God is a loving Father who lets us make our own decisions. When we decide to return to Him and confess our sins, He compassionately forgives us. He receives us with open arms and gives us all He has and restores us to our place in His kingdom as sons and daughters.

This word picture, also stressed that when a wayward brother or sister returns to the Lord; we must rejoice. We must have the right attitude and humbly help restore them to the body of Christ. At times in life, we may occupy the role of the father, the prodigal or the older brother.

Jesus used another parable to show us more about relationships. The Good Samaritan shows us how we are to treat our neighbors or fellow man. Here Jesus tells about a man who traveled from Jerusalem to Jericho. Along the way he fell among thieves who stripped him and left him near death. A priest came and passed by on the other side. Also, a Levite did the same when he saw the wounded man. Lastly, a Samaritan came by and had compassion on the injured man. He bound up his wounds, set him on his own beast and brought him to an inn and took care of him. The Samaritan also left extra money to pay the wounded man's bill. Jesus asked the lawyer, "Who was a neighbor?" The lawyer answered, "He who showed mercy." Then Jesus told him to go and do the same. (Luke 10:30-37). Jesus' parables utilized life and nature to teach his followers truths.

## The Plant Kingdom

The Lord, Our God, still communicates with us today through nature. He created the plant kingdom of herbs, grasses, vegetables and trees, as a source of food, but also, to teach us about Him.

A plant starts with a seed and requires a growing process. As a child I helped with the planting and growing process of many different seeds. Our first task was to prepare the soil by cultivating it. We loosened the soil and turned it over so it could accept the seeds we planted.

God also has to prepare the soil in our hearts to receive the seed (His Word). This often requires a breaking up process which isn't pleasant. God sometimes permits disappointment, sorrow, disaster or tragedy to touch our lives as a cultivation process. "If you have been experiencing trouble or heartache, God may be softening the soil of your life so the seed of His Word can grow in you. Don't fight it. Let Him have His way. Allow Him to produce patience and maturity in your heart."[1] One day we may thank the Lord for preparing our soil to receive His Seed.

As a child, I enjoyed planting watermelon seeds and watching them grow. I always marveled at this process of creation. William Jennings Bryan, famous American lawyer and creationist says, "A watermelon speaks volumes about God. One little seed in the ground, with the help of sunshine and showers gathers 200,000 times its own weight. It forces all the material through a tiny stem and builds a watermelon. The outside is covered with green, inside is a rind and red juicy fruit dotted with other seeds. Each seed is capable of creating fruit again. God speaks His wisdom and power through this marvelous creation."[2]

We can't create a melon. Neither do we fully understand what instructs the melon seed to grow, but God does. We are also like that seed and can produce much fruit that is sweet to the taste of others.

To be productive, the seed must first be planted and lie dormant before it springs up in a different form. "Truly, truly, I say to you unless a grain of wheat falls into the earth and dies, it remains by itself alone, but if it dies, it bears much fruit" (John 12:24 NAS).

Tulip bulbs lie dormant in the winter and burst forth with new life in the spring. It is a reminder of what Christ did for us on the cross. We too must die to self, if we are to bear fruit. It is so appropriate the new life of flowers comes around the Easter season.

We as humans are much like flowers. Our fleshly life, our will (the seed) must be buried with Christ before we can be raised to resurrection power as a tender shoot springs forth from the ground. We are born to newness of life with Christ. "Therefore if any man be in Christ, he is a new creature . . ." (2 Corinthians 5:17). The newness we experience is shedding our will and letting it be replaced with God's spirit and His will. This isn't the end of the growing process.

Much must happen between the time a new plant shoots forth and the harvest. The plant must be watered and cultivated continually to yield a crop. Moisture gives the plants a freshness and vigor. In a spiritual sense the watering is prayer and praise. It refreshes a Christian just as water does the plants. If done regularly we will grow stronger and begin to produce fruit.

As the plant begins to grow, so do weeds. Weeds have been humorously referred to as any plant that isn't growing in the right spot. If there are weeds growing next to plants, we pull them out. However, we must use wisdom to know the difference between plants and weeds. We must also use caution or we will accidentally pull up plants with the weeds. In the spiritual realm, the plant can be viewed as the new nature in Christ and the weed as the old sin nature. The old nature will always try to rear its ugly head. We must deal with it like we would weeds in a garden if we expect to harvest anything. Sometimes we have to let the tender plant grow for a little while to assure that it is solid enough to withstand the pulling of a weed that appears next to it. Other times the weeds are spaced further away from the plant and it is no problem to eradicate the weeds. We must always try to pull the weeds out at the earliest possible point. The longer they are permitted to grow, the tougher it is to pull out all the roots.

A tree seedling is a perfect example. When it is pulled immediately it is easy, but let it wait and it's an impossible task. It is the same with our old nature or sin. It must be pulled out by the roots immediately. If left it gets such a hold in our lives that it chokes out, Christ's nature in us. Weeding is a continual process that must be done if we expect to see that one hundredfold harvest.

## Root Systems

The weeds we don't take care of in time require rooting out with a shovel, or hoe. So it is in our lives with persistent sins or self will. A simple confession will usually pull up small weeds but it doesn't always take care of the persistent roots. These tenacious roots must be cut out.

The gardener usually has to dig out the roots. This growth underground, can be dug out by God (our master gardener). We need to take authority, "In the Name of Jesus," over the root problem and bind it from our lives. Then lose Satan from his assignment against us and release the power of Jesus to heal the problem.

At other times God has to discipline us and sometimes permit us to pass through trials and hardships. The master gardener may utilize some or all of these tools to dig or surgically cut out the roots.

Sometimes the root systems erupt at unexpected places. We had a tree outside our garage and didn't think much about it until the cement flooring of the garage cracked lengthwise. Roots usually aren't seen much from the top of the ground, but they go down deep and can do severe damage.

"Bitterness is a root that often has its beginning in rejection."[3] Bitterness can take hold quickly, and if not dealt with swiftly, can go down deep to the very core of our being. It can choke out the love, peace, joy and gratitude in our lives. It can leave us with an attitude of revenge and vulnerable to physical illness.

Bitterness isn't the only root we must be on guard against. Unforgiveness, selfishness, self-pity, pride and fear are also root systems and need to be dealt with promptly. Rooting out the subconscious hurts is like trying to dig up the roots of a tree. We need the help of the master gardener, and then we need to be willing to let Him dig it out His way.

## Time in the Valley

The discipline we experience from the master gardener leads us from the mountain top to the valley. Most of us are like the people Moses lead. We murmur and complain when we are in the valley. Often it seems that we spend more time in the valley than on the mountain top. "Why do we stay in the valley so much?" This question was asked at a meeting with graduate students at Oral Robert's University. "One young man replied, 'It's because the soil is better in the valley and that's where the grass grows."[4]

The same is true spiritually. It's in the valleys that we have the soil of adversity to help us. We grow much quicker in rich soil. The valley isn't a bad place when we remember to praise the Lord and let Him work in our lives. We can experience "Victory in the Valley." We can grow (as a planting of the Lord) and begin to produce fruit.

## Lessons from the Trees

Just as there are fruits in the spiritual, there are juicy seed bearing growths in the natural. Most fruit come from trees. However, not all trees are fruit producing. These tall woody plants, differ considerably in appearance, growth rate and value to man.

Each tree grows according to the Father's plan. We learn much by observing how trees survive the storms. A heavy snow storm that comes in early fall, before the leaves drop, can wreck some trees. The pine and the elm trees handle a snow storm differently. "An elm holds its branches rigid. As it becomes weighted down, eventually its limbs break. But when a pine or evergreen is loaded, it simply relaxes, lowers its branches, and lets the burden slip away."[5]

We need to learn to be a pine tree and let our heavy weights slide away. "Cast thy burden upon the Lord, and he shall sustain thee . . ." (Psalm 55:22). It's only by letting God have our burdens that we can bear the weight of them.

The apostle Paul, who experienced many trials and adversities, gave a three-fold method for handling difficulties: 1. "Be anxious for nothing. 2. Pray about everything. 3. Give thanks for everything" (Philippians 4:6). This is the way to a victorious life that isn't broken.

Strong winds often break tree branches and sometimes destroy the whole tree. What causes some trees to stand while others are destroyed? Tanya Tucker's song "Strong Enough to Bend," says the tree can survive the storms and winds because it bends. The lyrics, likens that to a love relationship and says, "Our love will last if we're strong enough to bend." Bending means we are flexible. We can see the other person's point of view. We are willing to forgive when we've been injured, or to ask for forgiveness when we've inflicted the pain. Yes, if we are willing to bend, our relationships will last and can bring honor to the Lord. Flexibility makes us like a tender tree. We can bend and sway with the wind and not break like a stiff old branch.

How well a tree survives the storm depends on how well its root system is anchored in the soil. One person told about an ice storm that damaged one of the two birch trees in his backyard. One survived the storm and the other one was completely uprooted. The toppled one had been growing at an angle. Consequently, the root system wasn't anchored in the soil as it should have been.

The author gives us a biblical example of Samson. Samson leaned more to his own lusts instead of to God's will and married a Philistine woman. He was later uprooted or fell because he was a leaning Christian. He hadn't been obedient to the Lord.[6] "Therefore let him that thinketh he standeth take heed lest he fall" (1 Corinthians 10:12).

The storms of life can easily make a person or a tree fall. One morning after a bad wind storm, I assessed the damage. Our weeping willow tree had broken off a few feet from the ground. The tree broke close to the area where woodpeckers had bored holes through the trunk. The tree wasn't solid enough to withstand the storm. I knew there was a lesson here. I asked the Lord to show me what it was. He said, "That tree is like some people's lives. It's full of the holes of sin. With sin in your life, you can't withstand the storms or adversities of life. Your life must be solid in me."

We need to be solid like the vines that sometimes grow up the side of oak trees and cling to them during the fierce storms (temptations). Although the wind beats, the tendrils hold tight to the tree bark. If the vine is away from the wind, the oak tree protects the vine. However, if the vine is on the exposed side, the wind presses the vine more closely to it. Sometimes we are like the vine sheltered by God. Other times he allows us to be exposed so we will be pressed closely to Him.[7] We can learn from the vine and cling to the Lord. We can withstand temptation so sin doesn't overtake us. Deadly sins don't leap on us they creep on us.

The psalmist implores God, "Direct my footsteps according to Your Word; let no sin rule over me" (Psalm 119:133b). It's only when we keep sin out of our lives that we will be able to grow and flourish as most trees do. The Word of God likens us to trees often. "The righteous will flourish like a palm tree, they will grow like a cedar of Lebanon, . . . They will still bear fruit in old age, they will stay fresh and green" (Psalm 92:12 & 14 NIV).

In his book 'As a Tree Grows,' W. Phillip Keller tells us about the cedars of Lebanon. They are unique trees of breathtaking beauty, massive size, rich fragrance and high - quality timber. The cedars of Lebanon are used as a symbol of all that is to be desired in Christian character. A tiny cedar seedling, by growing steadily and surely, matures into a mighty monarch of the mountain forest. But the tragedy is that some never get much beyond being tiny, stunted seedlings. They are alive; they are true trees; but they virtually stand still. There is no growth.

A writer compares the lack of growth of the little cedars to not putting on an annual growth ring. He indicates that many of us as Christians aren't putting on growth rings spiritually. Often this is because of unfavorable growth conditions. To be able to grow spiritually we need to have favorable growth conditions of Bible study, fellowship, prayer and disciplined obedience to Christ.[8]

Christian growth requires that we trust and become like leaves on a tree. Leaves on a tree are attached to a limb which is an extension of the tree trunk. The tree trunk is anchored in the earth by a strong root system. The leaves don't worry about falling when the branch moves and sways with the wind. But we as Christians often wonder if we can trust the Lord in what he has told us to do. We feel like we are out on a limb for the Lord. When we find ourselves on a limb and the branch begins to sway, we need to go back to the basics. We need to check and find out whether we are attached to the trunk of a tree which is firmly rooted.

When grounded in the Lord, we will be able to withstand the winds of change. As one minister reminded us, we can become like a tree that takes in waste (carbon dioxide) and produces something good (oxygen). We will begin to draw our food from the root system, God's Word. It is at this point that we will adapt to our environment and flourish like a palm tree.

## The Birds of the Air

God speaks eloquently when he shows us how beautifully all nature adapts to its environment. "Look at the birds of the air; they do not sow or reap or store away in barns, and yet your heavenly Father feeds them . . ." (Matthew 6:26 NIV). It amazes me when I look at the birds and see how God feeds all the different varieties that inhabit the skies.

God has designed baby birds to open their mouths wide and make a lot of noise in anticipation of being fed. I have been privileged to see this scene many times in a gazebo in our back yard. A bird built a nest and raised her young in a large spider plant. The birds wait eagerly for mom to come back. They had their mouths open widely, ready to eat. God spoke to me through this event and His word. "I opened my mouth, and panted: for I longed for thy commandments" (Psalm 119:131). Much like these birds, He wants us to be eager for His Word.

Each species of bird, knows how to build their nests and care for their young. The humming bird has one of the smallest nests. It can measure as little as an inch across the top. The eagle's nest is large and can span several feet. Most nests are anchored to structures, trees or rocks that are high off the ground. This is to provide safety for the eggs and eventually the young birds. God speaks to us through the birds and tells us we need to build high with Him (utilize faith) for our protection.

When I look at a bird nest and see the intricate weave of string, straw, branches, mud, briars, and feathers, I know there is a God. How else would each species have the instinct to adapt to their environment and utilize the common materials they find within their world? As children of God we need to realize God has supplied all our needs. We need to learn how to utilize all he has placed under our dominion just as the birds do.

One of the birds we can learn from is the sparrow. "Are not two sparrows sold for a penny? Yet not one of them will fall to the ground apart from the will of your Father. And even the very hairs of your head are all numbered. So don't be afraid; you are worth more than many sparrows" (Matthew 10:29-31 NIV).

Pastor and Author A.J. Gordon, tells us how a sparrow survives adversity. When this bird's nest is pulled down it, rebuilds again. However, if the nest is pulled down several times, the sparrow seeks a new and higher location where it will be less vulnerable.

Gordon observes, "Christians aren't always that wise. They form dwelling places of happiness and hope that are built on the values of this world, only to see them pulled down time and time again. Yet after each interval of tears, they begin building all over again in the same way. They fail to set their sights heavenward."[9] The Lord is sad when Christians fail to learn from life's difficulties and failures. Neither are we pleased with ourselves when we don't learn from difficulties.

Just as God knows when the sparrows nest has been pulled down, he also knows and permits adversity to touch our lives. God allows trials and difficulties to cause us to rebuild on Him and His Word.

## Soar like an Eagle

When we begin to build on God and utilize faith, we will be able to soar like an eagle. "But they that wait upon the Lord, shall renew their strength, they shall mount up with wings as eagles; they shall run, and not be weary; and they shall walk, and not faint" (Isaiah 40:31).

An author tells us about the fascinating flight of an eagle. "These majestic birds can soar for a long time without a single wing beat. They ride upon the currents of the wind, taking advantage of updrafts of warm air. The eagle must spread their wings to make use of the air currents."[10] We too must be ready to spread our wings of faith if we expect to be able to soar above the daily trials and problems of life. The flight of the eagle must be an exhilarating one.

An evangelist portrays an eagle's habitat and life. The eagle may weigh up to 26 pounds, but it can carry a kangaroo. The eagle is a lofty bird who builds its nest in the cliff of rocks. It is usually born in one place and then moves to a special rock it claims as a fortress for protection. We need to be like the eagle and get to the rock of Jesus.

The mother eagle builds her nest in a high place. This nest is made with sticks, briars, thorns and thistles. Then the mother lines the nest with rabbit fur and feathers, which she has plucked from her own tail, to make it soft.[11] Then she lays her one to four white eggs mottled with brown. She uses the same location year after year.

The mother and father eagle both take turns sitting on the eggs. The dad also acts as a watchman, a protector and hunter. He takes his responsibilities seriously. Fathers can take their place as the leader of their households just as the male eagle does.

The mother eagle feeds and nurtures the young birds after they are hatched. When the baby eagles are ready to leave the nest, mom starts nudging them. But since the nest is so soft and comfortable, they don't want to leave. Consequently, the mother eagle backs up to the nest and starts pulling out the fur and feathers. When there's nothing but briars and thorns left in the nest, it becomes so uncomfortable the babies are ready to fly. The mother eagle is utilizing tough love and discipline by not allowing her young to stay where it is comfortable. Mothers can use both sides of love to help their babies grow and fly.

We as Christians are just like the baby eagle. We'd rather stay in our comfortable surroundings than to try to fly on wings of faith. When the baby eagles begin to fly, they get onto their mother's back. She flies for a while, then she flips over and the babies start to fall because they aren't anchored or grounded. But just before the babies hit the ground, dad swoops down and picks them up. They go through this a couple times before the babies learn to fly.[12]

There is a great parallel in our own lives. Sometimes God has to permit things to happen that shove us out of our comfort zone. We have to take wings and try to fly. Often we flounder and think we will hit rock bottom. But just before that happens, our loving Heavenly Father, like an eagle, swoops down and picks us up. He is so patient and often has to do this with us.

There is another time in the life of an eagle when they are vulnerable and need protection. Eagles go through the molting process annually until they are four-years-old and have their adult feathers. During the molting process of maturity, the eagle flies down into the wilderness. When they descend to the valley, they lose their sense of direction. We are like that too, when we get out of the will of God. In the wilderness, the eagle, as well as us, becomes prey to the enemy.

The eagle stays down in the wilderness for two or three weeks and loses its strength. We can lose our strength while in the wilderness. The eagle walks around and finds it has no strength. Its beak and claws swell up. Its feet can burst from a touch. The eagle can't even lift its brow. The wilderness is a dangerous place for it to be. The eagle's powerful beak builds calcium around it and it can't open its mouth. The eagle seems like it is all but dead.

Then we see help on the scene. The older eagles, who have survived the wilderness, fly over and drop meat to the weak eagle. We as Christians need to encourage our brothers and sisters with the Word while they are in the wilderness. The eagle is a meat eater. We are like that eagle. If we can't eat meat, we can't get any strength.

At this point, the eagle can't eat the meat yet. So it rubs its beak in the blood of the fresh meat. It helps to soften the eagle's beak so it can again eat meat. We need to do as the eagle does and get back into the blood of Jesus. It softens us, helps us repent with a sincere heart.

Once we've repented, we can eat meat again like the eagle. We can only come out of the wilderness by the meat of God's Word. Every day the eagle gets stronger. Soon it's ready to fly. It starts to flutter its wings. If we get into the meat of the Word we can soar like an eagle.

When the eagle begins to fly, hawks tail it closely. The eagle peels off and flies into the sun. This lofty bird is equipped with an extra lens over the eye that allows it to fly directly into the sun and its enemy can't follow it. If we fly toward the Son of God, the devil can't follow us. We need to determine, like the eagle, we are coming out of the wilderness and flying directly into the Son of God's arms.

Remember when the eagle was in the wilderness it had bitter calcium on its beak. It was bitter to its mouth but sweet to its soul. There is nothing in the wilderness for the eagle or us. We are meant to soar like an eagle. Not all the Word (meat) tastes good. But the eagle ate it and got out of the wilderness.[13] We need to eat all the Word of God and get out of the wilderness.

Just as the Eagle goes through the molting process and leaves behind its feathers of immaturity, we need to leave behind those things that bind us and cause us to stay in the wilderness. The eagle must go through this process annually until it is four-years-old. We too may have to be in the wilderness several times until we learn how to stand on God's Word and take the wings of faith. We are to soar like an eagle above our problems, not muddle through with a murmuring spirit.

Author Everett L. Fullam, tells us how an eagle deals with death. "When an eagle senses it is about to die, it leaves its nest, flies to a rock, fastens its talons on it, looks straight into the setting sun, and dies." If we can see beyond this life, we will be able to run to Jesus (our rock). We can fasten our faith on him and look straight into the Son of God's face, confidently knowing Jesus is with us, when He calls our name. We can learn from the eagle how to take this final journey of death.

## Other Winged Creatures

Another winged creature that teaches us a lesson in faith is the bumblebee. The author tells us that scientifically it is impossible for a bumblebee to fly. Their body is too large for the wingspan size. When the bumblebee has its wings folded up it, can't fly. But when they stretch their wings and begin to fly, they can be menacing.[14] When we stretch our wings of faith, we can be menacing to our enemy and his plans. We can be victorious. Jesus says unto us, "If thou canst believe, all things are possible to him that believeth" (Mark 9:23).

We can believe for victory in our lives because God has created all nature to thrive in their habitat. He has also created us with survival instincts.

God speaks to us through another one of His creations, the osprey, who is well adapted to its environment. "These fish-hawks, as they are commonly called, are twenty two to twenty five inches long. They have a five to six-foot wingspan. They live near water, returning to the same nest year after year. The fish hawk drives off all competitors and reserving their lake or section of ocean for themselves. Their long, pointed wings give them both the power to dive, and the control to hover. Keen eyesight lets them see several feet below the water's surface. And their claws are perfectly designed to help them hold firmly the fish they grab."[15]

Isn't it marvelous how God has created the fish-hawk perfectly for its habitat? We can learn much from the osprey. It utilizes its God given abilities, of power and control to survive daily. It drives off all its competitors and reserves the lake for itself. We as humans need to learn how to use what God has given us (His power) to meet our needs and to victoriously drive off our enemy (Satan).

## Lessons from the Geese

God continually speaks His power and truths to us through nature. Most of us have observed geese in flight as they fly south for the winter. There are several things we can learn from watching the geese. First, as each goose flaps its wings, it creates, an "uplift" for the birds that follow. By flying in "V" formation they are able to travel farther and more efficiently by traveling on the thrust of one another.

When a goose falls out of formation, it suddenly feels the drag and resistance of flying alone. It quickly moves back into formation to take advantage of the lifting power of the bird in front of it. When the lead goose grows tired, it rotates back into the formation and another goose flies the point position.

Another lesson we can learn from the geese is encouragement. Geese honk, when they are in clouds, fog or at night. Honking helps keep the flock together and helps them keep up their speed.

When a goose gets sick, wounded or shot down, two geese drop out of formation and follow it down to help or protect it. They stay with it until it dies or is able to fly again. Then they launch out with another formation or catch up with the flock.[16]

Through the geese we learn several lessons. One is the importance of working together and traveling on the thrust of another. We can also begin to share leadership and responsibilities within our homes, churches, and places of business. And one of the most important things we can do is to stand with others and encourage them in difficult times. Everyone thrives much better on encouragement. It brings strength and unity to the Body of Christ.

## Insects Teach Us

As Christians we need to look to God's creations. Even the little insignificant insects hold a lesson for us. "There are four things which are little upon the earth, but they are exceeding wise: The ants are a people not strong, yet they prepare their meat in the summer; The conies are but a feeble folk, yet make they their house in the rocks; The locust have no king, yet go they forth all of them by bands; The spider taketh hold with her hands, and is in kings' palaces." (Proverbs 30:24-28).

According to Proverbs, the ants, conies, locust and spiders are not strong insects, they don't have leaders but yet they are able to store food, build homes and invade even the castles of kings. How are these small weak creatures able to survive so well? How do the ants build an underground colony? This feat, "Requires communication and cooperation." Ants are experts at teamwork. Their wisdom is seen in their ability to work together.

We humans need to learn the lesson of the ants. If we work together, we can be more efficient and accomplish more without the risk of a few people getting too tired and suffering burnout.

> This poem expresses it well:
> "Has God assigned a heavy task;
> a job too big for you?
> Enlist the aid of willing hands.
> Their help will see you through."[17]

## Safety in Numbers

We as humans don't practice togetherness like the animal kingdom does. Unity helps many species of animals efficiently accomplishing a task. It also provides protection for them. Wolves run in a pack to make their kill. Cattle and buffalo often travel together as a herd. Fish swim in a school. All these animals know by instinct that there is safety and efficiency in numbers.

We as Christians need to grasp this fact of nature and incorporate it into our lives more. "As iron sharpens iron . . . one man sharpens another" (Proverbs 27:17 NIV). Not all of us have the same talents, but each of us can excel at what we do best. By pooling our skills we can have a more efficient society and reap an abundant life.

## Dealing with Danger

All of God's creations are made efficient for survival. When danger comes, a turtle withdraws into its shell. A chameleon changes its color. A porcupine bristles. A skunk sprays forth a pungent odor. Cattle or buffalo stampede when danger threatens.

How do we humans deal with danger or problems? Some of us withdraw like the turtle. Others of us change with the situation like a chameleon; we aren't true to our convictions. And still others are defensive and bristle like the porcupine. While others spew forth profanity, hatred, and bitterness, like the skunk does. Others panic and let fear and the enemy chase them like a herd of stampeding beasts. But, none of these coping behaviors are going to bring inner peace or help us deal effectively with our problems.

A better way to handle difficulties is to realize we can't change some situations and we can't change ourselves, but Jesus can. The buffalo and cattle don't try to change the heat of the day. They search for a marshy, low area in the ground that naturally retains rain waters (a wallow). They come to the cool refreshment of the water in the heat of the day.

The deer longs and pants for the cool water. "As the deer pants for the water brooks, so my soul pants for Thee, O God" (Psalm 41:1 NAS).

A television documentary and a minister helped me understand the deer's behavior better. The deer pants when it runs. Most usually a predator is chasing the deer. The deer longs for the water because they know safety awaits them there. The deer's predator loses their scent at the water's edge.

We need to come to the cool water of Jesus in the heat of the chase, so the enemy will lose our scent. When we come to the water, God can begin to equip and change us to deal with life's dangers or problems better.

The Ermine (a weasel like creature) reacts differently to danger. This animal has snow white fur in winter. The ermine instinctively protects its white coat against anything that would soil it. Hunters take advantage of this trait. The hunter finds the ermine's home in a cleft of a rock or hollow of an old tree. Then they smear the entrance and interior with grime. The hunters set their dogs loose to chase the ermine. The frightened animal flees toward home but doesn't enter its home because of the filth. Rather than soil its white coat, it allows itself to be trapped and captured while preserving its purity. Purity is more precious than life for the ermine.[18] This animal speaks to us that we need to keep ourselves separated from the filth of this world at all cost.

## Man's Best Friend

Animals tend to deal with life better through use of their instincts than we do through exercising self-will. Dogs are one of these animals.

God used our pets to teach valuable lessons. Our dogs give us unconditional love. They forgive us quickly even when we hurt them accidentally. Dogs find a quiet spot, lick their wounds and recuperate. They know how to relax. Dogs live in the present, not the past or the future. Our dogs make the most of each adventure, especially their walks. They see, smell and taste the good and bad along the way.

Dogs know they deserve love and are never embarrassed to ask for or receive it. It takes so little to make our dogs happy; just a touch from their Master's hand is enough. Maybe we would be happier if we practiced what our dogs teach us. Dogs read body language much better than we humans do. They quickly learn and adapt to the routines of their master. Instead, we as humans, expect others to adapt to us and our needs within and outside the home.

## Homing Instincts

Cats and dogs that have wandered away from their home will often return, even years later. God has given great homing instincts to many animals and they heed them.

A writer compares the homing instinct on a spiritual level. The wayward child of God doesn't seem to heed their instincts to return to their master. In our rebellion we exhibit less sense than the animals. Our loving creator has given us every reason to come home to Him. He offers love, lasting protection and fullness of joy. Away from him there are temporary pleasure and despair.[19]

God's Word reminds us that animals observe the homing instincts. "Even the stork in the sky knows her appointed seasons, and the dove, the swift and the thrush observe the time of their migration. But my people do not know the requirements of the Lord. How can you say, we are wise . . .?" (Jeremiah 8:7-8 NIV)

We humans are the only species created with a self will. At times, we utilize it for destruction. True wisdom comes from returning to our maker and letting His instincts guide and change us into the image God intended for us.

## Change Creates Growth

The caterpillar is an example of how God changes one of His creations. It is an uncomely creature that can't get very far on its own. It needs help to become different. When it is time for a caterpillar to change, it crawls to a safe place and attaches itself. Then a cocoon begins to form around it. The butterfly must struggle to free itself from its cocoon. It uses one of three methods to become free. The butterfly wiggles, uses its jaw teeth or it spits an alkaline solution forth to break out of the cocoon. Then the butterfly must wait till its wings dry before it can fly. The change has made it a beautiful creation.

One way we can handle problems is to be more like the caterpillar. We can attach ourselves to God and let Him wrap us in a cocoon of love. Then wait on the Lord and let Him make us into something beautiful. Time, change and effort on our part can cause us to burst forth as a butterfly, a new creature in the Lord.

The Lord often uses time and change to perfect all His creations. God can utilize lakes, rivers, seas and streams as ways to teach us a truth about stagnation versus change. A lake (the Dead Sea) has no source of water flowing into or out of it. It will soon become stagnant and support no source of life. However, if fresh water continually flows in and out of a body of water, it will be a place of cleansing and life can flourish. The Sea of Galilee is like that. We can consciously choose to be like the Dead Sea or the Sea of Galilee.

If we take in the Word of God and receive His blessings but greedily horde it for ourselves, we will become stagnant. We will become unproductive and of little assistance to other people. There will be little fruit for others to feed on. However, if we open our hand and give of what we have been given, it frees up more room for a fresh supply of anointing to flow through us. Fruit can be produced that will feed others. In turn, we will also be refreshed by letting God's power flow into and out of our lives.

Keeping our selves open to the Lord requires that we be ready and able to accept change. Most usually without change there is little growth whether it is in a body of water or in a human life.

A good example of how change can affect nature is the damming of the Colorado River. This body of water snaked its way thirteen hundred miles to the ocean without any seeming benefit to mankind. Then a huge dam blocked the river's current. The dam supplied water to many people. Sometimes we are like the rivers. Our lives don't yield power until we have barriers block our path. God doesn't bring barriers our way but He allows them to help us become more powerful for Him.

## Change Can Produce Barriers

Change can become a definite barrier for people. We can react to it with anxiety, worry or fear. "Worry is a thin stream of fear trickling through the mind. If encouraged, it cuts a channel into which all other thoughts are drained." [20] "For God, hath not given us the spirit of fear, but of power, and of love, and of a sound mind" (2 Timothy 1:7). God doesn't want us to cut a channel of fear that drains us of all power. But he wants to see us cut channels of love that can move the iceberg of fear.

Our lives parallel icebergs floating in arctic oceans. Some icebergs are tiny while others are gigantic. The small ones are subject to surface winds, but the huge ones are carried along by deep ocean currents. Similarly, our lives are subject to the surface winds, everything that is movable. We are also subject to the deep ocean currents, (the sure movement of God's purpose).[21] "We are hard pressed on every side, but not crushed; perplexed, but not in despair." (2 Corinthians 4: 8 NIV). When we trust the Lord, we won't be moved by the surface winds but we will be carried along with the deep currents of God's love and power.

## Ride Out the Turbulence

To feel the mighty working of God's power, we need to learn how to ride out the turbulence that often enters our life. Turbulence always reminds me of airplane travel. When least expected air pockets are hit and the ride becomes rough. What do pilots do to counteract this turbulence? They tell the passengers to fasten their seat belt, and they take the plane up a little higher. They just keep moving up until they move above the storm. When turbulence hits, just move up a little closer to Jesus.

One of the most natural, but turbulent times, humans face is the process of parenting children. We don't prepare and train for it like we do a career. Yet parenting is one of the most important occupations we can perform.

If we listen, God will speak to us through the parenting process. A little baby needs love and constant nurturing till it is old enough to begin to do a few things for itself. When the little tyke is able to do small tasks, the parents try to exercise great self control and let them do all they can for themselves. The same is true in the spiritual sense. The Lord will not do for us what we can do for ourselves.

## Roots and Wings

I've often heard it said, there are two things we need to give children, "Roots and Wings."

A writer gives us 10 commandments for producing good character or "Roots" in children:

1. *Teach them, using God's word.* "Hear, O Israel: The Lord our God is one Lord: And thou shalt love the Lord thy God with all thine heart, and with all thy soul, and with all thy might. And these words, which I command thee this day, shall be in thine heart: And thou shalt teach them diligently unto thy children . . ." (Deuteronomy 6:4- 9).

2. *Tell them what's right and wrong.* ". . . God forbid that I should sin against the Lord in ceasing to pray for you: but I will teach you the good and the right way" (1 Samuel 12:23).

3. *See them as gifts from God.* "Lo, children are a heritage of the Lord: and the fruit of the womb is His reward" (Psalm 127:3).

4. *Guide them in godly ways.* "Train up a child in the way he should go: and when he is old, he will not depart from it" (Proverbs 22:6).

5. *Discipline them.* "Correct thy son, and he shall give thee rest; yea, he shall give delight unto thy soul" (Proverbs 29:17).

6. *Love them unconditionally.* Be like the father with the prodigal son. "And he arose, and came to his father. But, when he was yet a great way off; his father saw him, and had compassion . . . ." (Luke 15:20).

7. *Do not provoke them to wrath.* "And, ye fathers, provoke not your children to wrath: but bring them up in the nurture and admonition of the Lord" (Ephesians 6:4).

8. *Earn their respect by example.* "He must manage his own family well and see that his children obey him with proper respect" (1 Timothy 3:4 NIV).

9. *Provide for their physical needs.* "If anyone does not provide for his relatives, and especially for his immediate family, he has denied the faith and is worse than an unbeliever" (1 Timothy 5:8 NIV).

10. *Pass your faith along to them.* "I have been reminded of your sincere faith, which first lived in your grandmother Lois and in your mother Eunice and, I am persuaded, now lives in you also" (2 Timothy 1:5 NIV).[22]

These, 10 commandments, if utilized by parents (from birth to maturity) can help instill natural and spiritual roots in children. These roots are what anchor a child and help them grow to maturity. It helps them weather the storms of life. They know which way to bend and sway to keep from being broken by situations. The roots we have instilled in our children act like pebbles on a pond. They have a rippling effect and reach out from generation to generation. That's why it is important to send down the right roots.

Roots alone will not cause a child to succeed. They must also don a set of wings. How can we give wings to children? By realizing we have built a firm foundation (the roots). Then we have to encourage the child to try endeavors using their wings of faith. Whether they fall or fail, we pick them up, help them with unconditional love and send them on their way again. Only when we release our children, can we see them soar to new heights. They need roots to know what is right and wings to tackle tasks. These are two things our children need.

Our Heavenly Father speaks to us through the child rearing process and tenderly tells us that he utilizes these same 10 commandments. He tenderly guides and disciplines us through His Word. He provides all our needs and loves us unconditionally. He instills roots in us first, and then he asks us to don our wings, and fly by trusting Him and His Word.

God has adapted us for victorious living in our environment just as He has all other creatures. The animal kingdom lives in harmony within the world God has given them. Because we are of utmost importance to Him, He desires we do the same.

## Everything Beautiful

"He has made everything beautiful in his time . . ." (Ecclesiastes 3:11 NIV). The lush green vegetation, mountains, rivers, seas, skies, birds, beasts and man, speak eloquently of God as our creator. No wonder Jesus used the backdrop of nature to quiet our souls and instruct us about God. We have only to look to the beast, the fowls of the air, to the earth, the fishes of the sea and hear God say, "I love you, enjoy the beauty, take dominion and run my world well. I've given you roots, wings, instinct and wisdom to accomplish my mission."

## CHAPTER 4

# *Insights and Object Lessons*

"If any of you lack wisdom, let him ask of God, that giveth to all men liberally,
and upbraideth not; and it shall be given him"
(James 1:5).

Our Father God is the best source of wisdom because he created the universe by speaking it into existence. He implanted instinct in animal and man. But to people alone, he imparted a self will, a soul and a searching spirit. Man's inner being hungers after wisdom.

Often I seek The Lord for understanding in relationships with family and clients I counsel. It is such a comfort to know, foresight is only a prayer away. Daily I remind myself of a goal to use discernment. "She opens her mouth with wisdom; and in her tongue is the law of kindness." (Proverbs 31:26).

Wisdom is the power of judging rightly and following the soundest course of action, based on knowledge, experience and understanding. Given this description, most of us possess wisdom in varying degrees from time to time. However, we realize our imperfections and try to avoid mistakes by pursuing prudence.

## Society Defines Wisdom

Our society tends to define wisdom through formal education, life experiences and age.

The same philosophy was prevalent in Job's day. His friends tried to apply their understanding to Job's situation but they had no answer. Elihu, a younger man told them why their reasons weren't helpful to Job. He said, our years should teach us wisdom. Great men aren't always wise and our elders don't always understand judgment. He concluded, there is a spirit in man from his creator that gives understanding. (Job 32:7-10).

This friend's opinion was correct. Age and knowledge alone aren't enough to produce good judgments. We must be instructed of the Lord to have true wisdom. God's Word instructs us that the discernment of the world won't stand. ". . . Hath not God made foolish the wisdom of this world? . . . Because the foolishness of God is wiser than men; and the weakness of God is stronger than men" (I Corinthians 1: 20 & 25).

## God's Wisdom

God's Word says that man's understanding can't compare with His wisdom. Yet we know that discernment is important in making right decisions. It behooves us to learn what Godly prudence is. The Lord tells us to not glory in our wisdom but rejoice that we know Him. He is the creator that exercises loving kindness, judgment and righteousness in the earth. (Jeremiah 9: 23-24).

Scripture tells us not to think that our knowledge, power or wealth can sustain us or make us intelligent. It's only in knowing Jesus as Lord of all that we should boast or glory in. "The fear of the Lord is the beginning of wisdom . . ." (Psalm 111:10). God isn't telling us that we are to be afraid of Him, but He is saying to reverence Him. We are to love and respect Our

Maker so much that we will obey His commandments. This is where true godly understanding begins and surpasses man's knowledge.

The Word of God tells us to pursue wisdom. "Wisdom is the principal thing; therefore get wisdom: and with all thy getting get understanding . . . Hear, O my son, and receive my sayings; and the years of thy life shall be many" (Proverbs 4:7-10).

Solomon (a wise king) knew there were many benefits to seeking godly wisdom. He realized that his position and knowledge wouldn't be enough to make right decisions. So he asked God for discernment not riches or power. He wanted to govern the people under him with wisdom and knowledge. (II Chronicles 1:10).

We need to follow Solomon's example and ask for wisdom. "For the Lord giveth wisdom; out of his mouth cometh knowledge and understanding" (Proverbs 2:6).

God imparts His wisdom to us in many ways. I like to refer to these interpretations as insights.

When I speak about insight, it means I have a better understanding about something. It is a penetrating mental vision or discernment, where underlying truths are seen. It is the sudden grasping of a truth or a solution.

Often we can capture some insight on a given situation or problem. We normally understand it with our intellect or head but can't quite get it to our heart.

## Object Lessons

The Lord understands our difficulty in grasping truths. That's why He utilizes object lessons as a way to communicate with us. This instruction is conveyed by means of a material object or practical illustration.

Our Lord is so gracious to us and imparts wisdom by intertwining insights and object lessons. He used the parable of the birds and the lilies to help us understand how we are to live life free from anxiety. We aren't to worry about our life, what we will eat, drink or wear. Our heavenly Father feeds the birds. We are much more important than the fowls of the air. (Matthew 6:25-28 & 30).

If we listen faithfully, we may hear the Lord instruct us with an object lesson as He did Jeremiah. He went to the potter's house and began to watch the craftsman work with the clay. The pot he was making was marred. He reshaped it as it seemed best to him. (Jeremiah 18:1-3).

Often I have observed people working on pottery wheels and saw how they used their hands to smooth and shape an object like a bowl. But since it was a lengthy process I never took time to see it from start to finish until I visited a potter's house in Japan.

When my son, a friend and I walked in, we were warmly greeted by a potter and his wife. As I looked around, I saw many finished items of clay, some of which were Buddhist idols. I felt like running from the place, but I knew God was instructing me to stay, pray and let Him give me insight through this object lesson.

The potter had a huge mound of clay in the center of his work table. He took small pieces and worked them into a teapot, a cup and a bowl. Then he asks me to try my hand at fashioning an object. I chose a tea cup and rice bowl. Neither item I made resembled either item. But the potter encouraged me. He took my work and reshaped it. He moistened it with water when the clay became too dry and reshaped it into a cup.

This scene sounds similar to Jeremiah's experience. ". . . Then the Word of the Lord came to me, saying, 'cannot I do with you as this potter? . . . Behold, as the clay is in the potter's hand, so are ye in mine hand . . .'" (Jeremiah 18: 6).

Neither the potter Jeremiah visited nor the one I visited destroyed the marred vessel of pottery. The potter's reshaped them until they were things of beauty. Our creator has a right to smooth and reshape us until we are a useful earthen vessel. We don't have the wisdom to tell Him how it should be done. Since the potter can reshape me as it seems right, then I need to let Him reshape others, not try to do it myself.

The Lord also instructed that if I would pray for the Japanese craftsman (prayer is the moisture that makes the clay more pliable) He would reshape him according to His will. God can reshape any of us if we will become clay in His hands. To be soft we must become God centered and not self focused. We have to completely yield ourselves to our maker before we can become a vessel of honor in His hands.

Clay naturally yields to the potter's hands. This was demonstrated well by Joe Smith. He presented the "Potters Parable" at the Passion, Play site in Eureka Springs, Arkansas. God spoke many important truths through His Word and this object lesson.

As the potter set the clay upon the wheel he showed us the parallel to our lives. "I waited patiently for the Lord . . . He brought me up also out of an horrible pit, out of the miry clay, and set my feet upon a rock . . ." (Psalm 40:1-2). Just as the clay is set on the rock, we must be established on Jesus.

Until the clay is centered on the potter's wheel, it fights against the maker's hands. At this stage the clay is like us when we are self-centered. As soon as the clay was centered, we saw a rapid change. It no longer fought against the potter's hands.

Then it was ready for the creator to begin shaping it. He pierced the heart of the vessel by putting his hand down the center of it. He worked until the inside (heart) of the vessel became large. This is what God does with us. Then the potter built the vessel up from bottom to top. Only he could see into the vessel. We saw only the outside of the vessel. Man looks at the outward appearance, but the Lord sees the heart. (1 Samuel 16:7).

Before the clay vessel can be used, it must be fired. Without firing the heart would fall apart. The clay vessel is fired in a kiln. It takes a high temperature of about 2400 degrees for as much as twelve hours. Sometimes the vessel gets so hot it appears to begin to melt down. This firing fuses the many tiny particles of clay together. After firing, light reflects on the face of the vessel. It is the same with us, we feel like we are going to melt down when we are going through fiery trials. But after we have been through the fire, we are useful vessels and reflect the light of Jesus on our faces.

The designer made many different vessels from clay. Out of the heart of one vessel all the others were created. Jesus created us out of His heart. He wants us to be like a cup that is poured out and refilled again to serve others.[1]

The potter stressed that the nature of clay is a desire to yield to the hands of its maker. We need to have the same desire to yield to our potter and let him reshape us.

## Construction Site

This process of being reshaped often hurts and takes much time. While we are molded, we may look much like a construction site to others. As I drove by such a place, God utilized it as an object lesson. The place was a mess. There was a half-finished structure with dirt and building supplies scattered around it. At this stage, I could see no beauty in it. The Lord reminded me that this is often the way we view people, His works. We forget who the master carpenter is and that He always completes the work He starts.

## Limp Gloves

So often in this process of construction, we feel inadequate to do what God has instructed us to do. God used a pair of gloves as an object lesson for one woman. The gloves were lying limp and useless - until the woman slipped her hands inside them. At that moment she realized that God didn't want her to think about her limitations. He wanted to put His power into her and work through her, just as her gloves became useful when she put her hands into them.[2] "God is able to do exceedingly abundantly above all we ask or think, according to the power that works in us" (Ephesians 3:20). God's wisdom and power working in us make us useful to Him.

## Pressure Cooker

Sometimes God has to let pressure, and trials descend upon us, so He can make us more useful to Himself. Gay Hyde (a musician) used the metaphor of a pressure cooker. God speaks through the pressure cooker and says, "I get things done more quickly by putting you under pressure." It isn't very pleasant being in a pressure cooker. It's a time when we have to trust His wisdom.

We need to learn to wait on God and seek His wisdom more. His Word tells us to "Be still and know that I am God . . ." (Psalm 46:10). I'm beginning to understand what it might mean to be quiet. It means to quit striving in my own energy to figure out situations or make things happen the way I want them to. We need to release our problems to Our Father and let Him figure them out.

## Letting Go

The Lord used an object lesson to help me understand the necessity of letting go, so He could work. One day I was visiting a woman who was nearly bed bound. She needed to use the bathroom. A nurse aid assisted her to the stool. All was well until the woman was to be transferred from the stool back to her chair. The woman was holding onto a hand rail next to the commode. The aid had both arms around the woman's waist, and asked her to let go of the rail. However, the woman didn't let go because she was afraid of being dropped. Finally the aid said, "I can't help you until you let go." At that moment, her words exploded in my head. God spoke to me! "Let go of the problem with your son. I can't help you until you do. I can't heal the relationship between you both until you let me have him. Let go of the un-forgiveness, the old hurts and let me work in your lives. My way is better than yours. Give your son time and space so I can do it my way."

Our maker doesn't ask us to let go (trust him) unless He has us (or the situation) in His hands. That was a very powerful object lesson. I could choose to believe Him or try to change it myself.

Author and speaker, Joyce Meyer, relates we can either believe God to produce change, or try to achieve it ourselves. We can be a believer or an achiever. Both God and we can't be in control. We must determine who is going to be the one doing the work. Whose job is it to be the master carpenter? If I am honest with myself, I will determine it is God's job. I know He can do a much better job than I can. So what is our job? Jesus tells us, "The work of God is this: to believe in the one he has sent" (John 6:29, NIV). Our job is simply, to believe. Meyer asks this piercing question. "Will I be a believer and let God do the work, or will I be an achiever by trying to be in control myself?"[3]

Trying to be in control ourselves is like pushing something versus pulling it. If we let God be in control, it is more like pulling an object. U.S. Army General, President Dwight D. Eisenhower often used the concept of pulling and pushing to demonstrate the art of leadership in a simple, but powerful way. He would lay a string on a table and say, "Pull it, and it follows wherever you want it to go. But push it and it goes nowhere"[4]

This principle of leadership applies to the home, church, and business place. Leadership that pull's, leads by example with democracy and respect for others. Leadership that pushes is autocratic and demanding. All people deserve to be listened to and treated fairly. Through this object lesson, God tells us to use our authority to pull the string of leadership in a respectful, democratic way. Then we will have His pulling power in our lives instead of our pushing control which causes conflict.

## Authority for Battles

There will be many battles we have to fight. We can be successful when we fight them in the name of the Lord. The Lord brought this insight to mind one day when I was making a business call. I didn't get results when I used my name, but when I utilized the name of the company I worked for, I quickly had what I needed. Just as there is much authority in a business name, there is all authority in Jesus name. Using the Lord's name is one way we can fight battles.

## Christian Soldier's Armor

Another way to win conflicts is to put on the armor of the Lord. We are to go out dressed for war like scripture instructs us to in Ephesians 6:13-18.

The Lord has given insights to many people through the object lesson of the Christian soldier's armor.

The Christian's, *Girdle of Truth* is put on by believing and obeying God's Word, making it part of our lifestyle. The girdle is like an undergarment we put on to make the breastplate fit better. If we don't believe and practice God's Word, it is like trying to wear the breastplate without the foundation garment of the girdle.

The old medieval armor had a breastplate to cover the vital organs of the body from the front. There was no protection for the back. Why? The foot soldier was never to turn his back to the enemy.

The Christian's *Breastplate* is the "Righteousness of God." Because of what Jesus did on Calvary, we can stand righteous before God. The King's children have availability to all the power vested in the name of Jesus and the blood of Calvary.

God never intended us to turn our back to Satan and run from him. God meant for us to stand our ground and face Satan head on. Let Satan do the fleeing. As we go in the strength of The Lord, we take possession of Satan's territory for God.

Next we must put on shoes. The *Shoes* of the Christian armor are the "Preparation of the Gospel of Peace." If we don't walk in peace, it's like walking without shoes. Our feet are vulnerable to thorns, stones, and many elements that could cause injury. Then our feet would become sore and infected. This greatly limits our mobility and leaves us prey to elements that could endanger our lives. No soldier would march without military boots. Neither can a Christian expect to be totally militant without shoes of peace to wear.

If we neglect reading, and meditating on God's word, we will have little peace or spiritual nourishment. This leaves us vulnerable to Satan's attacks.

Without the proper elements of physical nourishment, our bodies can become lean, weak, emaciated and even die. So without regular nourishment from God's Word, our souls can wither away. We must cover our feet with the preparation of the Gospel of peace.

Our *Shield of Faith* is held by a handle on the back of it. We can take up the shield to ward off the fiery darts of doubt and fear. We need to keep the shield of faith between us and Satan's attacks by reaffirming our trust in God. We need to constantly remember that, "Greater is He that is in me - than he that is in the world" (1 John 4:4). Satan is already a defeated foe. He was overcome at Calvary.

The Christian puts the *Helmet of Salvation* on his head. When our minds are guarded by the Holy Spirit and self discipline, our helmet of salvation will keep the darts of Satan from penetrating. We will be able to take captive our thoughts and make them obedient to Jesus. This enables us to think wholesome, edifying thoughts of faith.

The *Sword of the Spirit* is God's word that we have hidden in our hearts. It can literally slay Satan's power as the Holy Spirit brings the word to our conscious minds. We can wield the sword of the spirit by quoting God's word as we come against Satan in Jesus' name. Just as Jesus used God's word against Satan in the wilderness, we can use it in the same manner daily. We must pray in the spirit at all times for all people. This provides protection for our brothers' and sisters' backs which aren't covered by any armor.

Put on the whole armor. Stand firm, holding territory we have gained. Move forward into battle as stalwart soldiers. Be confident that victory awaits us when we are obedient.[5]

## Missing the Mark

There will be some battles we won't win. Often it's because of disobedience, not hearing God or not wearing our armor correctly. If we fall in battle; we miss the mark. We can go back to the Father and repent.

Often I have missed the mark. On one occasion, I asked God where I missed it and He showed me. Then I ask Him why did I miss it - was I in the flesh? And he said, "Yes for a moment, you took your eyes off me and looked to the natural. But it's never too late to go back to where you missed it, and in faith, try again."

Then God showed me that missing it is part of learning to walk. He took me back to the joy I experienced when my children were babies and learned to walk. They had to fall, to learn to walk. If I'd never let my children fall, they and I would have missed the joy of them learning to walk.

I knew those little faltering feet would one day not only walk, but also run. Our Father God has faith in us and knows that we are trying hard to imitate Him. We learn to walk in love and exhibit all the fruits of the spirit. His heart is filled with joy when He sees us trying.

Even when we fall, He is pleased that we are trying. He regards it as a natural growth process. God lets us learn by missing it and getting up and trying once again to walk to His outstretched arms. All the time, He's encouraging us just as a proud parent encourages their babe to come - "Walk to momma, walk to daddy."

What do we get when we walk to daddy (God) - a big hug? Our Father, envelope's us with His love and we're encouraged and go out and try it again. We know His love, encouragement and arms are at the end of our walk.

We can look at those times when we fall. We remember we need not feel despondent, but instead repent. View it with joy and say, "I'm learning to walk to daddy's outstretched arms."

Walking and falling is part of our growth. "Rejoice not against me, O mine enemy: when I fall, I shall arise . . ." (Micah 7:8). Repentance causes us to arise and grow in wisdom.

## Move On

There were many times I sought God's wisdom. He spoke through life experiences. One of the objects He used was a three story slide. After getting to the top of the slide, I was scared. I wanted to turn around and come back down. But that wasn't feasible, there were others behind me. I said I couldn't go down the slide. I argued with the man behind me.

Eventually, he pushed me. I had a hilarious ride to the bottom. It was so much fun. I climbed up the slide and did it again.

In life we must keep moving or we will block the path. Then no one else will be able to move and we all become stagnate. My stopping would hinder other people and slow their growth. This was an important truth from the Lord.

Faced with a decision, I wanted to stay where it was comfortable. I didn't want to move on. I had been involved in a good Bible study group. Then I returned to work. I knew I would no longer be able to attend the group. At this point, the Lord showed me, "You've had a time of sitting at my feet and learning, a time of being schooled. Now I want you to go out and put what you've learned to use to help others." I didn't want to keep someone else from growing. Nor did I want to grieve the Holy Spirit.

## Jump Rope Lesson

As I sought God, and His wisdom, He faithfully instructed me through object lessons. As the jump rope was untangled, the Lord spoke to me. "This thick cord symbolizes a person's life. The knots and tangles in the rope are like fear. It can become so tangled that it is of no use." Our lives are the same way. Let them become knotted up with fear and we are ineffective. We can't do anything for ourselves or the Lord. The Apostle Paul tells us, "For God hath not given us the spirit of fear; but of power, and of love, and of a sound mind" (2 Timothy 1:7).

When we get the knots out of the jump rope (our life) it releases the power. Then we can use this cord the way it was intended. When the Lord gets the fear out, He can use us in a more productive way. Jesus desires to rid us of things that are hindering us.

## Weighty Back Packs

God utilized a back pack as another object lesson. I returned to college after being in the work force for twenty five years. I lugged my books in a back pack like all the younger students. Strapping it on my back, I took off. Suddenly, I realized it was too heavy. And I began to think, I need to lighten my load.

The Lord spoke to me. "Will you let me take the fear, selfishness, and un-forgiveness out of your life? You won't have to pack around that stuff."

As I experimented with the back pack and took out things I didn't need, I ask the Lord to work on me. I begged Him to take everything out of my back pack (life) that was hindering Him from using me. Maybe one day, I could take the whole pack off and toss it. Then I wouldn't have to carry any excess baggage.

## Warnings and Blind Spots

I carried a lot of extra weight with me while commuting by automobile to and from school. The Lord used several rules of the road to minister insight to me. When we come to the yellow light, instead of trying to beat it, we need to heed it. The amber light is a warning to us. We know there will soon be a stop light. God was telling me, "When there are yellow lights in your life, which I or others point out to you, stop! Don't wait until it gets worse. Take care of things right now."

He also reminded me, when we are driving we have blind spots. We can't always see everything, even though we use mirrors. In the spiritual realm, our mirrors are the Word of God, prayer and other people's instructions that line up with His Word. It behooves us to heed the instructions. The Word of God says "A wise son heareth his father's instruction: but a scorner heareth not rebuke" (Proverbs 12:1).

Others see our mistakes before we do because they can see us from every angle. We can only see ourselves from the front. We can't see ourselves from the side or back. It is important to heed constructive criticism, especially when you know it is based on the Word of God.

When we see other people coming to that warning light, and they don't stop, we need to sound the alarm. If we say nothing, they may not see their errors. If the truth is spoken with love, we receive wise counsel. We can correct the situation.

## No Perfection Here

The Lord continually used insights and object lessons to counsel and instruct me. One day while making my bed, I saw a teddy bear sitting on the headboard of the bed. The cuddly stuffed animal looked strange because she was missing one of her eyelashes. Evidently it had fallen off in a recent household move. I grabbed for the teddy bear. I was prepared to pull off her other eyelash, so that she would look right again. But the

Lord stopped me. He said, "No, don't touch that teddy bear. I want you to remember, just as that stuffed object isn't perfect (with one eyelash missing), neither are you perfect." "I said Lord, you're right. I'm not perfect. None of us are." But we can grow more whole through listening to God and doing what He instructs us to do.

## The Battered Bride

If we heed wise counsel, we can get some of the snags, tears, and wrinkles out of our lives. God is calling us (His church) to be a spotless, wrinkle free, bride. (Ephesians 5:27).

That reminds me of a story about a battered bride. Her hair was disheveled. She had a black eye and limped down the aisle, with one shoe on and one shoe off. Dirt covered her dress. It was torn and wrinkled because she was beat up, before she arrived at the church. There was nothing of beauty in the battered bride to bring to the bridegroom. But, there is much elegance in a well dressed bride. The Lord desires us to be spotless and wrinkle free.

But today, we often resemble the battered bride more than we do a clean pressed one. In effect, Satan has batter us with sin.

The bride's garments are coming apart. When sin rips our garments apart at the seams, we need to mend them with prayer and forgiveness. When we do this the rip won't get any bigger. We can mend it and the garment will be good and useable again.

Washing (repentance) takes all the stain and the dirt off the bride's clothing. "If we confess our sins, he is faithful and just to forgive us our sins, and to cleanse us from all unrighteousness" (1 John 1:9).

## Grace Gets the Wrinkles Out

But what do we need to do to get the wrinkles out? The Lord reminded me about ironing clothes. First, we need a steam iron filled with water. Then we must turn on the heat. The water and the heat combined, and applied to the cloth takes out the wrinkles. The right amount of heat is often our trials and problems. The water is our tears, life and prayers of gratitude. When the two are mixed, it lets God's grace flow. At this point we have put the Lord in control. Steam is His grace. That is what gets out the wrinkles.

We all know that cold water doesn't take out wrinkles. Cold water is ingratitude, bitterness, questioning. When we do that we usually turn away. We are left with some of the wrinkles in our garment. We know the Word says that Christ's bride is to be without spot or wrinkle. So we need to let gratitude come forth in the midst of our trials and see God's grace smooth out the wrinkles in our life.

When we are obedient and let the Lord work on the imperfections in our life, we grow stronger. If we don't let the Lord work, then the joy and the light often goes out of our life.

## Prepare Your Lamp

That's much like a lamp that hasn't been properly prepared. Matthew 25:1-13, tells us the parable of the ten virgins. Five of the young ladies had oil in their lamps and the other five didn't. When the cry went out that the bridegroom was coming, the ten virgins trimmed their lamps. But the five foolish ones had no oil. They ask to borrow oil from the wise ones. But, they refused to give oil to the foolish virgins because they had nothing extra.

As I think of that parable, the Lord reminded me of a message shared from a Bible Study group. Picture an old-fashioned kerosene lamp. It has a globe, a base, a wick, and in order for it to burn it must have oil.

The teacher instructed us that the globe is our heart. It must be clean for people to see the light of God. To keep the globe clean we must walk in repentance. A dirty globe reflects little light. It indicates there is bias, judgments or resentment. The light inside can't be seen for what it is. This globe must be transparent. "Keep thy heart with all diligence; for out of it are the issues of life" (Proverbs 4:23). The globe is a protection or guard for the wick. We need to watch what goes in and comes out of our heart. God is our hedge, just like the globe is a protection around the wick.

The lamp can't burn without fluid. Oil is the Word of God. The fuel is poured into the base of the lamp. That base is our mind. Out of the base comes the wick. It becomes saturated with oil.

The wick represents prayer. Godly communication helps the oil flow up from the base. The flame that burns from the wick is the spirit, or fire of God which produces light.[6]

75

As a child on a farm, I used a lamp daily. We had to trim the wick often to keep the globe from becoming sooty. So, in a spiritual sense, we must let our wicks be trimmed. The trimming of that wick is the purging by God. That's often painful and difficult. It is essential if we are going to be a vessel that shows forth God's light to a dark world.

Author F. B. Meyer states, "It is not for you to ignite the flame, to supply the oil, or trim the wick. Your simple duty is to guard against anything that may obstruct the outshining of the light of God from your soul. See to it that everything that might hinder the effect of your testimony and mar your influence is put away. Christ will see to it that your light will achieve the full measure of His purpose." [7]

It requires faith in our master, to allow Him to purge us at will. God's wisdom helps us burn bright. It assists us to make the right choices in difficult situations. We are to be a guiding light to others. Lord, make me a light house. Help me burn bright and be a witness to others.

## Swim for Your Healing

I knew I needed healing before I could be an effective witness. So I asked the Lord to restore me physically and take all the baggage out of my life. Then God said, "You will swim for your healing." I retorted, "Lord, I don't know how to swim." He instructed me, "You can learn." I responded "Okay Lord, then you will have to teach me." That took a lot of faith for me because I was over forty years-old. I'd never learned to swim as a child because I was deathly afraid of deep water. So I said, "Lord, take my fear away and teach me to swim."

God used swimming as an object lesson and taught me many things. First the Lord instructed me that I needed to have someone teach me to swim. During the swimming instructions, I learned the importance of going with the flow. It was important to relax and not fight the water. It lifted and buoyed me up. It took a certain amount of rhythm to move my arms, legs and to breathe at the same time.

Through this, the Lord showed me there needs to be balance in all areas of life. Stability is so important. If there is no rhythm, you are struggling. The water can't freely carry you along. Many times while swimming, I lost my rhythm and took in a mouthful of water. The Lord showed that is similar to falling, being disobedience or sinning. We must immediately recognize the sin and get it out of our lives. That is much like getting a mouthful of water; spitting it out and going on; and not letting it sink you.

After swimming for a few months, the Lord instructed me again. One day I came to the deep end of a twelve-foot pool. The Lord said to me, "Things are different now. You are able to swim without tensing up like you are afraid." I responded, "Well, I know I can swim; I've been in deep water before." And the Lord said, "Yes, in the natural you have been in many difficult situations. This situation you are going through is no different. You know how to swim. You know what to do. Do it." So I took that insight about swimming in deep waters and looked at it carefully.

Yes, spiritually, I knew what I needed to do. It was to have faith and put my trust in God. He would buoy me up. His spiritual laws are like the natural laws. If I was relaxed and used what I knew, I could glide through the water and not sink. Yes, I'd be able to swim no matter how deep the water was. I just needed to totally put my faith in God's spiritual laws. I needed to realize the financial and job problems were beyond my control. It was only by relaxing in the Lord and letting Him buoy me up, that I would be able to swim in any and all deep waters of life.

## Ride the Waves

A vacation to Myrtle Beach, SC, was used by the Lord as an object lesson. My husband and I enjoyed the walks on the beach and watching kids and families in the water riding the waves. Finally, we got brave enough, and went into the ocean. We tried to ride the waves or let them crash on us. It was fun and there was a metaphor from the waves. Waves always come in sets of two or three. That's the way loss, and problems hit us.

My husband was standing sideways letting the waves hit him and ready to catch me if I fell. I was facing the waves straight on. I almost got knocked off my feet several times, but my husband didn't. It was then I felt the Lord say to me, turn a little to the side. Not too much, because you still need to see the waves as they come at you. When I turned just a little to the side, I was able to withstand the waves nicely and really enjoyed it.

The Lord shared an analogy, problems or losses will come at you like the sets of waves. You need to see them coming so you can be prepared.

When you face the waves, head on it's like trying to do it in your own strength. But when you turn to the side you are aware of your surroundings while still looking to me, your rock, and to your support system, family and friends. When you are looking to me, the waves will not knock you off your feet. You will have a sense of joy, accomplishment and victory.

## Insights

God imparts wisdom to us not only through object lessons but through insight, deeper understanding into what His Word means. The Bible is powerful and discerns the motives of the heart even before we do. (Hebrews 4:12). It goes to the very core of the matter.

## Build My House

One morning while having a quiet time, I read "My house remains a ruin while you build yours" (Haggai 1:9). He was saying, "When you are doing your work and business; you are building your own house. But when you take time for me, and my work, you are building my residence. Trust me, if you will put me first by reading the Word and praying each morning, I will order the steps of your day; so you accomplish the necessary tasks. To do my work means to be flexible enough to give up your schedule, will, control and let me have my way with your day."

I said, "Okay Lord, I'm going to try it." I began to practice this, especially on my days off. When I had so many things to do, it seemed impossible to accomplish them all. I said, Lord, I don't have time to spend thirty minutes, an hour or maybe more in prayer and the Word. I've got so much I need to do. I don't need to just go through the motions, but I want to do it out of love. You need to get honor and glory out of it. So, I'm going to ask you to order my day.

## Prove the Lord

I began to prove the Lord by putting him first. I gave Him my best time early each morning. I read the Word and prayed. When I did that, I noticed God ordered my day well. He would arrange parking places right in front of buildings where I needed to stop and take care of errands. He directed me to the right places, at the right time. I didn't have to wait in the Post Office. The people God wanted me to talk to were brought across my path. I was able to spend time ministering to them and still get the things done I needed to do. The Lord showed me that when I spent time with Him, His efficiency flowed through me.

Many times when I felt overwhelmed with numerous tasks, I would say, "Lord, you promised me that if I would put you first, as a part of building your house instead of building mine, I would get done what I need to do. Now Lord, I've given you the best of my time this morning, I ask you to bless the day and help me accomplish those things I absolutely need to get done." Not once has that failed to happen. The Lord has prospered or multiplied my time. His work is much more important than mine.

## Children Trust

Another important insight God imparted was, we need to become as little children. Jesus called the little children to Him, and told the crowd that unless we become as little children, we wouldn't make heaven our home. (Matthew 18: 2-3).

Children are usually very humble and dependent. They trust us even when we unintentionally hurt them. They are able to forgive easily and trust again. The Lord spoke, "That is the way I want you to be. I want you to become childlike so I can work in your life."

The Lord instructed me with more insight from a story. A little boy said, "Salt is what spoils potatoes when it is left out." Salt is like gratitude. When thankfulness is left out it spoils life.[8] Children have a spirit of gratitude. They often give a spontaneous hug, thanks and are off playing again. The little boy in the story spoke his mind without covering up his feelings. This is the way the Lord wants us to be. He desires we be honest and truthful.

Children usually trust their parents that everything is going to be all right. We need that childlike faith so we can trust our Father God.

A story is told of two young boys who lived by a dense forest. One day they wandered away. As evening came the boys became confused and got lost. When the youngsters didn't return, their parents frantically searched for them. The parents found the boys the next day. Very much relieved the mother and dad asked the boys what they did when they realized they were lost in the woods. The older boy replied, "When it got dark, I knelt down and asked God to take care of Jimmy and me. Then we went to sleep."[9]

This is a beautiful example of a child's strong faith and trust. When we can simply ask the Lord for help and then leave it in His hands, we can go through the darkest night. This is possible because, "He that keepeth thee will not slumber . . ." (Psalm 121:3). Childlike faith and complete trust helps us to take God at His Word. When we become like children turning our hearts to the Lord, and trusting, we will be ready for revival.

## Steps to Revival

This insight on renewal was given to my mother through reading of Scripture. The Lord wants us to turn our hearts to Him.

Our Father says, "Therefore now turn ye even unto me with all your heart, and with fasting, weeping, and mourning. And rend your heart . . . Blow the trumpet in Zion, sanctify a fast, call a solemn assembly: Gather the people, sanctify the congregation . . ." (Joel 2:12- 13 & 15).

Turning to the Lord with our hearts, fasting, praying and mourning signifies Godly sorrow. Rendering our hearts signifies ripping away sinful desires and habits, rebellion, and self will.

Gathering the people (unity) and sanctifying the congregation shows a need to pray for forgiveness and cleansing of our souls and lives. Three crucial ingredients for revival are prayer, unity and brokenness or repentance.

Restitution is part of repenting. If we are truly sorrowful, we need to restore relationships, ask forgiveness and forgive others. This is like preparing the soil for planting. We eradicate weeds and break up the soil. Then the newly planted seeds can send out their tender roots and gather the nourishment needed for optimum growth and an abundant harvest.

Now that the seed is sown, we need to water the seed with our prayers and praise. "Rejoice in the Lord", Joel says in verse 23. "And I will restore to you the years that the locust hath eaten" (Joel 2:25). We will be plentifully fed, be satisfied in God and praise Him for dealing wondrously with us.

We will know that He is present with us and that He is our God, our supplier, and our keeper. We will not be ashamed because of our allegiance to Him and our dependence upon Him.

"And it shall come to pass afterward, that I will pour out my spirit upon all flesh: and your sons and your daughters shall prophesy . . ." (Joel 2:28). God will pour out His Spirit upon all of His children, showing wonders and signs through our lives. He will glorify Himself in us, and edify the entire body of Christ. Then we will have renewal. Revival is always preceded by prayer, unity and brokenness, a desire to be Christ like.[10]

## God is Light, Mass and Energy

My desire is to be more Christ like. But before that happens, I must know Him. An insight helped my understanding of God.

Shirley Boone shared an insight on *Richard Roberts Live Television Show*. This analogy was given to her daughter Cherry. She had gone to a synagogue with a Jewish friend. When she returned, her peer said, "I can understand how you say we worship the same God - the God of Abraham, Isaac, and Jacob. I can even understand why you think that Jesus is the Messiah. But I can't understand your worshiping three Gods -God the Father, God the Son, and God the Holy Spirit. The Scriptures say, "The Lord our God is one Lord" (Deuteronomy 6:4). Cherry, only fourteen at the time, told her friend, to remember what they had studied in science class. "Everything in all of creation is made out of light, mass and energy, and one cannot function without the other." Cherry went on to explain, that's the way God is. God the Father is the Source of all light (truth), Jesus was the mass form, and the Holy Spirit is the energy form. They're all one, interrelated. Cherry stated to her mother, "I know God gave that revelation to me."

This insight has really helped me understand God better. It also shows me that God and science can't be separated. Light travels fast, and is everywhere, just like God. Mass comes from light, just as Jesus came from the Father. (John 3:16)

Light also comes from mass just as God could be seen in Jesus. Christ is the mass form. Mass can be converted to energy. Jesus went to heaven and sent us the Holy Spirit. The Comforter is the Holy Spirit or the energy.

By looking at scientific principles explained to me by my son, I saw how Cherry's insight was backed by the Word of God. If we need wisdom as Cherry did to answer her friend, we need only ask of the Lord.

## Three in One

I needed wisdom to answer a question posed to me. Is God three in one (trinity), or is He Jesus only? I wrestled with this question before the Lord. I believed God was the Father, the Son (Jesus) and the Holy Spirit. But I wanted to make sure I had the truth and that it had me.

I sought the Lord for the truth. He was faithful and instructed with His wisdom and insights. "Then God said, 'Let Us make man in Our image, according to Our likeness . . .'" (Genesis 1:26, NAS). We are made in God's image with a spirit, body and mind. We are three parts in one body. Then God is three in one. God is the spirit, Jesus is the body, and the Holy Spirit is the mind or conscience.

The reason Jesus always prayed to God was so the Spirit could control the flesh. "Do you not believe that I am in the Father, and the Father is in Me? . . ." (John 14:10, NAS).

The Father was in Jesus and worked through Him. During Jesus ministry on earth, people saw His body, not His spirit or mind. Therefore, Jesus is the central figure. His body redeemed us. That is why His name is above all names. "God exalted Him (Jesus) and bestowed upon Him the name which is above every name, that at the name of Jesus every knee should bow . . . and that every tongue should confess that Jesus Christ is Lord, to the glory of God the Father" (Philippians 2:9-11, NAS).

## God's Creations Have Three Parts

The Father continued to instruct me through insight that all of His creations are made with three parts. Our earth is made of sea, sky and land. Time has three parts, past, present and future. If we break time down further, we have years, months and days. We refer to the day as morning, noon and night. Within our days we have hours, minutes and seconds.

God has given us time to use for Him in work, sleep and play. He has created food for us to eat but we must grow it. The growing of plants requires a time of planting, cultivating and reaping. The plants we reap are made up of leaves, stem and root system.

Everything God made has three parts. Our lives and every phase of our lives have a beginning, middle and an ending. God has created great balance and reason in all He made. I am thankful for His discernment through insight.

True understanding comes only from the Lord. We must let him speak to us through His Word, prayers, insights, and object lessons. We must be sensitive to listen to every way God communicates with us.

Wisdom after all, is knowledge of what is true or right, coupled with just judgment and correct actions. It is our learning. The reason of the world will not help us to swim in deep waters. It's only the prudence of the Lord that will cause us to be victorious, to be able to plunge out in faith into that water that is over our heads. "The fear of the Lord is the beginning of wisdom . . ." (Psalm 111:10).

CHAPTER 5

# *Situations or Events*

"For I know the plans I have for you, declared the Lord, plans to prosper you
and not to harm you, plans to give you a hope and a future"
(Jeremiah 29:11, NIV).

God often talks to us through situations or events in our lives. If we will
be sensitive to listen, we can discern His voice and know His plan for our
lives. God's greatest design for us began when He sent Christ to earth
to live.

## God's Plan for Jesus

God's plan for Jesus' life was fulfilled in His earthly ministry, on the
cross, in the tomb and the resurrection. He recognized God's plan for His
life. Christ said, "I glorified Thee on the earth, having accomplished the
work which Thou hast given me to do" (John 17:4 NAS).

In the Garden of Gethsemane Jesus wrestled with and submitted to God's directives for His life and death. "My soul is deeply grieved, to the point of death . . . My Father, if it is possible, let this cup pass from Me, yet not as I will, but as Thou wilt" (Matthew 26:38 & 39 NAS). Jesus went to the cross and proclaimed, "It is finished" (John 19:30 NAS). The Lord had accomplished all He needed to do for our salvation. His death and resurrection gave us victory over sin, death and hell. (Revelation 1:17 – 18)

## Abraham's Call

Just as God had a mission for Jesus, he also has plans for all people who have lived or will live. There was a design for Abraham's life. The Father asked Abraham to leave his family and promised He would bless him. He promised that through Abraham's life all families of earth would be blessed. (Genesis 12:1-3).

Abraham questioned when he had no children. "And Abram said, behold, to me thou hast given no seed . . . And God . . . said, look now toward heaven, and tell the stars if thou be able to number them: and he said unto him, so shall thy seed be . . ." (Genesis15:3 & 5). God's blueprints for Abraham's life were fulfilled and he became the father of the Israelites.

## Joseph's Rescue

The Heavenly Father continued His plan for Abraham's seed through Joseph. He was sold into slavery by his brothers. Then during the famine, his siblings meet him again but didn't know who he was. He invited them to come near and explained that God sent him before them, to help preserve life. And now he had been made a ruler in the land of Egypt. (Genesis 45: 4-6&8). The Almighty's plan for Joseph's life was fulfilled. He was used to rescue the Israelites from a famine that ravaged the land.

## Moses a Leader

God again continued His plan for the Israelites through Moses. "Come now therefore, and I will send thee unto Pharaoh, that thou mayest bring my people the children of Israel out of Egypt." (Exodus 3:10). Even though Moses was afraid, he listened to God through the events of his life. Therefore, the Lord was able to use him as a leader to deliver the Israelites from slavery in Egypt. Some of the situations these great men of God faced looked impossible. So they listened for their maker to reveal Himself and His way. God turned the events into good and His plans were fulfilled.

The Lord always has a design for our lives, even though we can't see how it can possibly work. It was very difficult for Abraham, Joseph, Moses and many other servants of the Lord to comprehend how His promises would be fulfilled.

## Abraham Tries to Help God

We want to be in control of our lives and make things happen. The Lord reminded me in Genesis when he promised Abraham a son. Many years went by and there was no son. Abraham decided he needed to help his Creator. He and his wife, Sarah, took the situation into their own hands. Sarah offered her handmaid to her husband. He slept with her and the maid bore him a male child. (Genesis 16:1-4)

The Lord instructed Abraham this wasn't the way His promise was to be fulfilled. God's plan was for Sarah to bear a child. "And the Lord visited Sarah as He had said, and the Lord did unto Sarah as He had spoken. For Sarah conceived, and bare Abraham a son in his old age . . ." (Genesis 21:1-2).

The Lord spoke through Abraham's life. We must remember not to get ahead of God's plans. We need to let Him be in control, because He does know best.

## Road Blocks

Other examples, from the Word of God, have been very powerful and instructed me. The Bible story of Balaam and his donkey was one of those. Numbers 22 tells us that Balaam had been conferring with the Moabite Princes and they wanted him to return with them. Balaam had refused. Then he prayed about it and went to sleep. "That night God came to Balaam and said, 'Since these men have come to summon you, go with them, but do only what I tell you'" (Numbers 22:20).

The next morning Balaam got up, mounted his donkey and rode out with the men. As they went along the road, an angel of the Lord stood in the path. The donkey wouldn't go forward. That happened three times. Finally Balaam beat his donkey. Then the Lord opened Balaam's eyes and showed him, "And the ass saw me, and turned from me these three times:

unless she had turned from me, surely now also I had slain thee, and saved her alive" (Numbers 22:33).

Just as there was a road block in Balaam's way, the Lord may allow a blockage to enter our lives. The hindrance is put there to keep us from going down that particular path. Often the Lord is saying, "I want you to turn around and go down another path." This is one of the ways he guides us. It is simply by letting situations arise in our lives that we don't understand or we have no control over.

## Parable of the Mule

A perfect example of a situation with no control was, the "Parable of the mule." A story is told of a farmer who owned an old mule. The mule fell into the farmer's well. The farmer heard the mule 'praying' or whatever mules do when they fall into wells. After carefully assessing the situation, the farmer sympathized with the mule, but decided that neither the mule nor the well was worth the trouble of saving.

Instead, he called his neighbors together, told them what had happened . . . and enlisted them to help haul dirt to bury the old mule in the well and put him out of his misery.

Initially, the old mule was hysterical! But as the farmer and his neighbors continued shoveling and the dirt hit his back . . . a thought struck him. It suddenly dawned on him that every time a shovel load of dirt landed on his back . . . He would shake it off and step up! This he did, blow after blow. "Shake it off and step up . . . shake it off and step up!" He repeated to encourage himself. No matter how painful the blows were, or how distressing the situation seemed the old mule fought "panic" and just kept right on shaking it off and stepping up! It wasn't long before the old mule, battered and exhausted, Stepped triumphantly over the wall of that well! What seemed like it would bury him actually helped him . . . all because of the manner in which he handled his adversity.

That's Life! If we face our problems and respond to them positively, and refuse to give into panic, bitterness, or self-pity . . . The adversity that comes along to bury us usually have within them the very real potential to benefit us!

## God's Way works for Good

That's the Lord's way to use all situations to benefit Him and us. "And we know that all things work together for good to them that love God . . ." (Romans 8:28). When I don't see how it could work out for good, I seek God and say, "God I love you and you said it would work for good in my life. Please help me see the good and walk in it." It's then we need to seek Him and say, "Lord what is your plan for my life." He is the only one who can see the overall picture of how our whole life is to fit together from start to finish. We see only one small piece of the puzzle.

Sometimes we aren't sure where that little piece fits. It's not until we have gone down several paths that we are able to look back and see how part of the puzzle is fitting together. We need the Lord's wisdom to be able to make good choices and go down the right paths. It's so important to let the Lord instruct us because we can't see very far down the path. We need to let our steps be ordered by the Lord. (Psalms 37:23).

## Near Hopeless Situations

Even though our steps are ordered by the Lord, there will be times we find ourselves in bad or near hopeless situations. When I think about desperate events, I think about God's beautiful example of Shadrach, Meshach and Abednego. Daniel 3 tells us how the three young princes of Judah faced a despairing time. King Nebuchadnezzar decreed that they had to bow down and worship the image of gold or they would be thrown into a fiery furnace. They knew they would be dead if they didn't fall down and worship the idol. But they decreed they would not compromise. They would not bow down! They said, "If we are thrown into the blazing furnace, the God we serve is able to save us from it . . . But even if he does not, we want you to know, O King, that we will not serve your Gods or worship the image of gold you have set up" (Daniel 3:17-18 NIV).

The three men held firm to their convictions because they knew The Lord had a plan for their lives, and no situation was hopeless. They determined not to worship the idol, and they were thrown into the fiery furnace. However, that wasn't the end of the story. God delivered them. He walked among them and with them in the fire and delivered them. They came out of the fire without the smell of smoke or without a hair on their heads being burned. Because of this miracle the King gave praise to the

God of Shadrach, Meshach and Abednego. He decreed and commanded that, "No other God could save in this way" (Daniel 3:29 NIV).

They trusted the Lord and became mighty witnesses. It's a very good example of how a hopeless situation turned around for good.

## Big Picture Veiled

When God is in control, we don't have to see the big picture, but we wish we could. We just need to be obedient and let Him unfold His plan for our life, one step at a time.

There's been many times in my life when I've heard a word from the Lord. When I stepped out in obedience to do the task, it defied common sense. It seemed the road was blocked like Balaam's path was.

As a young child I wanted to someday go to college and be involved in Christian work or ministry. Those feelings and thoughts stayed with me. However, if I had my way, my life might have been different or a disaster.

I'm so thankful God had the complete puzzle of my life in front of Him and knew which way I should go. He guided me through many situations. Each event was a stepping stone to the next one. Each dilemma was an opportunity for me to hear Him speak.

At age five, I asked Jesus into my heart. I understood little of His plan for my life. I remember praying and feeling so good deep within my soul.

## Double Tragedy

Weeks later, double tragedy ripped that feeling of goodness and my childhood innocence away. A five-year old playmate was killed when her grandfather accidently hit her while backing out of his driveway. I didn't understand about my friend's death, and wondered if the same thing could happen to me.

Shortly after my friend was killed, another tragedy struck. My older sister, a younger sister and I were left alone to nap, while our farm parents pursued other tasks. Instead of napping on a day in late August, we made mud pies. While attempting to cook the pies, the house caught on fire. Fire fighters weren't able to respond in time because we lived 23 miles from the city. My mom and dad, with help from two gas well workers, tried to put the fire out. They couldn't retrieve material possessions from our burning home. Both endeavors were to no avail. Our house and possessions were soon mere ash. The only things saved from the fire were a Bible, wash hanging on the clothes line, and equipment stored in the farm buildings.

Night was falling fast, as the embers of the fire began to die out. A question plagued us, where would we sleep? A neighbor came to our rescue. My dad drove my mother and us children to the neighbor's house. We stayed the night, sleeping on the floor. My dad returned to our farm where he kept watch to ensure the hot ashes didn't reignite and set another building ablaze.

The next morning we returned to our farm. One of the first questions my older sister and I had was, "What happened to our monkey coin bank?" Our dad sadly told us that everything had been destroyed. He cautioned us not to touch any of the ashes because they could still be warm.

He understood our need to find the bank. He gathered long tree limbs and showed us how to poke around in the ashes. It was a sad sight; two little girls and a dad poking around in ashes looking for a child's bank and anything else salvageable. We found the monkey! Heat had melted the coins together. Dad suggested we send the money to the government and they would replace it. He told us the government couldn't replace five hundred dollars in paper money that burned in the house. It was gone!

## Rebuilding Our Lives

We began to rebuild our lives with what we had left on the farm. The partially finished barn mow loft provided a place to sleep. It was scary climbing the ladder to the loft and carefully walking around on the areas that had boards. We used a grain building that had a dirt floor to eat our meals in. A small kitchen table was received from a neighbor. We were very careful not to drop any food on the floor because it wouldn't be edible if we did.

Others in our community soon got word of our plight. A notice appeared in the local newspaper, and many people responded with clothes and food for us. However, we still didn't have a house to live in. The weather was getting colder and sleeping in a breezy barn loft was uncomfortable.

After two months, my dad and his two brothers found a house and an old shack that could be transported to our land. Soon the house was moved on a large truck to our farm. It was exciting seeing a house. My older sister and I climbed up on the truck and walked through the house. It looked grand! It even had light bulbs in the ceiling! We thought we would have electricity. But our dad regretfully informed us, it took more than a light bulb to make electricity. We would have a house, but no electricity.

Soon my dad, his brothers and other family members started constructing a foundation for the house and shack. Then they joined the two structures. That became our house. We were delighted to have a place to live. Our new house had a kitchen, living room, and a joined porch way that led to one bedroom in the shack. It was our house, but it didn't feel like the home we had lost in the fire.

It was devastating to lose personal belongings and a peaceful home. We were already poor and this added to our misery. However, I remember something positive out of the trauma. My mother dropped to her knees, and through tears thanked God that He spared all our lives.

Years later, the Lord spoke to me about this event. He instructed me through Jeremiah. "But thy life will I give unto thee for a prey in all places, whither thou goest" (Jeremiah 45:5). The Lord didn't spare our property. But he gave us our lives, so His plan for us could be fulfilled. God promises our lives for a reward, but not our property. God doesn't want us to hold onto material things, but to grip onto Him, His promises and His desires for our lives.

Often as a child and adolescent, I wondered what my life would be like. I day dreamed of whom I would marry and what I would do.

## Military Life

A few weeks after high school graduation, I married my high school sweetheart. He had enlisted in the U.S. Army and was stationed in New Mexico. After our marriage, we immediately moved and established our first home. It wasn't long before we welcomed our first son. It didn't matter that we had little money. We were just happy to be a family.

Changes came quickly for our little family. Soon we had our second son. Just five months after his birth, we got military orders for my husband to report to Korea. This was an assignment where family members were not permitted to live.

We packed up our few belongings and returned to our hometown in Kansas. Here my sons and I were close to extended family. It was a blessing having both sets of parents to assist me with my sons. It helped us adjust to my spouse's 13 month absence.

When my youngest son became critically ill with flu, asthma and pneumonia, it was a godsend having family close by. While he was hospitalized, the whole family provided practical and spiritual support. We notified my husband about our son's health problems. My husband wasn't able to come home from Korea until his assignment was complete. Fortunately he had only a couple weeks to finish his tour of duty. He was home shortly after our son got out of the hospital.

It was a difficult adjustment for both my husband and I after his return home from Korea. We immediately moved to Utah leaving familiar faces of family behind.

Changing our address, church and friends was a normal routine. There was excitement and tension with each household move.

After our relocation, I began to work outside the home. This is when the Lord began to show me how He was putting my life together. He gave me concepts of how things come together in the spiritual realm as well.

In one job, I learned two new computer systems. In the next job, I was able to use that information to help with a complete reorganization and change over to new equipment. In life, often one thing builds upon another.

God smoothed out the bumps in the road of life. He showed me how pain and losses of the past had accumulated a great weigh.

## Depression Encompassed Me

Somewhere in between all these losses, I spiraled into depression. I felt like I was dropped into a black pit with no way out. There were times when I felt hopeless and suicidal. However, my strong belief in God, love from my family, church and friends kept me from going over the edge.

Eventually, I was referred to a psychologist. He was very compassionate and helped our whole family address some of our problems. From then on, we all functioned better emotionally, and I beat the depression. I vowed to never let that black mood engulf me again. I didn't realize at the time that I was experiencing grief, and it can often result in depression.

After the blue mood lifted, the Lord instructed me to become a professional family counselor. But to comply, I would need to receive formal schooling. Initially, I dismissed the idea.

## Hooked on Learning

Getting a college education didn't seem possible until after a military assignment to Germany. There I needed to learn to speak German. The most viable way to understand the language was to take a college class. I quickly got hooked on learning. I was a college student.

The educational process was part of the Lord's plan. I wasn't sure of a specific direction. My heart told me psychology, so I could be a counselor. My head and the rational part of me said, that's not feasible, so choose business management.

## Stepping Stones

The business degree acted as a stepping stone and I was able to go into human relations work. What I learned in that field was very valuable. It prepared me for greater challenges.

Even though I couldn't see the whole picture, the Lord knew exactly what He was doing. He put me in a personnel job to acquire tools needed to complete an even more complex job. That is often the way our lives are. We go from the simpler, less involved events and situations, into more complicated ones. It's only because of what we have learned in the shallow water that helps us be able to swim in the deep water.

Another situation developed while living in England. I was unfamiliar with driving on the left side of the road, and I didn't read road maps well. Our pet dog was quarantined in a kennel several hours away from where we lived. At that time, every animal was quarantined in England for six months to combat rabies. The family chose to visit our pet every two weeks. Because of this experience, I became more familiar with driving, while enjoying the passing scenes. I also learned how to better read maps.

When my sister came to visit, and my husband was unavailable to escort us, the Lord had already prepared me. I knew my way around. I could read a map. If all else failed, I knew how to ask for directions from God and others.

My life was just ticking away, but it didn't feel like the Lord's plans were being fulfilled. All the while, the Lord was working to complete His will. Before God could totally manifest His wishes, He had to root out a lot of fears, inadequacies and prepare me for what He wanted me to do.

## Wilderness Time

Every servant God calls, goes through a time of preparation. His own son (Jesus) labored for thirty years in a carpenter's shop. He also spent forty days in the wilderness before He began His three-year ministry. Moses spent forty years in the wilderness. Why should you or I be any different? Sometimes much of our life is a preparation for the work God wants us to do.

The Lord showed me through Biblical examples not to lose heart when I didn't see His plan for my life being fulfilled immediately. Mark 6:45-52 tells us about an adventure the disciples had when Jesus sent them to the other side of the sea. During the night a storm arose as the disciples tried to reach their journey's end. They saw Jesus walking on the waves and didn't understand His purposes. His message was that they depend on Him. Jesus' purpose is always that we rely on Him and His power now. If I can stay calm in the middle of the storm, that is the purpose of God. "God's end is the process – that, I see Him walking on the waves, no shore in sight, no success, no goal, just the absolute certainty that it is all right because I see Him walking on the sea. It is the process, not the end, which is glorifying to God."[1]

## Step by Step

God said to me, "Just let me work in the process of your life. I will take you step by step through the journey. Let the whole trip, my plan for your life, glorify me."

Another part of my journey took me through dark valleys. I had prayed long and hard for a miraculous physical healing from a long standing painful ailment. But the Lord's plan for me was to have major surgery. After the operation, I was more sensitive to people who were physically ill, hospitalized, or bed bound.

Several other circumstances unwittingly helped me prepare for such a move. Growing up in a disadvantaged state was one of those experiences that added much to my empathy and understanding of the plight of poverty.

Another challenge increased my understanding of living on a significantly reduced income. While both our sons were still in college, my husband retired from the U. S. Army. This was a big adjustment for us socially, emotionally and financially. We transported our household goods back to Kansas. It was great to be around family again. However, the economy bottomed out, and we had difficulty securing well paying, jobs. Even though we had a loss of income, we never went hungry and our bills were always paid. All our needs were met. However, many of our wants went untouched. It was during this period that God began to speak to me. He showed me His Word. "But my God shall supply all your need according to His riches in glory by Christ Jesus" (Phil 4:19).

While going through this trial, the Lord ministered to me that we need to learn the difference between a need and a want. The needs should be satisfied. He taught me from this experience that good financial stewardship was essential.

Had the Lord called us to do work for Him at that point, we couldn't have done it. We had too many obligations and too little money.

Soon God provided rewarding employment for my spouse. We packed up our household goods and trekked across the state to our new home. Both our college sons were now close enough to visit often.

During such a visit, both sons encouraged me to apply for admission to the University of Kansas. I did so and was easily accepted. The youngest son helped me enroll. Had it not been for my sons' and husband's encouragement and support, I couldn't have returned to college.

It was tough being a student forty-years plus. I still harbored a desire to pursue a degree in psychology. However, I soon learned I would need a doctoral degree and would need to do research, which I wasn't interested in. So with much prayer, I sought guidance from the Lord.

Early in the educational process, God lead students, professors and academic advisors across my path. Some students suggested I discuss my career goals with the Deans of psychology and Social Work.

After talking with the Deans of both departments, they concurred, Social Work is a match for you. That was the Lord way of leading me. I immediately changed my major to social work. This course work was exciting and rewarding. I began to pursue a Bachelors Degree in Social Work with earnest.

## Road Block

While working in a social work internship in a mental health center, a roadblock was encountered. I liked the work and clients, but my spiritual beliefs didn't line up with my supervisor's. Eventually she relieved me of my practicum assignment near the end of the first semester of my senior year. This was done without a conference with the college liaison. It was devastating for me. But I heeded wise counsel from Christian friends and the school liaison. The School of Social Work Practicum Administrator asked me to prepare my own evaluation. It was reviewed by a school panel and I was granted full credit for the semester.

However, the roadblock of losing my practicum assignment left me in a dilemma. I still needed another internship to complete my course work so I could graduate. I found a placement with terminally ill patients. It was a rewarding experience. That spring, I received a Bachelor's Degree in Social Work, with honors. But He knew the way that I took after testing me. I had come forth as gold by relying on the Lord. (Job 23:10) The prior roadblock was more like a speed bump. It hadn't stopped me. I quickly caught up.

## Gator Aid

Roadblocks or problems often prompt us to make choices we normally wouldn't make. I'm reminded of a funny story. "Gator Aid" was used in a Florida training camp during World War II. The GI's had daily physical training which included an obstacle course. At the end of the obstacle course was an endurance test. Here the men had to grab a rope and swing across a broad, shallow pool. Under the hot sun the water looked so inviting that the men made a habit of making it only halfway across the pond - until an enterprising lieutenant made it the new home for a large alligator. From then on the recruits left the ground 15 feet from the water's edge and fell sprawling in the dust on the other side.[2]

Sometimes our behavior must be shaped by danger or unfavorable circumstances. Without God's loving correction and faithful discipline we would never develop spiritual strength and endurance. The psalmist

David said, "It is good for me that I have been afflicted, that I may learn your statutes" (Psalm 119:71).

I thank God he cares enough about us to teach us His ways. He knows what His plan is for our lives. If we will let him guide us, we can avoid many problems along the way.

## God's Guidance

Another part of The Lord's plan for my life was Hospice work. The experience was very rewarding. I encountered issues that cut across every area of life. Every issue of unfinished business surfaced. It was a valuable learning experience that profoundly touched my life. God gave me a broad base of training. He was preparing me to work with all types of people problems. I had no idea how to effectively deal with all the different issues.

When I entered graduate school, I wasn't sure which specialty to choose. After much prayer, the Lord instructed me to learn more about children and families.

A hospital internship gave me experience with children and adult psychiatric problems. It helped me understand many of the issues I had tried to deal with earlier in working with the terminally ill and their families. Another part of the puzzle was being completed.

After graduation, I received a job offer and returned to my former hospice work. Now, I had more training and knowledge to deal with many of the problems that had surfaced previously.

When I look back on this experience, I realize I don't have the wisdom to know where I need to be to fulfill God's plan. If I will leave the choices to the Lord, He will always direct.

I was able to understand the people and situations that came across my path better because of prior depression. Knowing how devastating this illness can be, I was able to empathize with others and help them work through it.

## Jesus Comes into Our Circumstances

God knows where He wants us and permits different things to touch our lives as part of His plan for us. When things happen that we don't understand, we are often tempted to try to change others or our circumstances. It's been helpful to remember what a wise person said. "The situation is mine, but the problem is yours God." It's only with God's help that we can change ourselves, our circumstances and influence others.

The Lord doesn't usually lift us out of our circumstances, but He comes into our situation like He did with the disciples in the boat. He walked on the water and joined them in their sea worthy vessel. (Matthew 14:24-25). Jesus came into the disciple's situation in the fourth watch or the darkest part of the night.

## In The Dark

Often, it is the same with us. "What I tell you in the darkness, speak in the light and what you hear whispered in your ear, proclaim upon the housetops" (Matthew 10:27, NAS).

God used this passage to touch me. I felt like I was in the dark when suddenly, I was faced with an investigation lodged against me. This was the first time in twenty-one years as a counselor/therapist that I had ever had this to deal with. It was scary. I wasn't sure what to do. So I looked at the verse again in Matthew10. "If you are in the dark now, remain quiet. If you open your mouth in the dark, you will talk in the wrong mood. Darkness is the time to listen. If you talk to others while in the dark, you can't hear what God is saying."[3]

As I meditated on the previous verse and what Chambers had written, I knew I had my answer. I was not to say anything until I came out of the darkness. But I was to ask for prayer from a few people who could storm heaven with me. I ask a select few to pray with me for favor with the investigating board, for justice and God's will to be done. That was all I ask for them to pray.

One woman praying for me, immediately said she saw a picture of me being extended the golden scepter of favor from the Lord. This was much like Queen Esther as she went before the King in the book of Esther. I kept this image in my mind and it helped me have peace about the situation.

Then I offered myself, my license and my counseling business up to the Lord. I gave it all back to Him because He was the one that gave it to me in the first place.

Next, with my husband's help, I drafted my explanation of the situation, addressing all charges in detail. After the defense was written and sent forward, I waited four months for an answer. I had peace while

I was waiting, but there were times I was tempted to be fearful of the outcome. During those times I prayed the answer to my prayer. "I thank You Lord, for favor with the board, for justice and for your will to be done." I also stood on several verses. One of the verses was "But He knows the way that I take; when He had tested me, I shall come forth as gold." (Job 23:10 NIV.) Another verse that kept me in peace and functioning daily was: "No weapon formed against you shall prosper. And every tongue that rises in judgment against you, will be put down . . ." (Isaiah 54:17 NAS)

Impacting the situation was the need to renew my state license. So I ask God, "Do you want me to wait or should I call the investigating board?" I immediately sensed in my spirit that I needed to wait on the Lord.

Just a few days later, my husband called me at the office and said, "You got a letter from the board. Do you want me to open it?" "Yes," I responded. Then he asks if I wanted to know what it said. I immediately told him that I didn't want to know because I had two more clients to see for the day and I didn't want to be distracted.

When I arrived home, I read the letter and it said, "The investigating board met and we could find no rule, regulation or statuette violated, that governs your work. And the board unanimously voted to drop all charges in the investigation." Wow, what a powerful answer to the prayers we prayed!

After that, I soon received my license renewal notice. One question stumped me. It said, "Have you been under investigation in the last two years." I wasn't sure how to answer since charges were dropped. I called the chairperson of the investigation board. She said, "Doris, answer the question 'no' because we dropped all charges." I thanked her for handling the investigation in a great way and told her that my faith had grown much through this ordeal. It felt good to give this investigator a faith filled testimony. It brought glory to the Lord.

Now I knew I was in the light again. It was time to share what I had learned in the dark. Yes, Jesus became light in my darkness.

## Trust God's Character

Sometimes, I forget the victories, and fret like the disciples in the storm. I stew about circumstances, and forget that Jesus is here to touch my situation. "Fretting is to want my own way and to calculate without

God."[4] Instead of worrying, I just need to trust the character of God when things don't seem right instead of blaming Him and everyone else. His heart toward me is love. (John 3:16).

God loved me so much that He gave His best gift to me. How could I question His plan for my life? I'm often doubtful when situations began to squeeze the joy and life out of me. "Every experience, I offer to Christ can become a gateway to joy. Gratitude comes from acceptance of the situation."[5] When I offer my situation to God, He can become the Lord of my circumstances.

## Broken Bread and Poured out Wine

Often I have asked God to use me in difficult situations. "God can never make us wine if we object to the fingers He uses to crush us with. If God would only use His own fingers, and make me broken bread and poured-out wine in a special way. But when He uses someone whom we dislike, or some set of circumstances to which we won't submit, we object. If we are going to be made into wine, we will have to be crushed."[6]

I don't like to be crushed, but the Lord has shown me that sometimes it is necessary. When we are crushed, others can drink from our experiences and we can be a blessing for them as they go through similar situations. That's what it means to be broken bread and poured out wine for others to eat and drink. God is with us through the crushing times. The Lord reminds that He will hold us in His right hand. He instructs us not to fear, because He will help us. He will make us a new instrument that will thresh the mountains and destroy the hills. (Isaiah 41: 13 & 15).

## Praise Levels the Mountains

"But Lord how will I thresh the mountains in my life?" The Lord spoke to me while I was doing dishes one morning. "You will have to take action and use a tool. The tool you are to use to thresh the mountains, in your life is *"praise."* ". . . Do you now believe?" (John 16:31, NAS). Yes Lord, I believe praise will work to level the hills.

God has been faithful and the mountains are being leveled one by one. He has used every situation or change in my life to help me grow and become more equipped to do His work.

## Don't Pick up Others Loads

Often we are eager to do work for the Lord and can easily do more than we need too.

A man asks God if he could do something for Him one day. God replied, "Well yes, just take your wagon and these three medium size rocks all the way up the hill for me." The man was so pleased he had a job to do for the Lord.

He started off with his wagon adjusted under his arms. He went up the path and met a neighbor. The neighbor asks him what he was doing. The man stated he was doing some work for God and taking rocks up the hill. The neighbor asks him if he could take a couple smaller rocks up the hill and the man obliged. Going on further, the man met a friend. This man also asked him to take a large rock up the hill. Again the man took on the extra load. Next the man met another neighbor and he asks him what he was doing. He replied "Taking these rocks up the hill for the Lord." The man asked if he could also take his rock up the hill. Again he deposited it on his cart. Suddenly the man realized the load was so heavy it was cutting into his arms and he couldn't budge it. He began to complain to the Lord.

"Lord, I thought you said this job was going to be easy, but I can't even pull it now. What do you want me to do?" God spoke to the man and instructed him to unload all the rocks out of his wagon except the ones He had asked him to take up the hill. The man questioned God. "Do you just want me to leave all of them here beside the road? "Yes", God replied. "I only ask you to take the three rocks up the hill, but you stopped and picked up other peoples loads."

The moral of this story is: we aren't to pick up loads others are supposed to carry. Set good boundaries or you will be over whelmed and not able to accomplish what the Lord has asked you to do.

## Test the Spirits

One day a woman was doing what she thought the Lord had asked her to do. She came to our house while I was cooking supper. I had never seen her before. She came in saying that the Lord had sent her. I said, "Oh, tell me about it." And she told me that unless I did certain things, which appeared to be legalistic, I would not make heaven my home. It made me feel a spirit of oppression. And peace evaded me.

After the woman left, I said, "Okay Lord, what are you trying to tell me?" The Lord sent me to His Word. "Beloved, believe not every spirit. But try the spirits whether they are of God . . ." (1 John 4:1). God's warning was to test the spirits according to His Word. The lady's message didn't line up with the Bible.

## Choosing Churches

I need to be very careful when listening to other people. This was good instruction because I would need to choose churches many times after household moves. I needed to evaluate a church according to the Word of God. Did their doctrines and teachings line up with the Holy Bible? Was there love present in that body? "By this all men will know that you are My disciples, if you have love for one another" (John 13:35 NAS). This experience helped me to rely on the Lord to choose a body of believers to worship with.

I had a dilemma. There were two churches with very similar belief and worship patterns. One was a tiny church in an old building that had been used as an automobile show room. But the Word of God was there.

Another church was in a nice church building. It was large and there was love there. I sought the Lord and He instructed me. "If both churches had the same physical facilities, where would you go?" And I responded, "Well, I'd go to the small church." The Lord said, "Okay, then that is where I want you to go, even though they don't have fine fixtures."

The Lord has used each situation and event to teach and lead me in the paths He wanted me to walk. "And your ears will hear a word behind you, this is the way, walk in it, whenever you turn to the right or to the left" (Isaiah 30:21 NAS).

## Missing It

There are times we don't listen to the Lord nor walk in the path He has commanded us to. When we miss it we need to go back and fix it.

Very often when I've made a mistake, I've had condemnation. When I receive criticism, it makes me stop and evaluate myself and the situation. One thing I have found most helpful is to go to the Lord in prayer and begin to tell him about it.

I was very pleased to find confirmation that this was an effective way to deal with criticism. I was instructed on criticism. One of the best ways to deal with it is first review the matter with God. The second way to handle criticism is to freely acknowledge that you've been hurt, and have bitterness, resentment and fear. Don't try to defend yourself, just let God be the Judge. Third, confess your weakness and inability to overcome the problem. Then fourth, ask God to personally intervene.[7]

Ordinarily, I ask God to work everything out for good because I know this is part of His promise for us. (Romans 8:28). Everything can work out for good if we look for the positives, from the Lord's hands.

## Our God Reigns

I've begun to realize the importance of prayer and letting God direct my life and order my steps.

One evening while in a counseling training class, a weather storm broke with much fury. We weren't sure what to do. We knew the area was under a tornado watch. We decided to take cover in the Hall ways of the church. We prayed and asked God's protection and guidance. We listened to the weather and storm report. One front had come through an area adjacent to us. The area had hail the size of grapefruit and ninety mile an hour winds with torrents of rain.

Another location had a crane fall on the emergency room of a hospital. We stayed put until we heard there was a slight break in the weather. But within the hour, another front was expected to hit our area.

At that point we all felt the Lord guiding us to make a run for it and get home. To stay out of the path of the storm, I would have to go north before heading west. I started north and drove out of the storm. Just as it was clearing, I saw the remnants of a sunset with black clouds in the west. At that moment, I heard the song "Our God Reigns," playing on the car radio. God was speaking to me through this situation and the song. He said, "I reign supreme. I'm in complete control." I knew then He would get me home safe; and He did.

## Putting Pieces Together

One day I was subpoenaed to court in a small town nearby. It was for a family I had been counseling with in foster care. We were requesting that the children and mother be reintegrated back together as a family. They wanted to make a fresh start. I ask the Lord to give us this. We successfully negotiated testifying in court. We had favor with the judge and he gave the children back to their mother. He gave her permission to move out of state and live with the children's aunt. I felt this was a great answer to prayer.

When I look back on many past situations and events, I realize how God spoke to me through them and directed my life. He was working on situations to bring about His purpose for my life. I now realize God set His plan in motion before I ever ask for His help or encountered particular problems or needs.

Truly God has shown me through situations and events in my life and the lives of others, that He has a plan for every one of our lives. His way is best. He has the wisdom and can see the whole picture. He knows how the puzzle should fit together to make a perfect picture.

If we give God our very best, He will always see to it that we get His greatest good. The Lord's best is truly His plan for our lives. Jesus is saying to us in all situations, "Listen I'm here and in control of your life. I want to be Lord of your circumstances" "For I know the plans I have for you, declared the Lord . . ." (Jeremiah 29:11).

# CHAPTER 6

# *People*

"But thanks be, to God: who always leads us in triumphal procession in Christ
and through us spreads everywhere the fragrance of Him"
2 Corinthians 2:14 (NIV).

God uses people daily to communicate His fragrance and message to us. Too often we don't check to see what aroma or impression we are leaving for others to see, hear or smell.

However, after visiting in someone's home or before checking out of a motel, or when moving, we double check to make sure we haven't left anything behind. Even criminals check to make sure they haven't left any clues at the crime scene to identify them.

# Something Left Behind

A robber thought he had committed the perfect crime. He assumed he left no clues behind. But he didn't count on someone remembering how he smelled. The odor he left behind was what helped convict him.

Yes, we leave something everywhere we go. Stuart Holden reminded a young man moving out of a boarding house. The young man said, he was double checking to make sure he wasn't leaving anything. Holden remarked, "There's one thing you will leave behind, young man, your influence."[1]

The owner of the boarding house was referring to the impression we leave with others. We always leave a little bit of our character behind. It's our fragrance, whether good or bad.

Most of us have a lasting effect on people we meet. It is much like the ripples created when a stone is tossed into a body of water. We usually can't see where it ends. So it is with our effect on others. We never know what our impact has been.

# Jesus' Fragrance of Blessings

God often uses people to communicate His message. When God sent His son Jesus to this earth, He sent a very precious gift.

Jesus left His aroma everywhere He went. People knew he had been there. When people heard that Jesus was coming, they would come for miles around and stay until evening. This type of situation prompted Jesus' compassion and the miraculous feeding of the 5,000 people. ". . . He took the five loaves and the two fishes . . . He blessed the food . . . And they all ate, and were satisfied . . ." (Matthew 14:19-20a NAS). God speaks to us about Jesus through the scriptures. We need to be like Jesus and leave an aura of blessings everywhere we go.

# Others Aroma

There are many Biblical characters that left their positive impressions behind. God speaks to us through them.

Peter left a big foot print, even though he didn't want anyone to know he was a disciple of Jesus'. ". . . You, too, were with Jesus the Nazarene.' But he denied it . . ." (Mark 14:67-68a NAS).

Peter had the fragrance of Jesus and others recognized it. His life spoke in a powerful way even when he denied Jesus. Later Peter repented. He was faithful and trusted His Lord.

## Abraham Listened Twice

Many other Biblical characters left their fragrance and have been used of God to speak to us. Abraham left the scent of listening twice to God when He tested him and asked him to sacrifice his son Isaac on an altar on one of the mountains, a few days journey away.

(Genesis 22: 2). Abraham obeyed God and took Isaac to the mountain. After Abraham had bound Isaac on the altar God spoke to him a second time.

An angel called to him from heaven and told him to not raise his hand against the lad Isaac. The Lord told him that he knew he feared Him because he didn't withhold his only son. (Genesis 22:10-12).

A minister pointed out that if Abraham hadn't listened to God twice in that situation, he would have killed Isaac. God's instructions for us may change, so we need to be sensitive to listen all the time as Abraham did. We need to be able to say, "Here I am," as Abraham did.

## Aroma Passed Down

Abraham's son Isaac followed in his father's footsteps of righteousness. Isaac's son (Jacob) dug many wells. He passed "the fragrance" down to his decedents.

Jacob's son, Joseph, carved out a positive reputation when he served as commissioner for Pharaoh in Egypt during a severe famine. Prior to being a commissioner, Joseph was a faithful servant while he worked in Potiphar's house. Joseph never compromised, even though tempted by the ruler's wife. (Genesis 39:7-9).

## Sisters' Fragrances

We have many Biblical accounts of seemingly ordinary people who had very different priorities. The gospel of Luke tells us how Mary would sit at Jesus feet and listen to Him, while her sister, Martha was distracted with meal preparations. ". . . But the Lord answered and said to her, 'Martha, Martha, you are worried about many things; but only a few things are necessary, really only one, for Mary has chosen the good part, which shall not be taken away from her'" (Luke 10:41-42 NAS).

Mary had chosen the most important thing, being with Jesus. She developed a relationship with Him. Martha chose to be busy cooking for Jesus. She had chosen to serve her Lord without companionship with Him.

Am I flexible enough to be like Mary? One of my friends was. She shared her philosophy reference visitors to her home. She said, "If you want to see me, come anytime. But if you want to see my house, make an appointment." The priority was placed on the relationship with people, not on how well kept her house was.

That spoke loudly to me about Mary and Martha. Mary understood the importance of a relationship with Jesus. Martha was concerned more with an image and everything being done proper. The Lord continually reminds me of Mary and Martha's priorities as a lesson on relationships.

A minister expounded on Mary and Martha's lives and how Jesus responded differently to them after Lazarus' death. They both said the exact same words to Him. "Martha therefore, said to Jesus, 'Lord, if you had been here, my brother would not have died . . ." Jesus said to her, 'Your brother shall rise again . . . Therefore, when Mary came where Jesus was, she saw Him, and fell at His feet, saying to Him, 'Lord, if You had been here, my brother would not have died . . . He was deeply moved in spirit . . . and said, where have you laid him? . . ." (John 11:21, 32-34).

Jesus' response to Martha and Mary was directly linked to their relationship with Him. Jesus responded to Martha with a promise. But with Mary, He took action. That connection meant the difference between life and death for her brother.[2]

In this passage of scripture, Jesus speaks to the Jews surrounding Mary and Martha. "Jesus said, 'Remove the stone.' Martha . . . Said to Him, 'Lord, by this time there will be a stench, for he has been dead four days'" (John 11:39 NAS).

As I studied this passage of scripture again, the Lord showed me more of His truth. Mary and Martha both called Jesus, Lord. Mary knelt at His feet often and Martha didn't. Martha often told Him what to do and then questioned Jesus. The Lord showed me that I am more like Martha. I'm busy doing instead of sitting at His feet getting to know Him. I also question Jesus when He speaks to me. I want to sit at Jesus feet and have a relationship with

Him like Mary. I want to say, "Yes Lord," instead of questioning Him. I want to get to know Jesus, His presence and fragrance more.

## Pass It On

There are many other examples of great people who knew Jesus and left a beautiful scent wherever they went. Paul proclaimed bold messages and was imprisoned many times.

He recognized the fervency and zeal young Timothy had. It was obvious that it was passed down through the generations. "For I am mindful, of the sincere faith within you, which first dwelt in your grandmother, Lois and your mother Eunice . . ." (1 Timothy 1:5 NAS). From this we learn the presence of a beautiful character can be passed down from the older to the younger generation. We need not slight the message even though it comes from a child.

Samuel, a young boy, was the vessel God used to communicate an important message to Eli. "And Eli said to Samuel, 'Go lie down, and it shall be if He calls you, that you shall say, 'Speak, Lord, for Thy servant is listening.' So Samuel went and lay down in his place. Then the Lord came and stood and called as at other times, 'Samuel! Samuel!' And Samuel said, 'Speak, for Thy servant is listening'" (1 Samuel 3:9-10 NAS).

Many people from Biblical times were messengers for Christ, and so are we. "We are ambassadors for Christ as though God were pleading through us" (2 Corinthians 5:20). As the Lord's agents, we are always to be communicating, Him to others. We never know how far our influence will ripple.

## Get Back On and Ride

Often the people, who have the greatest impact on us, are those we encounter early in life. I remember many things my dad said as I was growing up. They are etched in my memory. After falling off a horse, he instructed me, "Just remember, whenever a horse bucks you off, get back on and ride it." This advice made me tough and determined. I used this metaphor to propel me through many difficult situations in life.

When I had a car accident, I remembered what my dad said. I was determined to get back behind the wheel of the car and drive again. Whenever I made a mistake, I would remember this lesson.

## Mother's Scent

My mother left me with a life lesson. She told my sisters and me to treat others with understanding. A small plaque on a wall in our living room said, "Do unto others what you would have them do unto you." (Matthew 7:12).

My mother's insight was intertwined with the Bible verse, which left a lasting impression on me. As an adult, when faced with a decision on how to respond to someone who had mistreated me, I remembered my early teaching at home. I knew I couldn't treat them badly. I remembered being taught to love and bless others even if they hated or persecuted us. If they were hungry we were to feed them. In doing this we would be heaping coals of fire upon their heads.

(Matthew 5:44 & Proverbs 25:22). Treating others justly was what Jesus wanted of us. It is sometimes difficult.

## Love and Give it Your Best

My grandmother accepted me, just as I was. I felt important to her. Unconditional love and acceptance is what we need to convey to everyone that comes across our path in life.

My grandfather utilized stories to deliver powerful messages. He told the story of a retiring carpenter who built houses for his employer. One day the boss asked him to build him one last house before the he retired.

So the carpenter said, "Okay, I'll build it for you." The craftsman thought, this is my last house. My boss hasn't paid me like I think he should have. So, I'll just cut some corners and see if I can't save some money on this job. So he built the house not doing his best work.

After the house was built, he showed it to his employer. And the boss said, "Thank you for building this house. Now, I have a surprise for you. This house is yours. It's a retirement gift from me to you."

My grandpa used this story to illustrate that when we agree to a project we should do our best. It might be yours someday. "And whatsoever ye do in word or deed, do all in the name of the Lord Jesus . . ." (Colossians 3:17).

My parents and grandparents often reminded me, that if a job was worth doing, it was worth doing well.

## Morning Worship

One of the most important imprints my parents left with me was the regular habit of morning worship. Often we immediately did our farm chores of milking the cows and feeding all the farm animals. Then we trooped back into the house to eat. After breakfast, we dutifully had our morning devotions.

During worship, my mother would read a Bible passage. Then we children would say the Lord's Prayer. Mom and dad always ended in pray.

There were many times when I got out of the habit of worship. But I eventually came back to the Word and prayer. This heritage has given me more ability to discipline myself. This habit has shaped my life for good. I realize the importance of starting the day off with God and giving Him my very best.

## Children Catch Our Scent

God has put children in my path and spoken through them. He has also spoke to me through my own children and showed me, that they quickly catch our values. We can also learn much from our little ones.

When I taught Sunday school, God used children to speak to me in a powerful way. When I asked the children if they wanted to pray, a little five year old boy prayed and thanked God for making his grandmother well. Weeks later, I learned his grandmother had been healed. The little lad was learning the importance of giving praise to the Lord for His mighty works. That left a good fragrance for all.

During a Sunday school lesson, a small girl became ill. I asked if she would let us pray for her. She indicated, yes. Without being asked, all the children stood up and made a circle around and laid hands on her. These children were three to five-year-olds.

That experience spoke powerfully to me that what children were seeing in church and Sunday school was having a deep impact on them. No wonder Jesus said,

". . . Suffer little children to come unto me, and forbid them not: for of such is the kingdom of God" (Luke 18:16).

A couple relayed their children had been baptizing each other in a mud puddle in their back yard. These children could have been playing any number of games. However, they chose to act out a baptismal. God was speaking through those children and saying, "What you are teaching them, they are learning. They are taking it to heart. They are acting out what has been put into their hearts and minds." Those children had a powerful witness!

## Sweet Honesty a Child's Fragrance

In my private practice, as a therapist, I learned much from hurting children. One little girl was sitting on the floor using play dough. She cut hearts out of clay like they were cookies. The little miss looked up at me, and displayed a heart that was broken in two pieces. She said "My parents broke my heart." I told her I was sorry her heart was broken. We talked for a while and I pointed to a picture on the wall. It said, "God can heal a broken heart if you give Him all the pieces." She took the play dough and smashed it back into a round ball and rolled it out again. This time she said "God has healed my broken heart." I almost cried. She had so much faith and was telling me God was doing the work in her heart we couldn't do.

Children are so sensitive and open to listen. God often gets His message through them when He can't get adults to listen. Our minds are more cluttered, and we have more pride. We as adults have a tendency to look at children and say, "Oh God can't use them in a special way." Or sometimes we look at new Christians and wonder if God can use them.

## Don't Judge a Different Smell

The Lord spoke to me through His Word and used new converts, to say "Judge not, that ye be not judged" (Matthew 7:1). I'm not to judge others, but to simply accept them as they are. The reality of this truth came to me when a sister exclaimed, "The Lord has given me a word today. Don't judge me today by what I've done in the past."

He spoke to me through another individual who experienced some traumatic situations. The Lord said, "You don't know them like I do. You don't know how far they have come or how much farther I can take them. Don't judge them." He showed me, after I got to know them, that He could use them in very special ways. I decided that when I witnessed to someone, I was to pray for them, love them and spur them on so they could grow stronger in the Lord.

The Lord showed me that they now had a different fragrance. Their old crowds of friends were seeing them as a new and different person. It was a powerful lesson from Jesus. He instilled in my heart, not to count anyone out of His service or kingdom, no matter how they looked, sounded, acted, or responded.

While reading a devotional book one morning, I was nudged to remember many of the people the Lord had brought across my path. The author stated "The Holy Spirit reveals that God loved me, not because I was loveable, but because God's nature was love. Now, show that same kind of love to others. 'Love as I have loved you.' I will bring any number of people about you whom you cannot respect and you must exhibit my love to them, as I have exhibited it to you. God has loved me to the very utmost of His being. He has loved me to the very end of my sin, meanness, selfishness, pride and all the wrong that I've done. Knowing this will send me into the world to love others in that same way. I must love from the very depth of my being. Growth in grace stops when I get huffed at others or begin to judge them."[3]

I needed to love and accept others just as they are if I was going to continue to grow in grace. The Lord continued to speak to me, "Just give others my grace and remember I will complete the work in them."

## Secret Sister – Agape Love

In our congregation, we were beginning to learn how to reach out more in love and grace to others. A woman's agape club was formed. We encouraged each other and developed secret friendships. Names were drawn from a hat. We prayed and encourage through written messages and small gifts of love.

My agape friend surprised me with a couple of encouraging messages. One letter apologized for not writing because life had been so busy. She had little time with the Lord. She began to spend time with the Lord and was able to encourage me in a mighty way. She starts her letter by saying, "May the Lord continually bless you. Having the light of the Lord shine down on you is an uplifting of the spirit. Make the most of every day because the Lord will come as a thief in the night. We must prepare ourselves for His coming day. I glory in the time when the Lord will bring us home."

"Time goes by so quickly and the Word still hasn't reached all people. We need to learn to spread our faith to others because the Lord wants us to glorify him and bring others to him. The shepherd is coming for the sheep, and the sheep need to know the Lord is looking for them. Let's pray that we can give the Lord His just due. The closer we are to God, the more trying the times seem to be. However, the rewards are always worth any kind of trouble our enemy (the devil) may throw in our way. Remember this and let it lift your spirit. Then let it shine through. God will lead us home if we will just follow Him and let His son take us there."

She continued "Hang in there no matter how rough things are. We will conquer. The most powerful energy (God) is inside of you. Show it to the world, so those who are lost can see the glory they are missing out on and come, running back."

"The world is made up of many disobedient children who don't want to obey their father. Maybe as fellow brothers and sisters we can bring the light to their eyes. May the Lord bless you continually and shine a bright light in your path so you have a clear path home. In the name of Jesus Christ, I cast out the trouble that Satan wants to throw in your path today, Amen," your agape friend.

My friend's letter was very encouraging. It made me realize that no matter how a person acts, God is doing a work in their lives.

An added letter came from my secret sister, when I was grumbling that my prayers weren't being answered. I received a small gift. It was a plaque that read, "Prayer Changes Things." I keep that plaque setting on my dresser where I can see it every day. It is a definite reminder that prayer changes people, so prayer can change things. The Bible states, "For with God nothing shall be impossible" (Luke 1:37). We should never, ever give up on anyone.

She left me much of her fragrance. I'll never forget one of her notes that said, "Smile it makes people wonder what prayer God has answered for you."

I'm so thankful I didn't discount that relationship with her. She was obedient and let the Lord use her to teach me many things.

## It's Availability – Not Ability

Many others have left an encouraging aroma with me. An Olympic track and field athlete, Madelinn Manning - Mimms, spoke about her life and faith, during a church service. She told about emerging into life as a very sick child. She had an ailment and the doctors didn't offer hope that she would be able to walk. Eventually, with her mother's encouragement, she began walking. Then Mimms began participating in sport and physical fitness. With much prayer, faith and persistence, she eventually became a gold medal winner in the 1968 Olympics.

The message she imparted was, "God is not looking for *ability*, only for *availability*." What a truth! Many times when God calls us to do tasks, we say, "Oh I can't do that." Moses stated the same thing. He said, he wasn't eloquent and he didn't speak very well. The Lord asked him who made man's mouth. (Exodus 4:10-11). But Moses continued to argue with the Lord and eventually God gave him a helper, Aaron.

All of us have answered God in a similar way, or we've been tempted to. We've asked, "Why do you want me to do this?" Or, we've said, "I can't do that?" "God if you want me to do this, I need your help." I exclaimed that, when God ask me to write this book. "But God, I've not written much. I'm just an ordinary person." God answered me, "That is precisely why I want you to do the job."

Often God chooses an unlikely person to do the job. "But God hath chosen the foolish things of the world to confound the wise . . ." (1 Corinthians 1:27). If God was looking for ability only, many others could do the work. But God wants people who are willing to do His work. He will supply the talents and tools to get the job done. That's why availability is more important to God than ability.

This was the important message that Ms. Mimms spoke. And I was encouraged by her success and the obstacles she had overcome. Once again it shows us that God doesn't look at our ability because He can empower us to do great things.

## Encouragement – a Powerful fragrance

An Olympic, event on television inspired me. A sportscaster interviewed a gymnast trainer, Bela Korolya. He was quizzed about his success rate. He related that discipline and motivation are essential for success and victory.

His principle method of helping his students to be better was to encourage them. "You are doing well at what you are doing, but be the very best that you can be. Now go out there and give it a little something extra," he said.

As Christians we need to do the same. We need to live disciplined and motivated lives. We need to exhort others like Coach Korolya did. We need to tell them it's the little extra spurt that offers victory in our lives. This gem of advice spoke to me in a powerful way. I'm striving to implement it in every area of my life and encourage others.

I was reminded of the importance of written encouragement one morning while listening to the radio. A minister, Dr. David Jeremiah, talked about *"Encouraging the Write way."* He said there are five things that are important to remember about pinned encouragement. First, the written word is **deliberate**. It took thought to write it. Second, it is **definite.** It gets done. Third, pen on paper is **direct.** You often say what you really mean. Fourth, what's written is **durable**. It never dies. Fifth, it is **distance proof.** Written encouragement can go any distance.[4] That extra effort to encourage someone pays big dividends, now and later.

## Pray First Then Talk

There have been many people who have encouraged and helped me understand more about the need to help others. We need to pray for people before we talk to them about God. A musician, named Gay Hyde, stated "He who speaks to others about God, must first speak to God about others."

We need to be sensitive with wounded people and remember some may have been hurt by their religious experiences. However, they haven't been hurt by Jesus. A friend's method of assessing people's spiritual understanding was to ask a simple, but profound question. "Do you have Jesus in your heart?" This helped her know how to proceed with the helping process. I have used this approach to also cut through hurts and barriers. Immediately after asking if they have Jesus in their hearts, if they don't know the Lord, we then have the opportunity to introduce them to Him.

One of my Christian friends said that only Eternity will show forth the results of our work. We know all ministries are not the same. We are all called to plant, water and harvest. But, some people are especially gifted in one area. It takes utmost wisdom to know how to let the power of the Holy Spirit guide us.

## Guidance a Powerful Aroma

I needed guidance after a depressing dream. The Lord knew my need and he prepared a minister's heart. A righteous servant illumined me with the Word. If you don't have peace and the message doesn't line up with the Word of God; it's not from Him.

This minister was one of the first people that always pointed me back to the Bible. When I would ask him a question, he would always say, "What does the Word say?" He said, "If the Word doesn't back up what you read, hear, or dream, it's not of God. *Always return to the Word*!" It kept me out of Satan's snares many times.

There have been so many people God has used to guide me. A minister's wife told me about a time when her child was sick with a high fever. They had no money for a doctor's visit. She prayed and said, "Lord, heal my child." The wife said she was afraid to go to sleep because she thought her child might go into convulsions.

I quizzed her, "What did you do?" She said, "The Lord spoke to me and said, 'Okay you've prayed, you've asked for healing. Now, I want you to believe for that healing.'" At that point she hadn't seen any manifestations of healing. The fever hadn't dropped. Then the Lord said to her, "What would you do if you had those manifestations of healing and your son didn't have a fever." She said, "I'd go to sleep." The Lord said, "That is exactly what I want you to do, even though he still has the fever."

So she went to bed and slept. When the woman, awoke the next morning, her boy showed no sign of illness. That taught her she didn't have to see the manifestations of healing or see answers to prayers. She only had to pray and believe the Lord was working. That helped me grasp the Word of God.

## Relationship Spices

The Lord has used numerous people to teach me important truths. An elderly gentleman was facing some difficult decisions with his family and he said, "Ego (pride) and ignorance are two things that cause conflict." "Sometimes you win by losing." I pondered what the man said. I knew sometimes we have to put aside our pride, and lose a small battle to win the larger prize, peace in a relationship or home.

Another bed bound man always praised the Lord despite his illness. In response to others questioning him about not having an abundant life, he set the record straight. He responded from scripture, ". . . I (Jesus) am come that they might have life, and that they might have it more abundantly." John 10:10. He stated that "Abundant life is assurance of whose we are, knowing Jesus and having a relationship with Him." We can have an abundant life if we will live on the promises of God's Words.

He also said, "The world's and devil's report is on the left hand. God's report is on the right hand. I'm the establishing witness and determine how this trial is going to turn out by what I think, and what I speak." I can either agree with God's Word or believe the enemy. He also stated, "Satan pays attention to God's Word coming out of our mouths." Jesus taught us that from His temptations in the wilderness when Satan tempted Him and asked Him to turn a stone into bread. Jesus answered Satan and forcefully said man doesn't live by bread alone but by the Word of God. Matthew 4:4.

This godly man stated that, "The enemy works under pressure and the Lord works under love." He also stated we have to see things as already done, not how they may appear if we are to believe God's report. He reminded me of the verses about faith. "Now faith is the substance of things hoped for, the evidence of things not seen." Hebrews 11:1 ". . . Even God who quickens the dead and calleth those things which be not as though they were." Romans 4:17. As he said, *"were"* is past tense and means already done. He helped me understand this is one of the highest forms of faith to call something done even though we don't see it yet. It is praying the Word. This is truly believing and living God's report and not the messages of the world or the enemy. From that point on, I began to believe God's verdict about each situation.

Satan pays attention to the words we speak. We need to be aware of what we are saying.

This gentleman caught himself in mid sentence a few times and said, "Lord I repent for what I just said, I got my tongue twisted around my teeth." Then he finished the sentence with, "I am blessed."

## Aromatic Scent of Trust

Another dying woman who had several small sons,' related the same verbal message. She said, "I don't understand why I am going through this illness, but I still love Jesus!" She left such a powerful presence of Jesus behind. "No matter what we are going through, we need to love Jesus and completely trust Him."

Often it is very difficult to trust when a child is suffering. While serving as a hospice care team member, a terminally ill toddler taught me more about trust. She was mature beyond her young years. She had a sense of humor, was so accepting and didn't complain. Little things made her happy. What the little girl wanted was to be in her mother and dad's presence. The Lord spoke through this child saying we should have an overwhelming desire to be in our Makers presence.

We feel drawn to trusting, positive people. A fellow Christian, who was dying of cancer, was such a person. There were times when I felt depressed. I told myself that, "I should be in an upbeat frame of mind before I visit him." However, I would visit him anyway. He and his family would encourage me. I never heard them criticize anyone. Somehow they were able to convey positive information that spurred me to want to do better. Consequently, I always loved to visit them. I knew I would leave stronger and higher in spirits.

## Counter Negative with Positive

The upbeat person delights in praising others, pointing out their strengths and passing along good reports about them. Instead of condemning others they take more delight in commending people. They would rather build up than tear down others.

The story showed the difference in how two boys on a play ground dealt with a classmate. One boy said, "He is no good at sports." The other boy responded quickly, "Yes, but he is always fair." The critical one said, "But he isn't very smart in school either." The friend answered, "That may be true, but he studies hard." The boy with the mean tongue was becoming exasperated with the other classmate's good attitude toward the other kid. He said, "Well did you ever notice how ragged his clothes are?" The other boy kindly replied, "Yes, but did you notice they are always clean."[5] The lads give us a good example of how to counter every negative comment with a positive one.

The Lord knew I needed to learn more about countering negative with affirmation. A dear elderly woman taught me many lessons on life. Often this lady would remind me that, "You can catch more flies with honey than you can with vinegar." This statement was wisdom packed and taught me that being positive is more effective than being negative.

We need to refrain from speaking evil and speak only good things. "Let all bitterness, and wrath, and anger . . . be put away from you . . . and be ye kind one to another . . ." (Ephesians 4:31-32). This is how we can cancel out criticism. I believe many friends have practiced these principles.

Another friend taught me that it is more natural for us to tear down, rather than to build people up. Since it's not natural to build up someone, it is a real gift from God when we can esteem them.

It is easier for us to be negative than positive. Don't is one word, which we consider to have a nullifying connotation.

## Don'ts Can Be Good

There are four Don'ts that can result in good. First, don't doubt God. Jesus wasn't able to do mighty works because of unbelief or doubt. (Matthew 13:58) If we doubt, God won't be able to work through us like he wants to.

Second, don't limit God. All power is given unto Jesus. Therefore, we don't want to limit what Jesus can do in our own lives. Nothing is too difficult for God. If the devil is stomping on you, declare "No" to him today. In the name of Jesus, I have the right to stop you. You will not do this. We just need to ask in line with His Word and will.

Thirdly, don't compromise. Shadrach, Meshach and Abednego would not compromise their beliefs in God. (Daniel 3:1-28). Jesus walked into that fiery furnace and saved them. So we can be delivered from our enemy if we won't compromise.

Fourth, don't quit. "And let us not be weary in well doing: for in due season we shall reap, if we faint not" (Galatians 6:9). Yes, we will prosper if we don't pass out, if we don't quit trying. Just keep on doing what the Lord instructs even when you don't see results. Remember, a diamond is a piece of coal that didn't give up. Persistence leaves a good fragrance.[6]

## Gems of Delight

A Sunday school teacher set a life of example to follow. My desire was to be more like the Jesus I saw in her. She instructed us that it is very important to have the appropriate thing to say at the right time. If we don't, we're like a table that has three legs when it should have four. We aren't going to be very balanced or effective. We need to remember to do things that can minister grace to other people. She also instructed that people are very fragile. We need to treat them like fine china, not Tupper ware.

The teacher emphasized how important it is to have quiet time with the Lord. It's the time for recharging our batteries. Another way to put it is, it helps to keep us from overheating, and it lets the cream rise to the top of the milk.

There were many gems this dear woman had to offer. She dealt with condemnation versus conviction. She said that condemnation minister's hopelessness, despair and a sense of failure and heaviness. Conviction comes from God, and he ministers in one or two areas at a time. He puts His finger right on the spot. Our Father shows himself with meekness and with forcefulness. His cleansing is done with water, blood and fire. If the area he is working on is a soft area, he cleanses it with water. If it is a hard area, he cleanses it by fire. We need to understand the Lord corrects those he loves. (Hebrews 12:6).

## "If" – Not, "You Must"

When we are communicating or ministering to other people, we need to remember to deal with them like Jesus did, when He walked the earth. "Then said Jesus unto His disciples, If any man will come after me, let him deny himself, and take up his cross and follow me'" (Matthew 16:24) Another time Jesus said, "If thou wilt be perfect, go and sell that thou hast, and give to the poor . . ." (Matthew 19:21). The Lord gave the young man a choice just like He did His disciples.

Jesus was showing us that discipleship and relationships should involve choices. He allows us to use our self will. Jesus prefaced His statements with "If" not "You must." He always gave choices. The Lord convicted me that I need to always give choices and leave room for others to grow.

I practiced choices in giving my sister an option on a birthday gift. She chose an item that had a flaw in it. I immediately offered to give her another one. My sibling chose to keep the flawed item.

The Lord used the imperfect gift as an object lesson. He said, "I knew all your flaws and yet I chose you. I'm not sorry for choosing you. I knew

I could fix your imperfections." I'm so glad God knows how to fix our flaws or scars.

## Comfortable With Scars

One day I was reminded of how we look at scars. Several women talked about the trauma of their mastectomy. One said she felt lopsided until she had reconstructive surgery. Another didn't feel a need for reconstructive surgery. She stated, "I'm comfortable with my scars." That caused me to reflect, "Am I comfortable with my wounds? I thought about all the hurts we sustain on a physical, emotional, mental and spiritual level.

We have choices in regard to our short-comings. We can be miserable or we can be comfortable with our scars. If we give our wounds to God, he can heal them. Then the only scars in heaven will be Jesus' stripes. Our Lord is comfortable with the scars He suffered for you and me.

When God begins to heal our wounds, He heals one at a time. The ointment God uses to heal our wounds is a right relationship with Him and with others. His Word (Psalm) shows us how to relate to God. "Praise ye the Lord, O give thanks unto the Lord; for he is good; for His mercy endureth for ever" (Psalm 106:1). The Proverbs show us how to relate to people. "Let another man praise thee, and not thine own mouth . . ." (Proverbs 27:2). The Word tells us that we are to praise God and let others esteem us. It is difficult not to toot our own horn at times in our dealings

## Kindness is a Healing Oil

Good relationships require work and truth. Speaking the truth alone isn't enough. It must be combined with sensitivity. We always have the choice of using compassion and treating others as we want to be treated. Empathy is really kindness. This is the oil that mends relationships.

We need to be tolerant of others in our relationships. Friendships are two way streets with mutual respect and agreement. If there is a problem in an interaction, it's seldom one persons' fault. We have a tendency to close ourselves off from those who hurt us. "Loneliness is a very busy road." We humans have a desire to pick the speck out of our brother's eye. We see ourselves as okay and think the other person has a problem. We don't want to have a critical spirit. When we do that, the other person can't do anything right.

Jesus didn't withdraw from his disciples even though he knew he would be betrayed. It's interesting that, His disciples didn't say, "It's not I." But they examined themselves and asked, "Lord, is it I?" (Matthew 26:22).

## Change Me First

I'm trying to use this model when I have a relationship problem. I examine myself. I ask God, "What do I need to change to have a loving, smooth interaction?" I ask the Lord to change me first, then, He could change the other person, if He needed too.

In examining ourselves we have to be willing to be accountable versus defensive. We're not responsible to God for what others do to us. But, we're accountable to God for how we treat others. It helps to remember that God loves the other person just as much as He loves us. Others often irritate us because they mirror a part of ourselves back to us. We also have to be willing to forgive and to seek forgiveness.

## Cancel the Debt

Forgiveness is to pardon, cancel a debt, to cease to feel resentment against another. It offers a chance to recover from mistakes. It doesn't mean forgetting. Cancelling the debt releases us from bondage and bitterness. It means the past doesn't need to adversely affect today and tomorrow. Forgiveness is a choice I make to obey God, and to walk, in a higher realm by not allowing someone else's actions or attitudes to dictate my life.

When someone wrongs me I can choose to forgive (push cancel) or have a grudge (hit recall like on a computer). I can remember there is good about every person. I don't need to use the offense as another nail in their coffin.

## Bury the Hatchet

I remember a story about two men who let un-forgiveness destroy their relationship. Old Joe was dying. For years he had been at odds with Bill, who used to be his best friend. Joe sent for Bill so he could straighten things out. Bill arrived and Joe told him he was afraid to go into eternity with bad feelings between them. So reluctantly Joe apologized and told Bill he forgave him for all offenses. Things seemed fine until Bill turned to go. Joe called out to Bill, "Remember, if I get better, this doesn't count."[7]

This if often a picture of how we treat others. Often the forgiveness we offer to others is superficial and done with selfish motives. We say we've forgiven, but when the least bit of friction arises, we are quick to resurrect past grievances. We "bury the hatchet" with the handle sticking out, so we can easily pick it up again and use it to chop them over the head with.

True forgiveness buries the hatchet completely. It offers the glue that repairs broken relationships.

## Christ Restores

Forgiveness leads to reconciliation in relationships. Restoration should be in the same measure as the offense. If it was a private offense then private forgiveness is necessary. If it was a public offense then a public apology is needed. We don't want to use the offense as an opportunity to hurt others.

The primary goal is restoration. This is how Christ handled offenses. When Peter denied Him three times, Jesus sought him out. He forgave and restored Peter. The Lord asked Peter, "Do you love me." Jesus asked this of Peter, not once, but three times, the same number of times Peter denied him. (John 21:15-18). Peter knew he was forgiven. With the relationship mended, this disciple, soared to new heights. That's what forgiveness and restoration will do for us.

Jesus' method of forgiveness and other biblical accounts have helped me forgive others. Impetuous Peter asked the Lord, ". . . How often shall my brother sin against me and I forgive him? Up, to seven times?' Jesus said to him, 'I do not say to you, up to seven times, but up to seventy times seven'" (Matthew 18:21-22, NAS).

In answer to Peter's question, Jesus told a parable about a king who wanted to settle accounts with his servants. The king brought a man in who owed ten thousand talents. But he had no way to repay him. The ruler commanded the servant and his family to be sold and payment made to the king. The man pleaded with the leader to have mercy on him. The owner had compassion, released him and forgave him the debt. That same fellow went out and seized one of his neighbors who owed him a hundred days wages. He demanded the neighbor pay him back. The friend pleaded for mercy and insisted he would repay him. But the forgiven servant was unwilling to forgive his neighbor and had him thrown in prison. The other men saw what happened and delivered a report to the king. The ruler summoned the slave he had forgiven. He reminded him, he had forgiven him much more than he had to forgive his neighbor. The king was outraged and commanded the forgiven slave to be handed over to his torturers until, he paid all the debt. (Matthew 18: 23-35). "So shall My heavenly Father also do to you, if each of you does not forgive his brother from your heart" (Matthew 18:35 NAS).

## Forgiveness Model

This story of forgiveness coupled with what Jesus said on the Cross, "Father forgive them; they do not know what they are doing" (Luke 23:34, NAS), has been helpful to me.

The Lord instructed me, when I was having a difficult time forgiving, that I was to lace these two pieces together to create a Forgiveness Model. Remember others often don't realize how they have hurt us, or maybe they don't even know what they did. Much hurt is inflicted out of ignorance (not having all the facts). Forgiveness is a choice and a process that takes time and help from the Lord.

**Forgiveness Model**
**Father, forgive them their ignorance.**
**They don't know how bad they hurt me.**
**As an act of my will I choose to forgive you,**
**_____ for _____.**
**I release you from the heavy debt of un-**
**forgiveness I've had over your head.**
**You're free to go. You don't owe me anything,**
**because I didn't die on the cross for you.**
**But Jesus did. You owe Him everything. I'm releasing you to Jesus,**
**He can redeem you back to Himself. Jesus loves you!**

There is something about this model that gives us a sense of justice. Knowing there is righteousness from the Lord has assisted me to forgive myself and others. This model has helped many to let go of un- forgiveness and live a life of freedom.

## Forgiveness is a Healing Balm

"Forgiveness is the fragrance that the violet sheds on the heel that has crushed it," said Mark Twain. Forgiveness is something that all of us have difficulty with and must work hard on. God tells us it is possible to forgive any and all offenses because He has given us the ability to reconcile our differences. (2 Corinthians 5:18-19).

## No "Rent Free" Here

Without forgiveness we live in bondage. We are tied up with resentment and bitterness. Hanging onto resentment is letting someone you despise live rent free in your head. That gives the other person too much control over our emotions and reactions.

Forgiveness is the way out of bondage. It takes control from the enemy and gives it to the Lord. If we try to be in complete control in our relationships, we are doing the relationship and the other person a disservice. Yes, we must set boundaries in our relationships. The only control we will ever have in this life is when we let Jesus be in control of our strengths and our weaknesses. This is the ultimate control. Either we believe God is in control of everything or we believe he is in control of nothing. I choose to believe He is sovereign and oversees all things.

## Live in Peace and Love

God has shown me, it is not my responsibility to fix other relationships. But it is my calling to live in peace with others. "If it is possible . . . live peaceably with all men" (Romans 12:18). We are to try to resolve our relationship problems. Sometimes conflicts won't be resolved. It takes two to quarrel, and two to reconcile.

If we do our part and the problem still remains because the other person doesn't choose to forgive, there is still a plan we can follow. Romans 12:9-21 tells us how. Be affectionate.

Be prayerfully patient. Bless your persecutors. Be humble. Don't take revenge. We are to defeat evil, by doing good. Also, we must not harbor resentment or retaliate with the weapon of silence. It is imperative to allow God to work out the problem. We can follow this advice even when relationship problems aren't resolved. Our job is to be faithful, obedient and forgive all others just as Jesus forgave us.

We can truly say we have forgiven when we have good thoughts about the person who has offended us. We know we have forgiveness in our hearts when we can pray for the person to be blessed by the Lord.

The Lord has given us a commandment. "This is my commandment, that ye love one another, as I have loved you" (John 15:12). "By this all men shall know that ye are my disciples . . ." (John 13:35).

I desire that all my relationships be built on the foundations of the Lord's love. The Lord gave us His love and desires us to pass it on. His love and forgiveness is a great fragrance that we can leave behind in all relationships.

## Sweet Smelling Jewels

A dear woman left me with an aroma of Christ. This gem has helped me in all my relationships. She stated, "Don't compare yourself with others. Comparison will bring either pride or discouragement; and neither is good." This woman was a godly wife and mother. She declared that the Bible says older women should instruct younger women. (Titus 2:4).

Wives need to make it easy for their husbands to do the will of the Lord. Women aren't supposed to be the Holy Spirit in their husband's lives. We need to love them and let them take their rightful role. One of the best things a mother can do for her children is to show love to their daddy. We need to get our priorities straight and realize home is a very important place to teach lessons and set examples.

We glorify God when we are doing His will and in our proper positions. May we be able to say what Jesus declared, "I have glorified thee on the earth: I have finished the work which thou gavest me to do" (John 17:4).

## Aroma of Friendship

There are many other people that spurred me to greater growth in the Lord. "Iron sharpeneth iron; so a man sharpeneth the countenance of his friend" (Proverbs 27:17). I'm thankful for the way friends and acquaintances have helped me grow.

I AM THANKFUL FOR MY FRIENDS

God, when I consider all my blessings, I am especially grateful
for my friends.

As these dear ones share joy and laughter with me. I am
    reminded of your love and care.
Through a sense of humor and ability to help me look at the
    light side of life,
They radiate your goodwill. I am thankful for my friends' love,
    warmth, and concern.

God, I am thankful for the many ways my friends share light
    and guidance.
I enjoy the times we exchange ideas and inspire one another.
I appreciate their wisdom and loving support . . .

God, thank You for making my friends just the way they are.
Thank You for their unique personalities, faith, and dedication.
Thank You, God, for my friends!

## Jesus Carries My Load

God has used many people to speak to us, when we least expect it. While my family and I were traveling, we saw an eighteen-wheeler whiz by. As he passed us, I saw this message on his mud flaps: "JESUS CARRIES MY LOAD." "How neat," I thought! Yes, the truck driver was leaving his influence all along the highway. He left an important message. The Lord will carry all our burdens.

Just as that truck driver left his peaceful aroma to all on the road, we can do the same. God speaks to us, and says our influence needs to be a godly one. When we cross other people's paths, the aromatic scent of Jesus needs to linger in their nostrils and draw them to Him. I thank God He uses us to spread His fragrance everywhere. (2 Corinthians 2:14).

# Four Keys to Unlock A Sad Heart (Grief)

## 1. Think

Think about your memories of what you have lost. Memories are a journey we take in our minds. We relive it in our heart. Memory is a way of holding onto the things we love, the things we are, and the things we never want to lose. Take a memory trip and remember the good times.

## 2. Write

Write, or journal your thoughts or draw pictures. Now remember to write two things you are thankful for everyday. Writing slows you down so you can reflect, make sense of your feelings.

## 3. Talk

Talk about your feelings to the Lord and with other safe people. That safe person is one that will listen to you without offering solutions or criticism. They will let you say what you need to say, and never tell you to be quiet.

## 4. Weep

Tears are words that can't be spoken. Weep or cry, it is a God given right. It cleanses our souls and makes us feel better. Tears are jewels of remembrance of what we lost.

Here's an easy way to remember the four keys. Just remember the first letter of each key, T for think, W for write, T for talk, W for weep. That's T,W,T,W.

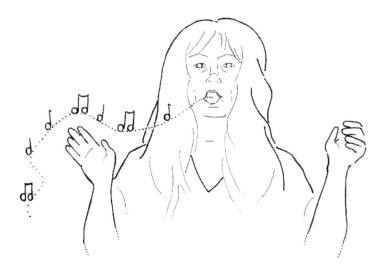

## CHAPTER 7

# *Music*

"And he hath put a new song in my mouth, even praise unto our God: many shall see it, and fear and shall trust in the Lord."
Psalm 40:3.

Music is a universal language that has been with us since the beginning of time. God instructs us many times through melodies and lyrics. The Bible shows us, ". . . I will sing praises unto the Lord" (Psalm 27:6). "Bring the music, strike the tambourine, play the melodious harp and lyre" (Psalm 81:2 NIV). There are many references in God's Word about making music with instruments and our voices.

Our creator gave us the ability and desire to sing. The love of vocalizing and making melodies was given so we could exalt him. Music is laughter of the soul that is translated into song. "Let us come before his presence with thanksgiving, and make a joyful noise unto him with psalms . . ." (Psalm 95:2). We are to make a joyful sound unto the Lord with all our being.

Many times after hearing a new tune, it rolls around in my mind and off my tongue, several days later. God impressed me with the importance of music. The lyrics and melodies we listen to goes into our subconscious and spirit.

## Praise Emerges From Distress

The Lord inspired people to write songs born out of great losses. God's Word tells us how Hannah's barren womb was a troubling distress to her. She prayed and cried before the Lord. Then after her son Samuel was born and weaned, she presented him to the Lord. Hannah sang this song of praise to the Lord.

> ". . .My heart rejoiceth in the Lord,
> Mine horn is exalted in the Lord:
> My mouth is enlarged over mine enemies:
> Because I rejoice in, Thy salvation.
> There is none holy as the Lord:
> For there is none beside thee:
> Neither is there any rock like our God"
> Samuel 2:1-2.

## Mental Anguish a Silver Lining

Many songs were also inspired by great trials in people's lives. William Cowper and John Newton were men who teamed up and wrote of their life experiences.

While visiting a museum in Olney, England, I discovered that Cowper had been plagued with mental illness. He was eventually admitted to an insane asylum, where he remained for eighteen months. Cowper wrote 67 hymns in the Olney Hymnal. Two of these great works *"O for a Closer Walk with God"* and *"God Moves in a Mysterious Way,"* came out of Cowper's mental anguish.

> *"God Moves in a Mysterious Way"*
> "God moves in a mysterious way
> His wonders to perform;
> He plants His foot steps
> In the sea and rides upon the storm.

You fearful saints, fresh courage take:
The clouds you so much dread are big with mercy,
And shall break, in blessings, on your head."[1]

This hymn ministers encouragement. It helps me remember that God's ways are higher than mine. There is so much I don't understand and God doesn't always explain His plans to us even though we may ask, "why?"

Another musical piece ministers comfort when I ask why my youngest sister was extremely ill with Multiple Sclerosis. The song, *"Trust His Heart,"* reminds us that all things work for our good. Often, we can't see how they could. It tells us that God is too wise to make any mistakes. Even if we can't see His plan, we must trust His heart of love for us.[2]

This vocalization helped me realize that God had a plan for each of our lives. He only allows trials and suffering to make us more like Him. Trusting His heart means I trust and understand His character, of love.

Even though my head understood that God uses tragedy to perfect us; often my heart couldn't grasp it. I was having trouble trusting The Lord, when a couple in our church lost their infant twins. During the memorial service, a vocal number ministered comfort to me. It helped me learn to trust Him even more. The song, asks a question, "Do I trust you?" It says the Lord knows my heart and He knows I'd rather die than lose my faith in Him. You were God before this situation. You will never change. I will trust you.[3]

This vocal number made me ask myself, do I trust you Lord? I concluded; I do trust God. Yes, I would rather die than lose my faith in the one I love. The song strengthened my resolve to trust. I also knew right then, the parents would trust God even though they were racked with pain. It would take a long time for the scars of their loss to heal.

## Scars Fade Away

We have many wounds inflicted here on earth. But when we get to heaven, there will not be any pain or blemishes. The only scars in heaven will be the ones in Jesus hands, feet and side. The following lyrics are like healing to the wounds.

*"The Only Scars in Heaven"*
When I think about the day when we'll stand in Heavens light;

When all tears are washed away and we're kneeling in His sight;
All the scars we gained in battle as we journeyed toward the prize
Quickly fade away when we look into His eyes.
The only scars in Heaven are the scars on Jesus hands.
A reminder of love freely given, love that never ends . . .[4]

This vocal piece projected healing and joy to me. It's great to think that we will be perfect in heaven without scars. Jesus' matchless love is the only thing that can heal our hurts here on earth. Sometimes others unwittingly cause us pain and it creates scars.

## Oh So Loved

Even when we are hurt, or are riddled with many scars, He still loves us. The Lord used the following song to help me understand how very much he loves each one of us.

*"I am Loved"*
I am loved, I am loved, I can risk loving you.
For the one who knows me best, loves me most.
I am loved, you are loved, won't you please take my hand.
We are free to love each other, we are loved.

I said if you knew, you wouldn't want me.
My scars are hidden by the face I wear.
He said, my child, My scars go deeper.
It was love for you that put them there.

Forgiven, I'm forgiven. And clean before my Lord, I freely stand.
Oh, I'm forgiven. I can dare to forgive my brother.
I've been forgiven. I reach out to take your hand.[5]

God reached out and took our hand in love. He wants us to extend that same love to others who have life's scars and don't feel loved. God's love is the only thing that can heal the wounds. Often when we have experienced traumatic situations, we have difficulty trusting others. It is hard to believe that people won't hurt us again. Regardless of the struggles in life, we can always rely on our Lord.

## Sorrows Roll, Like the Waves

Horatio Spafford knew how to trust without understanding. He was able to stand on the Lord's promises through many tragedies. He lost his only son. Later, his Business was destroyed by the great Chicago fire of 1871. Two years later, all four of his daughters drown, when the ship they sailed on sank, in the Atlantic. His wife was miraculously saved from the ship wreck. As Spafford sailed on another ship to meet his wife and console her, he was given comfort by God and wrote:

> *"It Is Well With My Soul."*
> "When peace, like a river, attendeth my way,
> When sorrows like sea billows roll -
> Whatever my lot, Thou hast taught me to say,
> It is well with my soul . . .
> And, Lord, haste the day when my faith shall be sight,
> The clouds be rolled back as a scroll:
> The trump shall resound and the Lord shall descend,
> 'Even so' - it is well with my soul . . .
> It is well with my soul."[6]

God used Spafford's lyrics to help me realize God is in control of my life. No matter what happens I want to be able to say, "It is well with my soul." He will bring me through any trial. My soul is at rest in God's care.

## Amazing Grace

The Lord's protection inspired John Newton, a slave trader, while he was in a fierce storm at sea. Fearful for his life he started reading a book, *"The Imitation of Christ"* by Thomas A. Kempis. God used this reading and the fear of ship wreck to bring the slave trader to Christ. Newton became a changed man and wrote many songs to include:

> *"Amazing Grace."*
> "Amazing Grace, how sweet the sound that saved a wretch like me!
> I once was lost but now am found, was blind but now I see.
> Twas grace that taught my heart to fear, and grace my fears relieved;
> How precious did that grace appear, the hour I first believed!"[7]

This song spoke volumes about how truly amazing God's grace is. It is impossible to describe it, except to say, it's God's Riches at Christ's Expense. Grace is something none of us deserve. However, I can continually thank Him in words and music for His blessings.

Each new composition puts a melody in our mouth. Words of praise and gratitude have blessed many people. Many of these lyrics were written out of a grateful heart after the Lord carried the writer through a difficult situation. Their song applauded how great and mighty God is.

Praise is an expression of approval, to laud the glory of God as in songs. It is most usually connected with The Lord. He deserves our esteem because He made us, died for us, and rose again. He reigns supreme.

The Word of God tells us that we should praise God in all things. "In everything give thanks . . ." (1 Thessalonians 5:18). We are to extol whether it is a time of peace, or in the midst of the trials. We don't thank God for the difficulty. We praise Him that He's in control and knows what is best for us. We thank God again when He brings us out of the trial.

The psalmist tells us how to extol God. ". . . I will praise the Lord with my whole heart" (Psalm 111:1). The object of our adoration is Our Maker. We are to acknowledge His power, wonder, and His works. Often it is a struggle to have gratitude through the uncertainties of life. The Lord asked me, "Will you worship me? Give me your heart, your all?" I had to conclude with, yes Lord.

God was prompting me to be willing to give Him something. This was a challenge to surrender myself as an instrument of worship. Take me Lord, my heart, my mind and all I am. Transform me into your image.

It is an act of worship to ask the Lord to change us. We are to bless Him all the while we live. God's Word tells us that we are to continually praise the Lord with all of our being. So often I fall short of magnifying Him. He instructed me I needed His power if gratitude was to be a continual way of life for me. Often my spirit is hungry, but my flesh is weak. Lord, light the fire in my soul and make me whole. I would only have his power, if He was breathing His life right through me, like a mighty wind.

When we praise, we are offering grateful homage to God in word or song. This makes my spirit want to soar with thanksgiving. I will lift your name on high, Lord. I'm glad you're in my life. You came from heaven to earth to show us the way. Lord you paid my debt. I will lift up your name.

Gratitude glorifies and exalts God. It puts a song in our hearts. When God saves our soul and redeems us, he becomes the new words and music of our lives. He is the melody and the harmony. He is the mighty God. I will return all the songs you have given to me, Lord. You are the tune I sing.

## Catchy Childhood tunes

Often I have been reminded of songs sung as a child. Those things learned when we are young, stay with us. There is usually a catchy rhyme or tune. Songs are one of the best ways to teach children important messages.

The Lord reminded me of a refrain sung as a child. He spoke to me about the importance of keeping our vessel filled.

> "Give me oil in my lamp, I pray.
> Give me oil in my lamp keep me burning,
> Keep me burning till the light of day.
> Sing Hosanna, sing Hosanna to the Lord of Lords."

God's message penetrated my mind through this piece of music. He emphasized the need to continually have the oil (of spending time with him in the Word and prayer) in our lamps. So we will keep burning until the light of day. The light of Day, refers to when we go home to be with Him.

The Lord spoke through another catchy rhyme, as a five-year old boy sang.

> "Freely, freely you have received, freely, freely give.
> Go in my name and because you believe
> Others will know that I live."

God captured my attention with this tune. He has freely given everything we need for a victorious life. We are to go and let others know about it. We are also to give freely out of our resources to help others. It's only in giving that we create more room to receive from God. We are made richer by giving than hoarding.

Another truth the Lord taught through a children's refrain was, Jesus loves me. This song says:

"Jesus loves me all the time, all the time,
Jesus loves me all the time,
He's my best friend."

The Lord speaks very clearly to us through this song. He loves us and is our best friend. We need to be communicating this message to all people.

God is so very good to us. Who else would ever be our best friend? This song, *"God is so good,"* was taught by a Scottish Family, the Cameron's. It's a really catchy tune that is so easy to remember.

"God is so good. He is so good.
He is so good. I love him so.
I love him so. He is so good to me."

## Good News

Our Father is so very good and can teach us through music. Often He sends others along to teach us new refrains. There's a song that really exemplifies that. It talks about those who bring good news to us.

"How lovely on the mountains are the feet of him who
Bring good news, good news;
Proclaiming peace, announcing news of happiness,
Our God reigns. Our God reigns" (Isaiah 52:7).

## Listen With Your Heart

God has used many people to bring good news and encouragement through songs. One musician brought hope as she sang.

*"Listen with your heart."*
"Today I tried to share with you that
My heart is an open door. . .
And though you hear the words I say,
If you'll read between the lines,
You'll find the words unspoken,
'Hold all the valentines.'
Listen with your heart and you'll hear love. . .
Someday, I'll learn to say it well. . .
But till that day I'll have to pray,

You'll hear me with your heart.
Listen with your heart and you'll hear love."[8]

As I listened to the refrain, the Lord spoke to me. We often listen with our ears and head, but not with our hearts. We don't always hear the real message others are trying to communicate, but God does. Listening with the heart is to feel another's pain and let it be part of us for a moment. When we can empathize, we are able to respond out of the depth of our being to others. This song taught me the importance of attending with my heart.

## Pride – a Prancing Horse

One powerful piece of music brought instructions for life.

> *"Not a prancing horse."*
> "Not a prancing horse, haughty and proud.
> Full of myself; swayed by the crowd.
> Lord willing to be, what you want me to be.
> With eyes not on man; looking only to thee.
> Let me flow with the spirit, not run ahead,
> Or drag behind, and may I listen,
> When I should be listening, and act when it is time.
> Not a prancing horse, haughty and proud,
> Filled with myself."[9]

This message from the song really sank in after I went to a state fair and saw show horses strutting. They were side stepping and prancing, their heads held high. The words immediately popped into my mind and I began humming it to myself. The Lord began nudging me. "I don't want you to be like that horse. I don't want you haughty, or proud. I want you humble. Pride has no place in my kingdom." Between the song and seeing the stallions, The Lord finally got an important message through to me. Pride often causes us to be inflexible.

## Sway With the Storm

God ministered a truth to me through a musical piece *"Strong Enough to Bend."* The song talked about a tree in the back yard that had never been broken by the wind. The reason it wasn't toppled was because it was strong enough to bend. The song writer likened this to us in a relational conflict. If we are flexible enough to sway with the storm, our relationships will last forever. Often we say something wrong we can't take back. We apologize. We have just swayed with the wind. We are strong and have just bent. The job of having a good relationship takes two. We can sway with the winds, if we are strong enough to bend."[10]

God's message through this song emphasizes that it takes more strength to bend with humility than it takes to be inflexible with pride. We will be broken when the storms of life come if we can't let go of pride and un-forgiveness.

## I'm Sorry

One day while listening to the radio, I heard lyrics that pricked my ego. The refrain reminded me of old injuries I had sustained. As I listened to the song, I began to realize that not only had I been hurt but, I had also wounded others.

> *"I'm Sorry"*
> "Sarah . . . Was five years old?
> I was eight, I was great,
> I lived across the street.
> We moved in before they did,
> Which gave me the right?
> To be mean, she was green.
> It would be quick defeat.
> Everyone laughed, cause she was meeker than us.
> Here came my chance to prove, that I was tough.
>
> Chorus:
> I'm sorry I pushed you down.
> I did not know what I was doing.
> I thought I'd grow taller, if I made you smaller
>
> Forgiveness finds me every time, I beg to be made new. . .
> Whatever I have done to one of these . . .
> You have said, I have done to You.
> When I hurt someone, it takes days for me to say,

'Jesus, what have I done?'
And so I come to you, my heart to bear.
Won't You hear me as I pray this prayer? . . ."[11]

It really hurt me to realize that every time I wounded someone, I had done it to Jesus. I don't want to continue to injure my Lord. Therefore, I must ask forgiveness of others, and extend that same forgiveness to those who have inflicted pain on me. I am not accountable for what others have done to me but I'm responsible for what I've done to them.

Forgiving others and ourselves is one of the most difficult tasks. We must have God's help to accomplish it. Forgiveness is the glue that mends broken relationships. It washes away the bitterness, hates and let's love flow freely within a relationship.

## Nothing Less Than All Your Love

A country love ballad spoke about material things we give to our mates. The lyrics said, "You can give me all these fancy gifts, but, *I'll accept nothing less than all your love.*" Material possessions aren't the most important things in our lives. They don't make us happy. The Lord spoke to me as I listened. He said, "I want all your love. I want a relationship with you. I don't want you to just do good things for Me. I want you to love Me, with all your heart." God's Word confirms this. (Matthew 22:37).

One way we can love the Lord with our life is to be a servant. Serving others is not our natural tendency. It is difficult and we must have God's help. The Lord really spoke to my heart in song. "Make me a servant humble and meek. Lord let me lift up those who are weak." Lord may the prayer of my heart always be, make me a servant.

## Edelweiss – All Alone

A musician ministered a beautiful message as she sang *"Edelweiss."* This is a plant that grows way up the mountain side, sometimes all by itself in a barren place. She states that even in hard times we are to be growing like this flower. Where no one sees us, may we serve not to be seen, but to please Our Lord.[12]

Many times we will be in situations, jobs or organizations, where we are one of the few Christians. We are to grow strong even though we are the only flower on the mountain. When we are in situations like the Edelweiss, we may feel lonely and like we are in a dry desolate area.

## Audience of One

Often in the desert area, we don't feel anyone appreciates us. We like to have an audience of people telling us we are doing a good job. We desire someone's applause. In a dry area of my life, God used a song to speak to me about the place applause should play in my life.

> *"Audience of One"*
> "It's such a strong temptation to live
> For man's applause.
> But I don't want to buy into the lie
> Cause I know that's not a worthy cause.
> So to keep things in perspective,
> I hung a sign up on the wall.
> The sign is nothing special but it
> Really says it all . . .
>
> I'll be content to serve an audience of one.
> Only His approval, counts when all is said and done.
> And this is my prayer when the race is finally run.
> I want to hear 'Well done'
> From the Audience of One . . ."[13]

The Lord ministered to me that only His approval of "Well done," counts for eternity. We don't need others applause. While we are performing for an audience of One, He is working humility in our lives.

## Bigger Things

Another musical piece says it well. Musician Gay Hyde sang *"He is Doing, Something Wonderful in Our Lives."* In the song, she relates God is doing bigger things than we will ever understand. He can see everything. We just need to be done with doubt and fear and trust his love for us. God is achieving more through some of the delays in our lives. We just need to keep expecting awesome blessings from his hand.[14]

If we make a habit of anticipating great things, we will see beautiful things in our lives and in others. The following song spoke an important truth to me.

> *"Something Beautiful"*
> "Something beautiful, something good,
> All I had to offer him was brokenness and strife.
> But he's making something beautiful out of my life."

## The Master's Touch

When we offer the Lord our brokenness and strife, He can make our lives beautiful. All it takes is the touch of God's hand to restore our lives and make them valuable.

> *"Touch of the Masters Hand"*
> "Well, it was battered and scarred
> And the auctioneer felt it was hardly worth his while
> To waste much time on the old violin,
> But he held it up with a smile . . .
> Now who'll start the bid on this old violin . . .
> Oh, give me one dollar, who'll make it two.
> Only, two dollars who'll make it three?
> Three dollars twice now that's a good price . . .
>
> From the back of the crowd a gray-haired man
> Came forward and picked up the bow.
> He wiped the dust from the old violin . . .
> Then he played out a melody pure and sweet . . .
> And then the music stopped.
> And the auctioneer, with a voice that was quiet and low,
> He said, what's my bid, for this old violin . . . ?
> One, give me one thousand, who'll make it two.
> Only two thousand, who'll make it three . . .
> The people cried out what made the change,
> We don't understand. Then the auctioneer stopped,
> And he said with a smile.
> It was the touch of the Master's hand.

> You know many a man with a life out of tune is battered and
> scarred with sin.
> He's auctioned cheap to a thankless world much like that old
> violin.
> Then the master comes and the foolish crowd,
> They never understand. Oh, the worth of a soul,
> And the change that is wrought,
> Just by one touch of the master's hand . . ."[15]

Yes, when our maker touches our lives, He changes us. God leaves the melody of beauty behind.

## Peace My Child

Peace and beauty often come after the storms of life. God used another song to remind me of the importance of peace in my life.

> *"Be at Peace My Child"*
> "Be, at peace my child, I am aware of you,
> Though, trouble may seem too much to bear.
> Be at peace my child. I send my angels,
> Each night, to watch over you.
> There will no evil thing come nigh you.
> Be at peace my child.
> I am God, creator of this universe.
> Place your care on me. Be at peace my child.
> These things I have spoken. Ye will find peace in me.
> In the world there is tribulation,
> But I've overcome this world."[16]

The Lord ministered to me through this refrain. He said, "I see and I understand everything you are going through. But be at peace because I am in control."

Another way we can be at peace is to take stock of all the gifts the Lord has given us. This old song challenged me to develop a better attitude.

> "Count your blessings, name them one by one.
> See what the Lord has done for you."

Adding up heavenly favors, gives us a grateful perspective on life. It helps keep us in peace.

## Fear Not, I'll Be There

Many of the songs are filled with God's Word and His promises. I'm so glad Our Father doesn't break His oaths. One of his promises set to music is:

> "Fear not for I am with you.
> Fear not for I am with you,
> Fear not for I am with you says the Lord.
> I have redeemed you. I have called you by name.
> Child you are mine.
> When you walk through the water I'll be there.
> When you walk through the flame, I'll be there.
> No way you'll be burned.
> No way, you'll be drowned, for I am with you"
> (Isaiah 43:1-2).

Because this is directly from the Word of God, it speaks powerfully to us. The Lord uses His Word to teach us to trust Him. In this scripture song He says, "Don't be afraid. You are my child, I know you by name and I am going to be with you no matter what you go through."

Sometimes we wonder when we look at ourselves, how God could have called us by name. He sees people and things differently than we do.

## Look at the Heart

The Lord nudged me through a song. The lyrics were based on the Bible story of David, a shepherd boy. He was anointed King of Israel.

The song, *"Shepherd Boy,"* has a powerful message. The musical piece relates, when others saw a shepherd boy, God saw a king. Even though our lives seem very ordinary, God can touch us and everything changes, when God sees a king instead of a shepherd boy.[17]

This song caused me to think about how God views us. He is more concerned about the motive of our heart, than He is our outward appearance. Man looks at the outward appearance, but Our Lord looks at the motive of the heart. (1Samuel 16:7). We make judgments on what we view. We don't see the potential in others that God sees. This is especially true when another person hurts us.

One morning, I was angry when a family member unintentionally hurt another person in our family. At that moment, I didn't see the potential God saw in her. I didn't understand what prompted the insensitive act. However, the Lord was merciful and later spoke to me through music. As we toured a Christian Broadcasting Studio, we sang a scripture tune in the chapel. The words cut deep into my heart.

> "Thou hast created all things,
> And for thy pleasure thou hast created,
> Thou hast created all things" (Revelations 4:11).

The Lord convicted me through this song and said, "Yes, I've created all things. I have created this loved one you are having problems with. I've created them for my pleasure. You need to learn how to love and accept them just as they are." It was beautiful the way Jesus helped me see my judgmental spirit.

## Clean My Heart

I responded with, "Lord I can't root out this evil, You are going to have to help me." Then another scripture song floated into my head.

> "Create in me a pure clean heart oh Lord my God,
> And renew a steadfast spirit within me.
> Do not cast me from your presence.
> But restore unto me the joy of your salvation
> And grant me a willing spirit, to sustain me"
> (Psalm 51:10-12).

This was part of my answer, first I needed to examine myself and admit my sins. Then I would be ready to let the Lord teach me how to accept others without compromising my values. My creator instructed me through another song.

It states, we have the power in Jesus name. Though Satan rages we won't be defeated. One of the reasons we have power is because of God working within us. "Greater is He that is within me than he that is within the world" (1 John 4:4). This is a beautiful scripture refrain. When we grasp this with our hearts, we will be victorious. Our Maker is greater than any other force. When we realize how awesome God is, our song of prayer will be: Lord I want to be more like you. I want to be a vessel you can work through.

## Nothing is too hard

I'm so glad His grace is new every day and He can use us. No matter what has gone on yesterday, I can worship God today.

> "This is the day that the Lord has made.
> I will rejoice and be glad in it.
> This is the day that the Lord has made."
> (Psalm 118:24).

The Lord gently whispered His truth through this refrain. He said, "I've created this day for you to serve and love me. I created it so you can make a conscious choice, to obediently do my will. Nothing will come across your path this day, that will be too hard for You and me to handle."

> "Ah, Lord God! Behold, thou hast made the heaven and the earth
> By thy great power and stretched out arm,
> And nothing is too hard for thee. . ." (Jeremiah 32:17)

We can reflect on this truth as we wage battles we don't know how to handle. Remember, nothing is too hard for the Lord. If we trust Him, He will give us success.

## He Misses Time, With Me

Victory will be ours if we have a relationship with Him in prayer. I hadn't considered how God felt, when I didn't spend time with Him. Then I heard this song, *"I Miss My Time with You."*

The song reflects on how God is waiting for us to come to Him so He can fill us with strength and wisdom for the battle of the day. Our Father says, He misses our time with Him. When His children are too busy to pray, it hurts Him. Yet, we are trying to serve Him. He will provide the power if I take time to pray. He won't have to say, "I miss my time with you."[18]

I don't want to hurt My Lord. I want to learn how to know Him better. When I am with God, then He can fill me with His strength and wisdom. This is one of the most important ways to victory.

The Lord tells us how we will be winners. We don't have to control everything. Turn it over to God. Let Him fight the battle. Then progress will be ours.

One of the ways we will have success in the battles, is to listen to what this song adapted from scripture says.

> "He hath shown thee, O man, what is good;
> And what doth the Lord require of thee,
> But to do justly, and to love mercy,
> And, walk humbly, with Thy God." (Micah 6:8)

## Secret Places

We must live justly and walk in humility. As we do this, we are dwelling with God in the secret places of life. His Word adapted to music says:

> "He that dwelleth in the secret places of the most high,
> Shall abide under the shadow, of the Almighty.
> I will say of the Lord, He is my refuge and my fortress:
> My God; in him will I trust" (Psalm 91:1-2).

God reminded me that the secret places are the times of peace, love and joy that we experience in our lives. It's His calm that keeps us in rest.

It's only when we are trusting in The Lord, that we can hear Him speak. We need to be able to step out and obey Him when He speaks. We must *"Step into the Water."* The refrain says, we must get out into the water if we are going to be set free.

God is speaking to us today. It is in the depths of His River where we see healing, salvation, and all we need. So "step out and be set free,"[19]

We must walk out in faith. This is like stepping out into the water and beginning to swim. Victory doesn't usually come until we are obedient.

We plunge into the water of life's circumstances, and trust the Lord to meet our needs.

## Time to Trust

Many times it is difficult to trust. Especially, when we pray and don't get a reply. Often, I have asked God what takes His response so long. He answered my question through a song.

> *"Time to Trust"*
> "There are times when we pray
> And we knock on heaven's door.
> It seems we can't get through, there's no reply;
> And there are times when we feel
> That the answer may not come,
> Then the Lord reveals the reason why.
>
> He's giving us time, time to trust,
> Time to believe the One who knows what's best for us;
> He's giving us time, time to trust,
> Turning our feelings into faith, so while we wait,
> He's giving us time to trust. . ."[20]

Learning to rely is a sure ways God gives us victory. An old hymn written in 1886, by Rev. John H. Sammis, says it well.

> *"Trust and Obey"*
> When we walk with the Lord in the light of His Word,
> What a glory He sheds on our way!
> While we do His good will He abides with us still,
> And with all, who will trust and obey.
>
> Chorus
> Trust and obey, for there's no other way
> To be happy in Jesus, but to trust and obey.

Through this song, God reminds us that trusting Him and obeying His instruction, is essential. It brings blessings and prosperity.

## Don't Dwell on Mistakes

Success comes by not ruminating on mistakes of the past. These lyrics from scripture ministers hope.

> "Remember not the former things,
> Neither, consider the things of old,
> Behold, I will do a new thing;
> Now it shall spring forth; shall ye not know it?
> I will even make a way in the wilderness,
> And rivers in the desert" (Isaiah 43:18-19).

Many times when we begin to dwell on the former things, we get discouraged. The Lord wants us to deal with our mistakes. We are to ask for forgiveness. Remember our errors only as a source of growth, not condemnation.

## Joined to the Vine

An important way we can mature is to pursue Our Maker. Then we will have a hunger to be joined to Him, our vine. A musician sang a refrain, *"Joined, to the vine."* She relates we weren't meant to struggle and try to draw on our own resources. We are to abide in the Lord and stay joined to him, like the branches are joined to the vine. We will need to be pruned and it will hurt. When we are disciplined it means, we are a branch that has stayed joined to the vine.[21]

It's not by our abilities but by God's strength and His Word that we stay connected to Him. We must come to the place where we can say with the song:

> "Thy will be done, Thy kingdom come,
> But most of all thy will be done in me."

## Arise Shine

When we sing this refrain, the Lord is ready for us to arise and shine. We are to be guiding beacons to the world.

> "Arise, shine, for thy light has come,
> The glory of the Lord is risen upon thee" (Isaiah 60:1).

He wants us to rise up and let His flame glow through us. As we let our light shine, we have strength to go in His Name. The song, *"Going in His Name"* gives us courage to go in the Lord's Name because he has called us. We are His temple. We are His mouthpiece, His hands and feet. Daily give Him your all so your weak flesh may let His strength shine through you. You didn't choose Him, He chose you. You're going in His name.[22]

## Yes Lord

As I go in His Name, I must be able to say, yes Lord. I will say yes to your will and to your way. My whole heart agrees. My answer is yes, Lord, from the bottom of my heart.

We say "Yes Lord," obediently because, Thou art worthy. God is worthy of everything we could possibly offer Him because He gave us His best gift, Jesus. This makes us want to praise Him with all of our being.

Through God's Word He instructs us; gratitude is the key that unlocks the door to worship and victory. 2 Chronicles 20, shows the importance of praise. An army put the praise and worshiper's ahead of the fighting troops. Their shouts of joy ambushed the enemy.

Every marching military formation uses chanting cadence. I ask why? God showed me that chanting encouragement lifts our souls and our morale. It helps us go forward. It shows the enemy that we have life in us. We are ready to do battle.

We don't win all the battles. When we suffer defeat, we can assess our losses. We can go forward in God's power to take back what was stolen. This refrain gave me determination to rescue what Satan had taken. The song talks about going to the enemy's camp and taking back what he stole from me. I need to put the Devil under my feet. Then I can come and give the Lord the highest praise, Hallelujah.

## Whose Report Will You Believe

When we go to the enemy's camp, he will try to make us believe it's not possible to recover our losses. It's then we must determine whose report we are going to believe. Will I believe God's Word or will I believe the account Satan tries to hand me? The Lord ministered through this song and challenged me to believe and speak His Word. The lyrics asked us what record we will believe. What is the Lords reply? God's Word says I am healed and free. I have victory. I will believe the report of the Lord! Positive affirmation is a part of our battle armor.

## Listen to the Words and the Music

God's praise can always be a new song in our mouth. It brings glory to His name. It also brings victory to us, His children. People will see and know we are trusting in the Lord.

God instructs us to live victorious lives through music. As we listen to the *"words"* and the *"music,"* of the songs, we will hear God speak to us. "I will hear what God the Lord will speak . . ." (Psalm 85:8).

## Chapter 8

# *Spoken and Written Messages*

"And it shall come to pass afterwards, that I will pour out my spirit upon all
flesh, and your sons and your daughters shall prophesy . . ."
(Joel 2:28).

Often God uses His servants and speaks in numerous ways to us. Our
maker gave us ability to use speech, a written alphabet and intelligence.
These abilities are to bring honor and glory to His Name. Our Father talks
to, and through us, in spoken and written language.

The Lord has often used revelations to get our attention. Prophecies
are a divinely inspired foretelling or predicting of future events.

God's word tells us the purpose of a prophetic utterance. "But everyone
who prophesies speaks to men for their strengthening, encouragement and
comfort . . ." (1 Corinthians 14:3 NIV). A prophecy instructs or exhorts

us. It helps us grow, to be encouraged and comforted in our daily lives. These messages are a Word from the Lord.

## Predictions

The first prophecy was given to Satan. God gave this prediction after the enemy had deceived Eve in the Garden of Eden. "And I will put enmity between thee and the woman, and between thy seed and her seed; it shall bruise thy head, and thou shalt bruise his heel" (Genesis 3:15). This message also says the seed of Eve, (Jesus) will bruise Satan's head.

Many prophecies were given about Jesus before He came to earth. One prediction tells where the Messiah will be born. "But you, Bethlehem . . . out of you will come for me one who will be ruler over Israel, whose origins are from of old . . ." (Micah 5:2 NIV).

Another for telling predicts Jesus will be born of a virgin. And He will be given the name of Immanuel (Isaiah 7:14).

The Word also tells us that Jesus would be despised and crucified with criminals. (Isaiah 53:3). Scriptures declare that Jesus will rise from the grave. "Because you will not abandon me to the grave, nor will you let your Holy One see decay" (Psalm 16:10 NIV).

## Fulfilled Prophecies

We see the fulfilling of these prophecies in the New Testament accounts of Jesus' life. After Jesus was born in Bethlehem, the Wise Men came from the east and asked where He was. (Matthew 2:1-2).

Predictions of Jesus' death and resurrection were also fulfilled. Two robbers were crucified with Him. One hung on a cross to His right, and the other one to His left. (Mark 15:26-28). ". . . You are looking for Jesus the Nazarene, who was crucified. He has risen! He is not here." (Mark 16:6 NIV). Many more predictions of the Bible have already been fulfilled.

## A Prophet Speaks with God and Man

Prophecies must have a messenger to deliver them. Gay Hyde (a musician) defines a prophets as, "One that speaks for God to man, and one who speaks to God, on behalf of man." He is an intercessor. The messenger has a big responsibility. They need to hear very clearly and know the message they are receiving is from God.

The Word in Joel 2:28 says, the ability to prophesy will be poured out on all people. Listen you may hear His instruction.

There are many biblical examples of messengers. Our Lord was often referred to as a prophet. Jesus asked a Samaritan woman at a well for a drink of water. Instead of her giving Him a drink, they talked and He offered her living water. "Sir, the woman said, 'I can see that you are a prophet" (John 4:19 NIV).

The chief priests and Pharisees didn't like what Jesus said about them. Consequently, they wanted to arrest Him, but didn't. They were afraid of the crowds because many people said He was a prophet. (Matthew 21:45). The Lord was more than a spokesman; He was the Son of God.

Other examples of prophets are numerous in the Word of God. The Lord spoke to Moses and told him he would be a god to Pharaoh. And He gave him Aaron as his spokesman. (Exodus 7:1). Samuel was also God's mouthpiece. "And all Israel . . . recognized that Samuel was attested as a prophet of the Lord." (1 Samuel 3: 20 NIV).

Elisha often heard from God and passed this information to Israel's kings. (2 King 6: 12).

## Messages Received

The Bible is packed with stories of prophets and ordinary people who were given messages from the Lord. Abraham received many prophesies from God. The Lord told him he would give his wife Sarai a son, and she would be the mother of nations. (Genesis 17:15-16 NIV). God began the fulfillment of this pledge when Isaac was born. (Genesis 21:2-3).

Rebekah (Isaac's wife) received a prophecy after she inquired of the Lord about why the babies were jostling within her womb. "The Lord said to her, 'Two nations are in your womb . . . The older will serve the younger'" (Genesis 25:23 NIV).

God fulfilled His prophecy to Rebekah. She was an ordinary wife. Yet, when she sought Her Maker, He spoke to her. The same is true today. When we seek to hear from The Lord, He will speak to us.

Prophecies may be given to other people for us, or given directly to us by God. Most of us receive messages both ways.

While at a church service, I received a prophecy from God through a minister. He proclaimed, "Father, in the name of the Lord Jesus Christ

I lay my hands upon my sister. I thank you for her. I thank you for the tenderness of her heart. Let's be quiet before the Lord. 'Oh, it's been a long way through the long tunnels and the corridors of time. My voice has come to you. There have been times when it's been so far away, so indistinct. You've wondered is that really the Lord? Is that really the power of God? Is it really the spiritual thing I've sought for?' - says the Lord.

'But I say unto you, yes. And I have called unto you even day upon day and hour upon hour. I have called unto you to turn your heart and turn your hands to me that I might use you,' - says the Lord. 'And I say that even now turn unto me and the gift that I have placed upon you shall come forth. The power of God shall be made manifest. You shall know great power and great victory and great authority. Stand up and use my name fearlessly and boldly,' says the Lord. Hallelujah!"

When this prophecy was given, someone was recording it. Later the Lord spoke to the woman who taped the service. He instructed her that I needed to be encouraged. She immediately transcribed the prophecy onto a piece of paper. My friend was obedient and delivered it to my door at 1:00 a.m., but didn't wake me. Along with that prophecy the Lord gave her a message for me.

My friend's exhortation said: "And a dozen 'Hallelujahs' from me! And the power of God shall be made manifest! May the joy of the Lord be your strength this Day. May your mortal body be quickened by the Holy Spirit that indwells you." "He who raised Christ from the dead will also give life to your mortal bodies, through His Spirit, who lives in you."(Romans 8:11b).

This prophecy and exhortation helped me realize that I can hear the voice of the Lord. It gave me strength and courage. I know God wants to utilize all of us to bring honor and glory to Him.

After a period of prayer, God gave an exhortation. It flowed so fast I could hardly scribble it down. It is something God wants His people to hear and take to heart. "Just trust me, I am your God. I love you with a heart full of pure love. My Child, be obedient, render your heart unto Me. It is by your obedience that My power will be manifest through you. Do not be afraid, I am your Lord. I uphold you with My right hand. Rest in me and the work I have for you will be accomplished, in My perfect timing.

Run unto me as a child would to their father; lean completely on Me. I am your only source of strength, your only source of power. Through

My Name you will know great power. By using it fearlessly and boldly, you will bring honor and glory to Me. I am creating in you a clean heart, which you have turned unto me, and I will use it mightily.

Your hands are precious to me also, an extension of My own. Let me use them completely and you will see great and majestic things happen. These things will be a blessing to many people.

I will be with you. I will never leave you, nor forsake you. You will never be put to shame when you use My name. It will lose the chains of bondage, and set people free so they can truly worship me as their Lord and Savior.

My power shall be made manifest through you. Never forget that. Hold it close to your heart. Remember my promises are all true and must be stood on. They will stand the test of time, fire and the power of the evil one.

Rest in Me, dear child. I have all things in My hands, and I truly reign supreme. I reign in and through your heart. Praise My Holy Name; for I am truly worthy. Don't question your worth at any time. Just know you are dear to Me. I have a work for you to complete, that only you can do. I have chosen you for this task.

I love you. Just keep following in My footsteps. I will truly guide you every step of the way your whole life through.

Honor, praise and glorify Me, and you will know a great reward. It will neither rust nor corrupt but will last for all eternity. What you do for me is all that will last and stand the test of time. Remember it is your heart and hands I want. Your service to Me is a sweet-smelling sacrifice, one that I am well pleased with.

Come unto me and rest in me. What I have said, I will do. I always keep my promises and complete every work I start. I am a God of finishes. I finish every good and perfect work. I am the Alpha and Omega. Trust no other. None other is greater than I. My greatness will never be used up but will last for all times.

My peace and strength I give unto you. Go and use this gift I have bestowed upon you. Use it wisely for My honor and glory. You will never be ashamed when you see how My name is glorified. You will be lifted up to soar on wings like an eagle.

My wings are wings of love, peace and joy. They will sustain you, no matter what happens, no matter how far or where you go. Just go in my name and do my work now and forever more. I will bless you my child and sustain you. Your family will know great victory by My power and My name also. I have given you them. They are gifts from me. Cherish and love them next to me. They are my dear servants too.

My peace I give to you; it rests upon your head this very night, rest well in it. Then wake with the morning light and be about my work. I shall guide you one step at a time. Just trust me, my child. Never have I failed you. Never will I leave you; never will I forsake you.

Always lift, Me high, that My name might be exalted above all names in heaven and on earth. As you lift Me up; I will exalt you higher till one day you will be with me in glory. Press forward to that mark. It is your ultimate goal. The only goal worth anything, in all Heaven and on Earth, is My lasting goal. Press forward. Be not weary in well doing of my work for I have your crown and reward waiting for you to claim. Press on my child, press on, your loving heavenly Father."

This prophetic exhortation really ministered peace, and is a message for every child of God.

## God's Promises are forever

Another exhortation I received came after a season of prayer. I was seeking answers from the Lord on the significance of the rainbow colors my sister was using in her wedding. The Lord spoke this message.

"My dear ones (My bride) you are the seed of Abraham. I have given all of you My covenants, My promises. They are from everlasting to everlasting. Just as I fulfilled covenants to Abraham, Noah, and countless descendants, I will fulfill covenants to you, My people. As you live by My spirit, you will know the fruit of the Spirit in your lives. The fruit will be manifest daily and draw others to Me. One day you will be my perfect bride without spot or blemish. As you await My return and our union as bride and groom, keep My covenants, stand on My promises, be ready for My return.

Look to the promise of the rainbow and remember it. It isn't just a promise to Noah that I will never flood the earth again. It is a promise that you will not have so many trials today, or in the future, that you are swept away and destroyed. It is My promise that I will sustain you through all your trials and you will come forth as gold, that pot of gold always looked for at the end of the rainbow. The rainbow was meant to make you look up and see my divine guidance through all the storm clouds. Just as you must have rain before a rainbow, so you must have sorrow, trials and uneven paths. Then you will grow and mature in me and manifest the fruit of the Spirit. It is essential, for you to become My people (My perfect bride).

Through each problem, each trial, I want you to look for the rainbow (My perfect will and timing for your lives). Cling to My promises. Let me show you their deeper meanings. The rainbow, and My promise to return as your bridegroom are to remind you, I want to develop the fruit of My spirit, in you.

My rainbow has seven colors: red, pink, orange, yellow, green, blue and purple. (Some rainbows substitute pink for indigo). You are my bride clothed in white purity of faithfulness and I am your bridegroom clothed in dark gentleness. I am Lord of all. I possess all riches, which I bring to this marriage, this union. I give you, My bride (My people), all things. I give you the fruit of my Spirit.

"But the fruit of the Spirit is love, joy, peace, patience, kindness, goodness, faithfulness, gentleness, and self control; against such there is no law." (Galatians 5:22-23 NIV).

| Rainbow Colors | Fruit of the Spirit |
|---|---|
| Red | Love |
| Pink | Patience |
| Orange | Kindness |
| Yellow | Joy |
| Green | Goodness |
| Blue | Peace |
| Purple | Self-control |
| | |
| Bride | |
| White | Faithfulness |
| Groom | |
| Dark or black | Gentleness |

The red in the rainbow is My love I am perfecting in your lives. Pink is for My patience I am working in you. Orange is My kindness you are showing forth. Yellow is My joy bubbling like a fountain and spilling over to others. Green is My goodness reaching out to all people. Blue is My peace I give to you so the world can see you tranquil through the storms. Purple is My self-control that comes after discipline, because I love you.

As in the rainbow, the red, yellow, and blue are the primary colors. All other colors come from these, so it is with the fruit of My Spirit. My primary fruit is love, joy, and peace; from these come all other fruits.

Out of love and faithfulness of My bride (red and white), comes patience (pink). From love and joy (red and yellow) comes kindness (orange). Joy and peace (yellow and blue) creates goodness (green). From love and peace (red and blue) comes self-control (purple). The radiance of the fruit of the Spirit is manifest in faithfulness (white), and gentleness (dark) represents all color, without reflecting it.

Without all these colors we wouldn't have a rainbow. The same is true with the fruit of the Spirit. They are all important and dependent upon each other to create balance. They make you My purified bride, ready and waiting for My return, and our uniting as bride and groom.

As you await My return, remember My promises, My covenants, be faithful to Me, be ready and waiting. I shall return and we will be united never to be separated again. Dear ones (My bride), I love you with a deep and everlasting love."

Jesus Christ your Bridegroom

## Master Puppeteer

Prophetic messages come in written or spoken form. As an evangelist prayed, he suddenly stepped back and gave this prophecy. He said, "I see a vision, your life is like a basket of leaves. The basket keeps getting turned over. You hurriedly rush and pick up the leaves. You put them in the basket and turn it right side up again. This keeps happening over and over. And the Lord is saying to you, 'Stand still and I will show you the path, says the Lord.'"

I sought God and asked Him, "What does this picture mean? Please instruct me! And He said, "The basket of leaves you see being knocked over is like a puppet, trying to control its own strings. It is awkward. And the

Lord showed me, I want you to be like a puppet. It doesn't try to control its own strings. You are going in your own power, not Mine.

When you do that, you are like a puppet that controls its' own strings. It's awkward. People laugh at the jerky movements of the puppet. I want you to let Me control the strings. Let Me be the master puppeteer. As I move the strings, it will be a beautiful sight with harmony and peace. People will delight to see it. There will be much beauty. And there won't be any more leaves dumped out of the basket.

You will know what path you are to take. You'll let me guide you. Trust Me with all your heart and I will direct you." (Proverbs 3:5-6). Truly the Lord was speaking to me.

## Sermons Speak Loud

God speaks to us through ministers who preach His Word. A sermon about courage resonated with me. "Have not I commanded thee? Be strong and of a good courage; be not afraid . . . for the Lord thy God is with thee whithersoever thou goest" (Joshua 1:9).

Bravery is necessary to conquer the giants and possess our inheritance. It takes courage to live in the presence of the Lord. Boldness is needed to break away from the world's image and walk humbly with our God. It is important to build personal relationships with the Lord in praise and worship. We need nerve to believe God and travel first class in all relationships.

Courage is important to help us enter the ministry the Lord has for us. We must remember, He will give us strength. (Philippians 4:13). The safest place is the center of God's will.

## Peace a Safe Place

Abide in God's leadership and peace will be your safe haven. When we rest in Christ, we can be channels for God to work through and touch others. A key to abiding in Christ is to trust in God. Also, don't lean on your own understanding. Christ has to be our whole life. Communicate daily with Him.

The Lord says, "Follow Me, I have plans for your life. Trust me while you are waiting." The next thing to do is to fear the Lord and shun evil. The fear of man brings a snare, but the fear of the Lord brings blessings.

Depart from evil, let the Lord help us have pure thoughts and attitudes. We can honor the Lord with our first fruits. Give Him our very best. When we do these things, we will abide in God and His leadership. As we begin to rest in the Lord, we will begin to see more successes and fewer failures.[1]

## Success and Failure

Special insight illuminated the path to look at successes and failures. First, we need to have a dream that is worth failing for. Next, we need to view success as something you can fail into. Some of the most successful people have been the most persistent. Success and failure are really the same coins. One is the head and the other is the tail. Also, learn how to fail in the right places. Ask yourself, what is the worst thing that can happen to me? Then learn to look for good in everything. It's hard to be afraid when you get paid for failure. Things turn out best for people who make the best of how things turn out. Remember, failure is necessary for growth. Then take a leap. "Faith precedes miracles and successes. We have to stay with no's long enough to get to successes."[2]

Sin often tries to enter our lives and disrupt success. "Sin will take us further than we want to go. It will keep us longer than we want to stay. It will cost us more than we want to pay. No sin can yield pleasure worth the penalty."[3] "The wages of sin are death, but the gift of God is eternal life through Jesus Christ our Lord" (Romans 6:23). We want to keep sin out of our lives. It produces failure, while life in Jesus produces success.

## Crisis or Opportunity

Another thing that determines success or failure is our attitude. We can look at a difficulty and view it as a crisis or an opportunity. Saul and all the Israelites saw Goliath as a great crisis to them. However, David saw the battle with Goliath as an opportunity. (1 Samuel 17:25)

The shepherd boy had a resume.' He applied his previous job skills of fighting wild beasts. David knew God had delivered him in the past. He had skills for the job at hand. He built on past experiences and went in the strength of the Lord.

King Saul wanted David to put on his armor. David put it on and decided it was too big and clumsy and he couldn't walk in it. What the Lord spoke through David's example is: we can't go in someone else's protective gear. We must go with our own preparation. For us to have our own armor, we must spend time in prayer and the Word of God. We must have our own relationship with the Lord.

David was prepared. He chose five stones. The five stones were: the name of Jesus, the blood of Jesus, the Word of God, prayers and praise.

After choosing the five stones, the shepherd boy approached the giant. The giant underestimated him. It's a mistake for us to under estimate our enemies. David was able to take Goliath's words and hurl them back at him. David was confident of his victory because he knew God was with him. He ran quickly to the battle lines, without hesitation. "Then said David to the Philistine (Goliath), Thou comest to me with a sword and with a spear, and with a shield: but I come to thee in the name of the Lord of hosts, the God of the armies of Israel, whom thou hast defied" (1 Samuel 17:45).

David took a stone out of his bag. He slung it and it hit Goliath in the forehead. The giant Philistine fell on his face and died. (1 Samuel 17:49). David only had to use the first stone, the name of the Lord His God.

Everyone else in the Israelite nation saw this as a crisis. David saw this as an opportunity for God's strength to triumph. He was prepared for the battle.

If we can deal with problems effectively, as David did, they won't become crises. There are many ways to attack the difficulty. Here is a simple four way plan to attack a dilemma. First, never accept anything except clear ideas. Second, divide the task into pieces. Begin with the simplest part and work to the most complex. Thirdly, check to see if anything has been overlooked. Fourthly, know your enemy and put on your fighting gear.[4]

One of the best ways to conquer trials and temptations is to resist the devil and his evil schemes. We must be in control of our thoughts before they capture us.

## Taking Thoughts Captive

I sought for answers on how to teach the concept of putting anxious thoughts under lock and key. The Lord gave this tool in a counseling session. It is an effective way to control our minds, one thought at a time.

# Cognitive Therapy Tool
# Taking Thoughts Captive

We are told in the Word of God to "bring into captivity every thought to the obedience of Christ." (2 Corinthians 10:5)

Thought:

_____

My Feelings:                    God's Truth

The *"Cognitive Therapy Tool"* can best be used by writing your thought down. Then move to *"My Feelings."* Examine your emotions and record them. Remember, while taking notes on your sensations, you don't live on feelings but by faith in Jesus. Then move to *"God's Truth"* and chronicle His report about your situation, use the Word of God. Capture the irrational perceptions. Then fling the truth back at your enemy, Satan. He will flee from your mind. You have just run off the bad thoughts.

Jesus took His thoughts captive when the devil tempted Him in the wilderness. "And (the devil) saith unto him, all these things will I give thee, if thou wilt fall down and worship me. Then saith Jesus unto him, Get thee hence, Satan; for it is written, Thou shalt worship the Lord thy God and Him only shalt thou serve." (Matthew 4:9-10).

Jesus literally told the devil to get lost and then he told him the truth of God's Word. This, we must do. We need to get so good at it, that we can do it in an instant. We must put God's thoughts into our minds and not let Satan put his in. Thinking produces actions. Wherever your mind has been, your body may go. If thoughts stay, imaginations come. We need imagery to be able to see ourselves as God sees us.

God has given us power to resist the devil. Another way to do this is: have an attitude of gratitude.

## Praise Ambushes Our Enemy

The Lord poured this message into me after reading (2 Chronicles 20: 1-26). King Jehoshaphat was faced with an impossible situation. He had three armies coming against him. He didn't know what to do. The ruler sought the Lord, prayed and fasted. The army of Judah heard a word from God. "You will not have to fight this battle. Take up your positions, stand firm and see the deliverance the Lord will give you . . ." (2 Chronicles 20:17 NIV).

The men of Judah knew they were descendants of Abraham and heir to all God's promises. They would not give up the land and blessing's God had given them.

King Jehoshaphat appointed men to sing as they went out to battle. They sang, "Give thanks to the Lord, for his love endures forever." (2 Chronicles 20:21-22. NIV) When they sang, their enemy was ambushed.

None of Jehoshaphat's men were killed. It took the men of Judah three days to clean up the loot. On the fourth day they set up altars and praised and worshiped the Lord.

The men of Judah accomplish this amazing feat. They took up their positions and stood firm and went out praising. We must be like these men. We know we are children of the Most High God, bought with the price of Jesus blood. We take up our position offensively by using the "Word of God, the Name of Jesus and the Blood of Jesus." We must also put on the "Armor of God" to stand firm.

Three more things we must offensively do to take up our place and be unmovable. We must take our thoughts captive by running the devil off with the truth. Secondly, we must praise God for everything we can. Praise loosens God's power on our behalf. It helps us think positively and focus on God's power and not our situations. Positive thoughts generate faith. Thirdly, we must speak positive self statements (using scripture). Our self talk must be truth and not deception or we will spiral down into the enemy's camp.

Satan doesn't have all power. He goes around like a roaring lion that has been stripped of his teeth. He is seeking whom he *"may"* devour. May, means that he must have permission to do it. We take authority away from Satan by using God's Word. Jesus took that force from Satan. The only way Satan gets that power back, is by our words.[5]

# Build Good Walls

When we grumble, we build walls. We are picking up bricks of bitterness and resentment. These enclosures are very dangerous. We get them so high we can't see out and no one can see in. We are left in the dark.

The best kind of wall we can build is God's wall. Our maker gives us the tools to build with. Brick by brick he helps us lay it. The first brick is praise. We bring His presence into our midst, and praise helps keep Satan out.

The second brick of God's wall is prayer. When we pray, we give up some of ourselves. We need to have that interlocking between praise and prayer.

The third brick is intercession. Give God the time and intercede for others. God does anoint His warriors. We are His mighty people when we intercede.

Our fourth brick is fasting. "Is not this the kind of fasting I have chosen: to lose the chains of injustice and untie the cords of the yoke, to set the oppressed free and break every yoke? . . ." (Isaiah 58:6, NIV). Fasting breaks the bondages in our life and the walls that we've built or that others have built.

The fifth brick is repenting. Lack of repentance is the veil that blocks the entrance to God. So if we don't use that brick we can't enter to the Lord. The Lord's love is the mortar that holds all these bricks together.[6]

God builds His walls so we won't be run over by enemies. It keeps the predators out and we are free to grow. The walls God builds will protect us through the conflicts of life.

# Depression an Internal Battle

There are two kinds of battles we fight, internal and external. The inner battles are often the toughest, because we can't see who our enemy is. One internal battle I fought was depression. I felt much like Elijah in (1 Kings 19:1-21). He was very blue and despondent. God spoke through this account to inform us how to conquer despair.

Depression often results from several things. We often use faulty thinking and are often afraid. Then we used faulty comparison.

When we compare, we usually look at the strong points of others, not their weakness. This can fill us with pride or make us feel like slug slime.

We need to look to the Word of God to view ourselves. Elijah also used faulty blaming. (I Kings 19:10 NIV). He blamed the Israelites for not keeping God's covenants. That, he reasoned was why he had to run for his life. It's a human tendency to blame others when we should take the responsibility for our own actions. Then, Elijah used faulty exaggeration when he said all of Israel had forsaken God and he was the only one left. Faulty blaming and exaggeration usually go hand in hand and sets us up for self-pity and depression.

Here are some things we can do to stay out of the trap of depression. When Elijah finally came to his senses, he listened to God. Then he rested in The Lord. He went to sleep under a tree. (1Kings 19:5) Then after resting, Elijah began to release his situation to God as he listened and followed God's directions. "The Lord said, 'Go out and stand on the mountain in the presence of the Lord, for the Lord is about to pass by.'" (1 Kings 19:11 NIV). Then, Elijah waited on The Lord to speak. First there was a powerful wind that tore the mountains apart and shattered the rocks. But the Lord was not in the wind. After the wind there was an earth quake. After the earthquake, there was a fire. When the fire died down, there was a gentle whisper and the Lord began to speak to him. (1 Kings 19: 11-14).

Elijah returned on his way and followed God's direction. (1 Kings 19:15).[7] He conquered his internal battle of depression.

## External Battles

When we face internal or external battles, it is of utmost importance to examine ourselves and the situations from Our Heavenly Father's perspective, not our own. Exterior conflicts are difficult. However, we usually know who our enemy is. The keys to effectively fighting our external battles are: pick up the sword, which is the Word of God, and go into battle. If we don't fight in the battle, we may be killed. There has to be intercession. We can't fight these battles on our own. We need the resources of others prayers. When victory comes, don't forget who brought it. Maintain the attitude, I will conquer. When I win the battle, I will give God the thanks. Keep a victory journal. This helps remind us of all the blessings and answers to prayer the Lord has bestowed upon us. God wants to cut short both our internal and external battles, so we can serve Him.[8]

One external battle that keeps us from serving God to the fullest is relationship problems.

We should never take either kindred tie for granted. Relationships must be worked on to keep the fire burning. Often we don't bond enough, and it results in external battles with those, we love the most. If we let conflicts go unresolved, we set ourselves up for defeat not victory.

## Prayer is a Key

The Lord impressed upon me, there are essential elements in a victorious life. One key is prayer. My communication with God needs to be a daily activity of listening and speaking. When we are hearing from the Lord, then faith comes. Communion with God turns on His light. We don't want to make a move until we have heard from God. We need to ask daily, "God what do you have for me today?" We don't want to arrive at a place where we don't have a need to seek God daily for His provisions or direction. We can't live on yesterdays Word, it must be fresh today.

Our power comes from waiting upon the Lord. If we don't tarry, what we set out to accomplish, may be a work of the flesh.

Prayer has to take first place in our life, next illumination comes. When we wait on the Lord, something will happen. "But they that wait upon the Lord, shall renew their strength; they shall mount up with wings as eagles; they shall run, and not be weary; and they shall walk, and not faint" (Isaiah 40:31).

After we hear from God and act on it, faith begins to work in us. We can stand on persistent faith. There were many who sought Jesus when He was ministering on earth. Jesus went out into areas of the country to rest. It didn't matter where He went, people always found him. If we seek Him, we will also find Him. As we listen and obey we will have victory.

## Warfare Brings Triumph

The Lord instructed through good teaching that spiritual warfare is a very important key to victory. The battle consists of five spiritual elements. First, the fight is worship. God dwells in our praise. Worship and praise are keys to victory. Second, warfare is waiting on God for victory. Our spiritual authority is in direct proportion to our dependence on God. Always do the next thing God tells you to do. Thirdly, the battle requires repentance and brokenness. When we identify with our city, nation, or land and confess its sins, we are raising a standard and standing in the gap. Prophets, Nehemiah and Daniel confessed the sins of the nations. We need to intercede. Someone has to ask God for forgiveness and to heal. Fourthly, warfare is overcoming evil with good. "Be not overcome of evil, but overcome evil with good" (Romans 12:21). Attack the circumstance with righteousness. When selfishness arises, use selflessness and humility. Confess your temptations and resist them. Counter attack, everything with good. Fifthly, the battle is travailing till birth. Daniel fasted for three weeks. We need to be able to stay with prayer until the answer comes. It means a humility and brokenness before God. And love settles for nothing less than victory.[9]

## Jesus Victory

Jesus waged warfare. In the Garden of Gethsemane, He said, "Father, if thou be willing remove this cup from me: nevertheless not my will, but thine, be done" (Luke 22:42). Jesus didn't let go until He won the victory, on the cross, in the tomb and arising from the grave. Jesus resurrection gave us confidence that we are on the right path. It gives us power over sin. With Jesus we can say no to evil. Grace carries the responsibility to choose not to sin. Satan can't get good hits in because Jesus took the wind out of him.

The resurrection gives us hope for a future. Our best pales in comparison to God's masterpiece. He is building a mansion for us. And lastly, resurrection also gives us joy. Death has been defeated. Jesus has risen. We have power. He is the only spiritual leader that tasted death and isn't in the grave. Jesus said He would die, rise again and come back for us. "I am He that liveth, and was dead; and behold, I am alive for evermore, Amen; and have the keys of hell and of death" (Revelation 1:18). Jesus took the keys of death, hell and the grave from Satan. It was because Jesus refused to quit in His darkest hour. That's why we can have victory. Jesus didn't give up on Friday, even though He had excruciating pain. He knew Sunday was coming. That's when God came through for Him.[10]

The resurrection speaks to me that in our darkest hour, we should never give up. "It's always darkest just before the dawn." The old saying rang true in Jesus life and death. Our Savior has victory for us.

## Moving the Target

Another key to victory is to set all of our relationships in order. Marriage and family relationships are of utmost importance. Our societal morals have changed drastically in the last few years. It has weakened our families and caused many problems in our world.

As I pondered the changing world and our morals the Lord spoke to me powerfully through a message. God's Word hasn't changed, but our morals have shifted. We don't believe in absolute rights or wrongs. We utilize situational morals. We look at the meaning of a situation, and how it makes us feel. We use that as our guide to make moral decisions, instead of using the Word of God as our absolute command. Changing our morals to fit the situation is like moving the target so we can hit the bull's eye. We are hitting the target only because we have moved it, not because we are better marksmen. The Word of God can stand alone without a compromise of situational morals. We are moving over to the ways of the world. We are practicing deceit when we move the target.[11]

When we practice deceit by moving the target, we will fall into moral decay. That is exactly what is happening today. We must leave the target (the Word of God) in place. This is our rule of conduct.

## Change Your Words

Scripture instructs us to utilize good morals. Our words need to showcase our character. Negative words make for negative conditions. If we are anxious to change what surrounds us, then we have to do it by changing our speech. We aren't at the mercy of our circumstances. But we create our own circumstances by the words we use. Desperation is a negative emotion, but calm is your sharper weapon. Peace can always be used to good advantage. It doesn't block the way to resolving a situation like despair does. One thing that pushes people into desperation is grief. When grief hits you, head on, don't give way to self pity. "Everybody in the world has something to overcome. Either by courage or the lack of it they have either gone under or risen above the catastrophe."[12]

One widow responded to her grief by saying that she realized she had to return to being an active person. She summed it up like this, "All of the water in the ocean could not sink a ship unless the captain permitted it to get inside the vessel." If we let grief turn into self pity, it can sink our vessel. We need to turn to the Lord with our sorrow and emotions.

How many times a day do you find yourself using these expressions: I need, I do not have. Instead, we need to say, "I have it, it is mine, it's here. It's more than enough." When our spirit can accept the Word, it becomes law. Before the law, the Word existed. Chapter's 1 and 2 of Genesis reminds us that God spoke everything into being when He created the universe. Our Creator's words are powerful, and so are ours.

We need to look at things with an optimistic mind instead of pessimistic. One of the first steps to empty out criticism and fill that vacuum is by inviting gratitude and appreciation in its place.

Positive words coupled with faith bring success in our lives. When we have faith, we have everything. And we can go anywhere and miracles begin to happen in our lives. However, if we don't speak the right words, we may have chaos in our lives.

## Attitude Check

Our attitude about life is very important. It is more important than facts, circumstances, what others say, your past, education or money. It has been said that life is 10 percent what happens, and 90 percent how you react.

An author gives us several ways to activate a positive attitude. "Be an ambassador of good words. Look for good and you'll find it. Fill your mind with good. Never surrender to negative emotions.

Use the principle of replacement. For example, replace anger, with love. Bar the suggestive, lewd, things from your mind. See the good in others. Determine to take an attitude of love and goodwill to others. Express appreciation to others.

Practice positive prayer. God is good and has a plan for your life. Affirm positives "God is my source, nothing is impossible with God."[13]

Everything we do needs to be done as unto the Lord. Christ is the greatest key to happiness in life.

## What Would Jesus DO?

A powerful message for living was gleaned from an old book. The purpose of this writing was to shock people out of the indifference of their

Christian practices. An author posed this question: "Ask, what, would Jesus do?" Then I challenge you to be guided by your best answer to that question.[14] The Lord instructed me to ask myself that question whenever I was confronted by decisions or situations, big or small. To know what Jesus would do, we need to know Him better and be faithful to Him.

## Apostle of Faith

Smith Wigglesworth was an apostle of faith. This giant of faith teaches us guiding principles. Wigglesworth believed, everybody has to be tested in some area of their faith. He was a great man of God. The two main factors in his spiritual life were these: He had reliance upon the spirit of God, and a confidence in the Word of God.

These were the foundations of his holy boldness. Wigglesworth tells us to be so soaked with the Word of The Lord that you are a living epistle, known and read of all men. Believers are strong only as the Word of God abides in them. He says, "You have to know your book, live it, believe it and obey it. Because it saves your soul, quickens your body and illumines your mind."[15] The Word of God is infallible. It must be implicitly obeyed because if you dare to believe, you must act in obedience. "But without faith it is impossible to please him . . ." (Hebrews 11:6). If we believe what God has said, there will be a performance. God speaks clearly to us through His Word.

## Jesus Commands

Jesus gave three great commands. "Pray ye, Do ye, and Go ye." None of those commands were optional. We can accomplish more by prayer than any other way. Talking to God is the key. Faith turns the key and opens the door.

We have a good example of an effective life. Jesus always prayed. We aren't as effective because we don't pray, like we should, and we aren't God-man. We have a tendency to pray so little and criticize so much. Prayer opens the way for God to use us and influence others.[16]

## Vessels God Can Use

We can become a vessel God can use. First, we must, accept the way God made us. Second, be emptied of self to make room for God. Thirdly, allow God to cleanse you, even if the process is painful. Fourth, be filled and constantly refilled with the Living Water of the Holy Spirit. Fifth, pour out your life in a ministry as God directs.[17]

Jesus wants us to model our lives after His life and ministry. His teachings were cloaked in steps of obedience, love, faithfulness, humility, righteousness, and forgiveness. Jesus died daily to His self will. The Lord's purpose was to do what pleased God. Our life's goal must also be to do the will of Our Father.

## God's Messages

Many spoken and written messages have imparted God's messages to us. The Lord's Word, prayer, dying to self-will, obedience and living under grace is so important in a relationship with Him. These are some of the keys to a victorious life that can be used by Our Creator. God has spoken to us many times through all of His creations.

All messages received from prophecies, sermons, written matter, must be put to the ultimate test. Does what I'm hearing line up with the Word of God? And do I have peace in my heart? If what you have heard agrees with the Lord's Word, and you have peace in your heart, then promptly obey. For God may choose to speak a number of ways. He may bellow thunderously through the big things or very quietly speak through a small voice or letter.

## Our Father's Letter to Us
My Child,

You are precious to Me and honored in My sight (Isaiah 43:4). I love you with an everlasting love. I have drawn you and continue My faithfulness to you (Jeremiah 31:3). I take great delight in you and quiet you with my love. I rejoice over you with singing (Zephaniah 3:17).

I created your innermost being and knit you together in your mother's womb. You are fearfully and wonderfully made (Psalm 139:13-14). By My hands you were made in My image. (Genesis 1:26).

I am faithful to all My promises (Psalm 145:13). I will never leave you or forsake you (Hebrews 13:5).

As all, you have sinned (Romans 3:23), but I am gracious and compassionate, slow to anger, and rich in love (Psalm 145:8-9). Because I love you, I gave My son Jesus to die on your behalf. He paid your penalty with His life (John 3:16). If you will confess your sins, I am faithful and just to forgive you (1John 1:9). If you repent, I will restore you (Jeremiah 15:19a). I love you as you are. In Christ you are a new creation, the old has gone, the new has come (2 Corinthians 5:17).

You can be confident that I will complete the work I have begun in you (Philippians 1:6). Cast all your cares upon Me for I care for you (1 Peter 5:7). I have come that you may have life and have it more abundantly (John 10:10).

This does not mean that you will not have tribulation. When you go through the deep water and great trouble, I will be with you. When you walk through the fire of oppression, you will not be consumed (Isaiah 43:2). I will work it all for good if you are fitting into My plan for your life (Romans 8:28). For this reason, praise Me in all circumstances (1 Thessalonians 5:18).

No eye has seen, no ear has heard, no mind has conceived what I have prepared for you (1 Corinthians 2:9). This life weighs heavy on you many times, and Satan will try to drag you down, making you feel condemned. But when you are in Christ there is no condemnation (Romans 8:1). In all things you can be more than a conqueror through My love (Romans 8:37).

Rebuke the devil in the name of My Son and he will leave you (Matthew 4:10). Nothing can separate you from My love (Romans 8:38).

With Me you have a kingdom that can never be shaken (Hebrews 12:28) and an anchor of hope for your soul that is firm and secure (Hebrews 6:19). Changes in your life can sometimes cause you pain and confusion, but I am the same yesterday, today and forever (Hebrews 13:8). Your heart can be at rest in times when you are down on yourself, for I am greater than your heart (1 John 3:19-20). I desire that you know the truth, that it may set you free (John 8:32). Indeed you are precious to Me and honored in My sight (Isaiah 43:4).

Love
Your, Heavenly Father

## CHAPTER 9

# "Inner Nudge; the Still, Small Voice Within"

"For God does speak - now one way, now another -
though man may not perceive it."
(Job 33:14 NIV).

God's Word clearly tells us that He speaks to us in numerous ways. Often we don't realize our maker is speaking to us. I've found that to be true, when I felt an inner nudge. Most of us have difficulty learning to discern the still small voice of the Holy Spirit. It's not strange that our creator would use our minds and inner ears to communicate His guidance and answers to us.

This poses another problem. What God has created, our enemy, the devil will also try to use. Conflict often arises because the inner sounds come from two sources. Those may come from the Lord, or Satan's voice. Each time we hear the inner nudge, we need to ask, "Does the utterance I'm hearing, agreeing with the Word of God?" If it lines up with the Bible, and we have peace about what we've heard, we can willingly and swiftly obey.

## Speak Lord

These internal nudges have been experienced since time began. There are many biblical accounts where God spoke to His servants in this manner. The child Samuel had no idea the Lord was talking to him when He called his name. Samuel heard a voice speak to him three times as he lay on his bed. Each time he answered, "Here am I," and ran to Eli. His spiritual mentor didn't hear the voice. We don't know whether the voice was audible or an inner voice. We know Samuel regarded the message. After Samuel heard the voice the third time, Eli (a priest in the temple of the Lord), realized God was speaking to Samuel. He then instructed the young lad to go lie down and wait for the Lord to speak again. If He talks to you again just say, "Speak Lord, for thy servant heareth . . ." (1 Samuel 3:9).

Often we have difficulty discerning God's voice. We have preconceived notions of how the Lord communicates with us. Our maker tries various ways to capture our attention.

## Still Small Voice

This was the situation with the prophet Elijah. Fear gripped him after he called down fire on the prophets of Baal. Immediately, he fled for his life to the desert. God spoke to Elijah and told him to go stand on the mountain.

The Lord used a strong wind, an earthquake and a fire to grab Elijah's attention. Then He spoke to Elijah with a still small voice. (1 Kings 19: 11-13). Often we expect the Lord to speak to us in the big things. Many times He whispers to show His character of gentleness.

## A Basket in the Reeds

Baby Moses' rescue from the Nile River, points to Our Maker's tender care over his life. Pharaoh's daughter and her maid servants went down to the Nile River to bathe. She noticed a basket among the reeds. The princess had an internal nudge or desire, to see what was in the basket. Curiosity overtook her. When she opened the basket, she saw baby Moses. She had compassion upon him, He was crying. Moses' sister, (Miriam) obviously heard an inner voice, instruct her how to respond to the princess. She quickly and boldly said: "Shall I go and get one of the Hebrew women to nurse the baby for you?" (Exodus 2:7).

## Burning Bush

Later in life Moses was in the desert tending his father-in-law's sheep. He saw a burning bush; that continued to burn. Moses had a nudge to explore the strange situation. As he moved closer to the fiery bush, God captured his attention and spoke audibly to him. God called to Moses from the burning bush. The Lord asked Moses to take off his shoes because the ground he was standing on was holy ground. God gave him the command to deliver the Israelites from Pharaoh and lead them out of Egypt. (Exodus 3:2-10).

Moses' life is a solid example of how God speaks to us through the small voice. These divine communications helped direct and protect Moses' life. Today the Lord still uses those same nudges and the little voice to instruct us.

We must be sensitive to recognize God's verbalization and obey quickly just as two missionaries' sons did.

The boys were playing in a tree in a jungle area. A poisonous snake appeared near a branch where they played. They hadn't noticed it. However, their father was nearby and noticed the snake crawling up the branch close to his sons. The dad spoke to the boys in a calm, firm voice, "Boys, drop to the ground, now, and run as fast as you can!" They did exactly as they were told, and ran to safety. Because the boys obeyed, they were protected from a poisonous bite and sure death.

Just as the missionary's sons obeyed their earthly father's calm voice, we need to listen carefully and immediately heed God's voice. There is seldom time to shoot up a prayer or reach for the Word of God. Our Maker uses the inner sound to guide us.

## Gentle Nudge

Most of us have had a gentle nudge. Often we obey without knowing why. Moments later, danger crosses our path.

My sisters and I were traveling on a road, when she had a notion to back off on the gas pedal, just before starting up an incline. As we crested the hill, we met an oncoming car in our lane. If she hadn't heeded the warning to slow down, we could have had a head-on collision.

The Lord instructed, "When you've been obedient to me, I'll take care of you." His guidance is always right on target.

An inner nudge protected my children and their friends during a family outing. We all piled in the car, after a swimming event and headed for home. At a streetcar stop, we looked both ways but didn't see anything coming. Suddenly, an inner nudge punched me in the ribs. I was instructed, "Keep your foot on the brake, wait a minute and look again!" I looked again, a train crossed right in front of our path. It was imperative that I heeded the gentle voice. It kept us from disaster.

## Blessings of Favor

Obedience always produces blessings. One evening my husband was air lifted to a hospital four hours away. The medical staff suspected he had a heart attack and possible damage.

I said a prayer and asked God to care for my husband and the nurses flying with him. I requested the Lord to direct us every step of the way. I knew I needed to listen carefully to His instructions. I wasn't alone because Jesus and our family pet traveled with me.

I called family members to alert them about our medical crisis. Suddenly, I realized there was no cell phone charger. I almost panicked. My portable telephone was about to die. I needed to be in contact with the medical staff all night. Quickly, I shot up a "Help me, Lord," prayer. God whispered, "I will take care of everything."

Half way there, I heard the Lord tell me to stop at a motel. It didn't sound logical to do so. But I pulled into a motel and immediately heard a still small voice loud and clear, "This isn't the right place." I immediately wheeled out and was directed to stop at the lodging across the street. After checking in, I had a nudge, "Ask for a cell phone charger." The chances of the motel manager having a device to fit my unusual Japanese telephone was remote, to say the least.

None of the chargers he showed me worked. Suddenly, the clerk remembered a guest that had left his charger and would return for it the next day. The clerk had me try the guest's electronic devise, and it worked. "Praise the Lord." I kept the cell phone on all night and was in contact with the hospital.

The next morning I gratefully returned the charger. When I arrived at the heart hospital, my husband was doing better. He was waiting for the doctors to finish their tests. Eventually, the doctors told us there was no damage to my husband's heart. We could go home. The trek home was joyfully and blessed with my husband's good health.

## God Still Speaks

When we listen to the inner nudges and obey, we are always rewarded. One young man wondered if God still spoke to us, mortals. He had been in a Wednesday night Bible Study. The Pastor had shared about listening to Our Father and obeying His voice. This gentleman contemplated, "Does God still speak to humans?" After the service he went out with some friends for coffee and they discussed the message. Several people talked about how the Lord had led them in different ways.

It was after ten o'clock when the young man headed home. Sitting in his car, he began to pray, "Father, if you still speak to us mortals, speak to me. I will listen. I will do my best to obey."

As he drove down the main street of his town, he had the strangest thought, "Stop and buy a gallon of milk." He shook his head and said out loud, "God is that you?" He didn't get a reply and started on toward home. But again, the thought, "Buy a gallon of milk." The young man thought about Samuel and how he didn't recognize the voice of God, and ran to Eli.

"Okay, Lord, in case this is you, I will buy the milk." It didn't seem like too hard a test of obedience. He could always use the milk. He stopped and purchased the gallon of milk. Then he headed home.

As he passed a street, he again felt an urge, "Turn down that street." This is crazy he thought and drove on past the intersection. Again, he felt that he should turn down that particular road. At the next intersection, he turned back and headed down the street. Half jokingly, he said out loud, "Okay, God I will."

He drove several blocks, when suddenly, he knew he should stop. He pulled over to the curb and looked around. He was in a semi - commercial area of town. It wasn't the best but it wasn't the worst of neighborhoods either. The businesses were closed and most of the houses looked dark.

Again, he sensed something, "Go and give the milk to the people in the house across the street." The young man looked at the house. It was dark and it looked like the people were either gone, or already asleep. He started to open the door and then sat back in the car seat. "Lord, this is insane. Those people are asleep. If I wake them, they are going to be mad, and I will look stupid."

Again, he felt a nudge to give the milk away. Finally, he opened the door, "Okay God, if this is you, I will go to the door and give them the milk. If you want me to look like a crazy person, okay. I want to be obedient. I guess that will count for something. If they don't answer right away, I am out of here." He walked across the street and rang the bell. He could hear some noise inside.

A man's voice yelled out, "Who is it? What do you want?" Then the door opened before the young man could get away. The man was standing there in his jeans and T-shirt. He looked like he just got out of bed. He had a strange look on his face and he didn't seem too happy to have some stranger standing on his doorstep.

"What is it?" The young man thrust out the gallon of milk, "Here, I brought this to you." The man took the milk and rushed down a hallway speaking loudly in panic. Then, down the hall came a woman carrying the milk toward the kitchen. The man was following her holding a baby. The baby was crying. The man had tears streaming down his face. He began speaking and half crying, "We were just praying. We had some big bills this month. We ran out of money. There was no milk for our baby. I was just praying and asking God to show me how to get some milk." His wife in the kitchen yelled out, "I ask him to send an Angel with some milk. Are you an Angel?" The young man reached into his wallet and pulled out all the money he had and gave it to the man. He turned and walked back toward his car, with tears streaming down his face. He knew emphatically, God still answers prayers and talks to us.

## Sensitive to Listen

Inner nudges come to us often if we are sensitive enough to listen for them. I walked into a hospitalized woman's room. She was emotionally devastated. She had received a cancer diagnosis. She immediately said, "I prayed that you'd come." That encouraged me. I knew I had heard from the Lord. My obedience was an answer to prayer.

## Everything Will Be Okay

One day I was sitting at my desk praying and crying. I struggled with how to ask my mother to move into town after being on the farm for sixty-four years. Her doctors stated she could no longer live alone, after having a mild stroke. She also had diminished sight and could no longer drive. Temporarily she stayed with my husband and me.

We had a family reunion to attend, on my husband's side. I didn't know what to do! We really needed time away. My mother also needed someone to care for her while we were gone. I sought the Lord and heard Him whisper, "Everything will be okay, listen to my voice." I immediately wiped my eyes and did as He directed. His instructions were to contact friends in the Women's Group at church. Schedule two people daily to come to our house. The ladies would help my mother with her meals and medications. Complete favor was granted. I quickly filled the schedule with helpers.

Everything was set in motion. My mother felt comfortable about the schedule. We were ready for the trip. The night before we were to leave, our air conditioner went out. We almost panicked. I shot up a prayer and reminded the Lord of His words "Everything will be okay!" And I retorted, this doesn't look okay to me. I heard the still small voice respond back, "This is just another one of those every things, and I am in control." Now instead of just saying "Everything will be okay," I want you to start saying, everything is okay, and it will be."

God's utterance instructed me "Call the repairman." I telephoned the work man. He volunteered to fix it that night. We left for the family reunion on schedule the next morning, with peace in our hearts.

I called my mother every day to make sure she was doing well. She was having wonderful visits with the women from the church. Half way through the week, my mother sounding like she was getting bronchitis.

Again I questioned the Lord and he assured me "Everything is okay." And I thanked Him that all was well. We called a doctor, and she prescribed medication for mom.

When we got home from our trip, I immediately took mom to the doctor. She stated mother had pneumonia. With God's help, we were able to treat it at home and she recovered nicely.

Through this experience, I began to be more sensitive to the still small voice of the Spirit. I began to trust Him more and relied on His Word. "(God) calleth those things which be not as though they were." Romans 4:17. My communication became "Thank you Lord, everything is okay."

## God's Plans Don't Change

Prayer is an important aspect of life. My husband and I had planned a Labor Day weekend trip. It seemed all of our plans disintegrated one by one. We looked for another plan. Suddenly, my husband suggested we go to a city in Colorado. I jokingly asked, "What's in that city besides the Royal Gorge Bridge?" And my husband quipped, the mountains. My first thought was that's strange. But then an insistent urge within me said, "I want you to go." So I said, "Sure, that's a good idea and a chance to relax." We loaded up and made the drive with our family dog.

As we arrived at our destination, we spotted a small motel and knew we needed to stay there. We checked in and had a wonderful evening in the mountains. The next morning we prepared to check out of our unit. Before packing up, I went to the ice room to fill a small water jug. As I stepped out of that room, I noticed a woman sitting on a bench nearby, crying. An insistent urge stated, "Speak to her." I argued with the voice but it became stronger. So, I asked the lady if she was all right. She said "No, my teenage son just died and I don't know why. You see, my ex-husband and I were divorced and the children were living with him. I have no one to talk to about this." She related to me, she had been down by the river walking and talking to God that morning. She petitioned Him, "Please, send someone to pray with me." At that point, I was very humbled. I could barely ask if she wanted me to pray with her. She said yes! We sought the Lord and talked some more. Then I went to my motel room and got a business card so she could call me. I handed the card to her and stated I would be praying for her and her family. She could call me anytime.

Then my husband and I went to eat breakfast. He picked up a newspaper while we waited for our meal. The front page of the paper had a picture of the woman I had just prayed with at the motel. She was comforting classmates of her son and holding a rose in one hand. Finally, we headed out for our day's activities. The scenery, music and activities were great.

After the festival was over, we drove back to the same motel and found no vacancies. The State Fair was in progress in an adjacent city. We checked a couple of lodgings and got the same report.

Suddenly I heard the quiet prompting. The instructions were to stop at a Best Western motel. We did, but got the same report, "no rooms." The motel clerk was so nice. While we went to the bathroom, she called one of her business friends that had an extra set of quarters, used for family visits. The woman asked us to give her thirty minutes to tidy up. Then we could have it for the night. We were delighted; it was an answer to prayer.

After getting settled into the motel, we went to eat supper. At the restaurant, we found information on a church to attend the next morning.

Sunday dawned bright and beautiful. We found the church with no trouble. Being early, I sought out a quiet place to read a devotional. When I entered the room, they were preparing for worship. A woman asked, if I had any petitions. I requested prayer for the lady whose son died. The people stated, they now knew how to help the mother and her family.

After the church service was over, my husband and I headed home. I marveled at how God used the still small voice to guide us the whole weekend. It was a divine encounter. I heard the unmistakable utterance of the Lord speak to me. He said, "When I want you somewhere, I will move heaven and earth to get you there." We can have much guidance when we are sensitive to listen to the Holy Spirits leading.

The nudge within is sometimes very faint. We can hardly discern it. Other times it is loud and clear. Many people think it is the subconscious or their own mind. They tend to ignore it. Others realize what it is and heed it, even though they don't understand it. Many instinctively know it is God's voice speaking to them. The still small voice within, is one of God's ways of communicating with us.

## Stay and Pray

While visiting in Jerusalem, with some friends, I heard a whisper as I got out of bed. The clear message was "Stay here and pray." I didn't understand it, nor did I want to hear it. We had planned to go to Joppa that day. I didn't tell anyone in our group. They might think I was silly.

After everyone was awake and we had breakfast, one of the women said she was feeling ill. She stated we needed to "Stay and pray" so we would be ready for the Lord's work. Then I told the others, "Yes, I received that message, but I ignored it, and I'm sorry." When we ignore messages, we need to repent, and ask God to help us be sensitive to His voice the next time.

## Questions and Choices

Other times the nudge is a searching question from the Lord. He expects an answer from us. After my military spouse retired from the United States Army, we moved back to our hometown. Many changes took place while we were away. The church we last attended was no longer there. This necessitated a search for another place to worship.

After visiting several places, I knew the choice was narrowed down to two. One was a small body of believers. They were meeting in an old automobile dealer's show room. The other church was a modern structure with good facilities. I prayerfully wondered where to attend. Then I heard the searching question, "If the little church looked like the big one, where would you attend?" My answer was, "Well, the little place of course." God said, "Then that is where I want you. Get your mind off the material things and worship me in spirit and truth."

Often it is difficult to stay focused on God when we are doing mundane chores. As I made my bed one morning, I reached for a stylish teddy bear. She was dressed with jewelry and eyelashes. One of her eyelashes was missing. I thought, I'll just rip off the other eyelash so the stuffed animal will look right. The Lord spoke to me, "No, don't do that. I want you to leave the bear just as it is. It will remind you, that you aren't perfect." That was a powerful message. The imperfect teddy bear reminded me of my flaws. My Maker uses this defect to humble me.

## Just Relax

Even after dynamic lessons, we often struggle to discern the Lord's direction. I was a non-traditional student. This was the first algebra course I'd taken in twenty-five years. There was fear in my heart about the upcoming semester, exam. The class had been a difficult struggle. The day of the exam, it started snowing. I checked the weather with a highway patrolman. He told me the road conditions weren't favorable. But he stated, if I drove slowly, the trip of thirty five miles could be negotiated. I decided to make the trip. A nudge began to form as a dread or apprehension. I brushed it aside, thinking it was Satan laying fear on me.

However, the very next inner voice was, "Wait until morning to make the trip. It will be lighter then. The instructor will let you take a makeup exam." I ignored that communication and started the trip to the university.

The roads were slick. I became fearful and began to pray. About a third of the way there, I hydroplaned. I knew I would hit the oncoming car head-on. The spirit within me stated, "You are going to hit the car, but you will be okay. You won't feel the impact. I want you to relax." This time I obeyed the voice. I relaxed, despite the normal instinct to stiffen up. Everything was slow motion. No impact was felt, but my glasses were knocked off. They were tossed in the seat next to me. The steering wheel was pushed toward my chest. I couldn't get the car door open. So I climbed across the seat. My only injury was a seat belt burn on my neck. If I hadn't obeyed the inner prompt to relax, I might have been seriously injured or killed.

The people in the other car all sustained injuries. Their vehicle was much larger than mine. It wasn't totaled, but mine was. It felt like I had an air bag in my car. But there wasn't one. The Lord was my air bag. He truly safeguarded me.

## Go Straight Home

Another time I averted danger by listening to the still small voice. I attended a seminar four hours from our home town. The instruction was, "When the meeting is over go straight home." During my travel, I was tempted to stop and shop. But again the inner nudge prompted me, against it. So I pushed on toward home. I breezed right on through a small rural town. It was beginning to get dark. It was very quiet with no signs of an approaching storm.

About thirty minutes down the road, I heard a weather report that the place I drove through had a tornado warning. Then my automobile radio went silent. I prayed for all in the path of the storm. I didn't think too much about it. We often have storm warnings in Kansas. The rest of my trip home was uneventful. I arrived home and went directly to bed.

## Massive Tornado

The next morning, the news was full of the report of the extremely powerful tornado that ripped through the city. The massive tornado was 1.7 miles wide. The path was bigger than the city itself. The wind exceeded 205 miles an hour. That town was 95% wiped off the map and the rest of it left in great destruction. I was shocked and humbled that God had protected me as I drove through the path of the twister, thirty minutes before it ripped the city to shreds and killed 11 people.

Had I not listened to the still small voice throughout that day, I might have been caught in the tornado's path and possibly killed. God is good and will protect us if we will hear His voice at all times.

## The Most High's Protection

Corrie Ten Boom, a survivor of a World War II German prison, tells about an incident of protection for another man held captive in a similar concentration camp. This prisoner was an Englishman who sustained himself with God's Word. He read this Bible verse. "He that dwelleth in the secret places of the most high, shall abide under the shadow of the almighty" (Psalm 91:1).

After reading this passage, he prayed, "Father, I see so many people dying around me. Am I going to have to die here too? You know Lord. I'd really like to work in your kingdom here on earth." After praying, this answer came to him in a still small voice. "Rely on what you have read, and go home."

So trusting in the Lord, he got up and went to the prison gate where a group of guards stood. They stopped him and asked him where he was going. He said, "I am under the protection of the 'Most High.'" The guard stood at attention and let him pass because Hitler was known to them as the "Most High." The man made it back to England and gave his testimony about what happened. He was the only one to survive that prison camp.[1]

## Hear the Whisper of God

We can definitely find refuge in the shelter of our mighty Lord, no matter what we are going through. The key to our safety is to abide in the shadow of the Almighty. Listen to every word He speaks. We must be very sensitive to listen to the whispers of God.

Not all situations are life or death. However, if our inner voices and nudges are heeded, we will be blessed.

We may be the answers to someone's prayer or our own. We must learn to become attentive and recognize God's voice, no matter how we experience it. Obey, without question, when we know it is The Lord's voice, just as the missionary's sons did.

We know it is God's voice, when it matches His Word. If you have peace, heed the utterance immediately. Ralph Waldo Emerson said, "Let us be silent that we may hear the whisper of God." "O My people, hear my teaching; listen to the words of My mouth."(Psalm 78:1, NIV).

## CHAPTER 10

# Dreams and Visions

"In a dream, in a vision of the night, when deep sleep falleth upon men . . .
Then, he openeth the ears of men, and sealeth their instruction."
Job 33:15-16.

God's Word tells us about dreams and visions given to men and women in the Bible. Some of these sleep images are symbolic and must have an interpretation. Other slumber messages are distinct. They have a clear meaning that is readily understood. Visions are similar to dreams. We often visualize them. Mental pictures predict something that may come to pass. It is seen, as if in a trance. It is often attributed to divine agencies. ". . . If there be a prophet among you, I the Lord will make myself known unto him in a vision, and will speak unto him in a dream" (Numbers 12:6). Most appearances from God are given to help instruct or protect us.

186

## Symbolic Dreams Need Interpretations

Pharaoh's dreams in Genesis 41 were symbolic and needed interpretation. In his sleep, the Ruler saw seven fat cattle eaten by seven lean ones. He also saw seven fat ears of corn eaten by seven lean ears of corn. The illusions perplexed him. So he sent for someone to interpret them. Joseph interpreted Pharaoh's dreams and stated there would be a famine in the land. They needed to prepare for it. Joseph gave him counsel, on how to prepare for the famine. The Ruler recognized Joseph's wisdom and put him in charge. God used Joseph and the sleep images to protect all of the people of the land.

## Dream Instructions

Understandable dreams were given to another man. Joseph was engaged to be married to Mary and he discovered she was with child. He was going to secretly put her away. ". . . Behold, the angel of the Lord appeared unto him in a dream, saying, Joseph, fear not to take unto thee Mary thy wife: for that which is conceived in her is of the Holy Ghost" (Matthew 1:20).

After Jesus birth, the Wise Men inquired in Jerusalem about where the Christ was born. Herod heard about this and was troubled. He gathered chief priests, scribes and the people around him and inquired of them. Where will Jesus be birthed? They all concluded by searching scripture, that Christ was to be born in Bethlehem. The King instructed the Wise Men to find Jesus and let him know the birthplace, so he could worship the Christ. (Matthew 2:1-8).

The Three Wise Men found Jesus in Bethlehem. They worshiped Him, presenting their gifts of gold, frankincense and myrrh. Before returning on their journey, they were given instruction from the Lord. "And being warned of God in a dream that they should not return to Herod, they departed into their own country another way" (Matthew 2:12).

After the gift bearers departed, Joseph was also advised of the Lord how to care for the Christ child. ". . . The angel of the Lord appeared to Joseph in a dream, saying, 'Arise, and take the young child and his mother, and flee into Egypt, and be there until I bring thee word; for Herod will seek the young child to destroy him" (Matthew 2:13). These visual images were given to protect Jesus because God had a plan for the Christ child.

Dreams from God didn't stop with the Old or New Testament. Today, people are still given instruction while they sleep. These images are for protection and direction about coming events.

## Power of the Blood

Author, Gwen Shaw shares a dream from her life. This night time trance helped her know how to deal with a coming event. On a Sunday morning she was awakened with a terrible nightmare that left her trembling. In this image she had been approached by Satan. He was so full of evil and darkness. She was repulsed by his presence. The enemy sneered at her and said, "I have power to harm you." She knew Satan was challenging her to go to war and she didn't want to. So she answered, "I know you have power to do me much harm. But you are afraid of the Blood." Then he answered, "I'm not afraid of the blood of bulls and goats." She didn't know what to say, but the Lord prompted her to answer, "No, but you are afraid of the Blood of Jesus." As she said that, Satan began to shake and said, "Yes, of that I am afraid." Then right in front of her eyes, he began to shrivel up and get smaller and smaller.

The author states she woke up fearful, knowing the devil was going to attack her. But she knew that God had given her the key to use – her Savior's Blood. She began praying and was later visited by an anointed woman. God sent the missionary to give support and confirmation about the dream Gwen had.

The next day when Ms. Shaw came home, her youngest son was ill. She began to pray and plead the blood of Jesus over him. She struggled in intercession for her son. Several days later he was healed.

Gwen relates, she almost gave up during those days and nights of fighting against Satan. It tested her faith, courage and ability to persevere. She might not have been able to persist for the deliverance of her son, if it wasn't for the instruction received in her sleep.[1]

The dream was an important way the Lord prepared her for what was going to happen. When the battle came, she would know what the key to victory was. It was important she knew victory would come.

When we have a revelation like that, it is a lot easier to stand when the battle is fierce. This is one reason the Lord gives us knowledge in our dreams.

## "Footprints" Dream – Vision

God often allows us to have sleep images to give us peace and help us through difficult situations. Often these illustrations help us decide which path we should take. One such beautiful vision/dream that has encouraged many people is *"Footprints."*

> "Footprints"
> I was walking along the beach with my Lord. . .
> When you saw only one set of footprints
> It was then that I carried you."
> By Margaret Fishback Powers

The author tells us that she wrote it after a walk on the beach. It was written at a time she was searching for directions at the crossroads of her life. This image gave her the needed confidence to make a wise choice.

The poem *"Footprints"* was first titled *"I Had a Dream."* The poem was lost, and found by another person and published[2] God speaks powerfully through this work. When we think we're all alone, that's when he carries us. This written work has brought comfort to countless people. It has also encouraged me in my struggles.

## Shook to the Core

There are times we wrestle to know if the sleep images are from God. Other times, we have a certainty they are from Him.

I wasn't sure whether this dream was from God or not. I awoke suddenly from a terrible nightmare. Someone informed me a family member had died. It shook me to the core. I said to the friend, "What do you think we ought to do?" She said, "Well, we have the power through Jesus name to command the person to arise. So we prayed and the deceased rose from the dead. About that time I woke up.

You would think I would feel good about the ending of the dream. But I was scared silly. I rolled over to try to sleep again. Then I said, "Lord, if this dream is from you, I ask you to give me peace about it." I went back to sleep and had the dream again but in a different form. The same people were involved. However, we went to the church this time and began the funeral. I was instructed, it was my job to walk up to the casket, and command the deceased to "Rise in the Name of Jesus." I said to someone, "How will I know when it is the right time?" They said, "You'll know because I'll slip in beside you. I'll take your hand, and walk with you." After the person slid in beside me, I commanded the person to "Rise in the Name of Jesus." And, they arose! Many people confessed the Lord and became His followers. What a mighty miracle, I thought!

After that nightmare, I never had peace. I lived in torment. This anguish continued for six years until a minister prayed me through the dream. During those six years, there were times when I thought I would lose my mind. There wasn't anyone I could tell about it. In the dream, I had been instructed, if you tell anyone, the miracle won't happen.

God spoke through a minister. He revealed this dream about death was Satan's trap. There was much deception in the dream. The pastor and I were able to take authority over it and saw victory. It has not happened, and will not. Death has been bound, and life has been loosed. And I am so very grateful that the Lord helped me through that time.

## Where Are They

Satan came at me much like he had come at Gwen Shaw when her son was ill. At that time, I hadn't read about her struggle. The Lord let me have the dream, but the end outcome wasn't from my Creator. It was the devil plotting against me. This image was a warning from God that Satan would try to attack with death.

Another night vision was a two part dream. In the first segment, I was frantically looking through every room in this huge mansion. I couldn't find one of my family members. Finally, I went to an open area outside the mansion and found all of my family except the one that was missing. I never found this family member in my slumber.

Later, the Lord showed me the mansion in my dream, was heaven. And he had allowed me to have this night vision so I would be serious about praying for our whole family's salvation.

## Satan's Attack

The second part of the dream was very scary. Satan came at me three different ways. The first time I couldn't see him, but sensed his evil presence. Just before he snatched me, I rebuked him in "Jesus Name." He left, only to return a little later.

In the second episode, the enemy was in the form of a person, but much smaller. He was green and resembled an elf. He had an ugly smirk on his face and hatred in his eyes. He was a repugnant sight. He grabbed for me, but missed. I opposed him, as I had before. But he kept advancing toward me. I berated him time and again, using the power and the "Name of Jesus." Finally, when he was a fraction of an inch from grasping me, I rebuked him again. This time he turned, put his tail between his legs and fled.

The third time, Satan came back, he was a black object. It became a cat. The feline hissed and lunged at me. I stormed at it in "Christ Name!" Then I reached out and grabbed the cat by the tail. As I snatched him, he turned into a black iron skillet. I held it up to my family and said, "Look family, the devil is dead. He is conquered. We're victorious in Jesus Name."

I didn't understand whether this sleep image was literal or symbolic. But I knew the Lord was telling me, I would face at least three major struggles. However, I would be victorious with each trial.

God used this dream to warn me to be on guard and fight against Satan. He would try to devour me several different ways. There would be times when I felt the Devil almost had me.

Years later, I realized the dream was symbolic. The first time Satan came at me, I couldn't see him but felt his presence. This correlated to the mind and the struggle I had with depression. It was an awful experience of being in a black pit of confusion.

The second time the devil tried to attack me in bodily form. That related to physical healing. I was disappointed when a blind woman wasn't healed after much prayer. I also had a health problem that lasted for twelve years. Eventually, I had major surgery and recovered well.

The third part of the episode completed the puzzle of the dream I had years earlier. Remember when Satan came as a black cat. That spoke of death. We had victory over death.

This dream had to be symbolic. If God had shown me outright, what the devil was trying to do, I would have been scared speechless. These instructions in slumber helped me to stand strong through several spiritual battles.

## I Love You the Same

The Lord allows night time comfort that helps us heal from grief. I had such a dream five months after my dad's death.

In my slumber, I saw people who had deceased, sitting at a banquet table eating. Other living people were unable to partake of the food. I couldn't eat either. Then suddenly, I saw my dad glide across the room toward me. He was wearing a long, off white robe. I recognize him in the spirit. Before he reached my side, he spoke and said, "Doris, you are okay now, aren't you?" I answered, "Yes." Then he said, "You understand death now, don't you?" I answered, "Yes," even though I really didn't understand death. It was as though he could read my mind. I asked him if he had time to talk. He stated, "Not long." I told him, "I love you." He said to me, "I love you the same." He put his arms around me. At that moment, he became Jesus Christ Himself. It was love like I've never felt before, or since. Then I told my dad, I saw him often in my memories. He said "Your mind never fails you." Then he floated away.

I had seen my daddy happy, dancing with joy and raising his arms in praise to the Lord. When he said, "Your mind never fails you," I knew he was telling me, "The way you see me in your visions is the way I am now." My dad had attained the love and perfection of Christ. He was happy and free. No more suffering! He had received the prize sought for all his life.

This was a marvelous revelation to me. My dad found it hard to trust in the Lord, and to praise him through the trials of life. Seeing him happy, praising and Christ like, was the healing touch I needed. From that day on, I grieved much less. I was certain he had attained his wholeness. What a beautiful release for me!

God used this dream to instruct me that death for a Christian was a glorious experience. Our journey here on earth is to prepare us for life everlasting, to reign with him. Earthly demise begins a new life. In heaven we can perfectly express all the qualities of Christ. This dream brought much peace and healing.

## The Lord's Warnings

God also allows slumber images to warn and direct us. My son had a dream the night before he took a flight back to Japan. He had visual images of being late to the airport and not catching his flight. After he told me his nightmare, the Lord instructed me to cover the dream in prayer. I said to my son, let's talk to God. That message may be a warning from the Lord. We sought our maker and bound all hindrances of evil or fear that could hinder his flight.

Later, I wrote a letter and reminded my son of God's faithfulness in getting him to his flight on time. We release the Lord's power to meet his needs. However, I never thought to request we get back home in a timely manner.

We left the airport and exited the freeway near a service station. The car died on us. We had it towed home.

That situation taught me, we need to heed warnings given in our sleep. Then take dominion over them in prayer. I'm very thankful the Lord gives us dreams so we know how to follow Him more closely and have fewer problems.

## I Know Her

A friend shared a slumber vision of me. She and her family were at their house. There was a slender, elderly gentleman there. She didn't know him or why he was staying at their house.

My friend and her family went to an event at a college. The older gentleman accompanied them. They were sitting high up in the stands, ready to enjoy an event. Then near the back, I jumped to my feet, and spoke the Word of God. Some people were mocking and not listening, but I continued to speak. When I stood up, the older gentleman with my friend said "I know her." After I finished speaking, I left.

My ally went looking for me. I was outside of the auditorium in the hallway and seven young people were kneeling down and receiving the Lord.

My friend was puzzled about this slumber message and decided to have it interpreted by a spiritual friend of hers. This is the interpretation of the dream. The older gentleman with us in the sleep event was the Spirit of the Lord. I was speaking to people who should be educated and should know the truth but did not. The spirit of the Lord knew my spirit. Seven is the number of completion. I was completing what God had called me to do.

The dream and the interpretation spoke powerfully to me. I had been concerned I wasn't walking in obedience to all the Lord was calling me to do. This was the encouragement I needed to keep on being compliant and wait on God's direction and His timing. This dream lifted my spirit.

## Use What Is In Your Hand

We may not always know the meaning of our night time visions. But God gives them to us for a reason. In one of my dreams, I saw a young couple. They were obviously struggling financially. There wasn't enough money to buy food. The only thing they had to sell was a dozen sugar cookies. These goodies were huge. The young man accessed the internet and advertised their product. The cookies sold. There was enough money to buy food and to replenish their business.

After that night illustration, I said, "God what does this dream mean?" The Lord said,

"The young man used what he had in his hand." The Lord showed me, we need to take what we have, and commit it to Him. It doesn't matter whether its time, talents, money, or resources; if given to the Lord He can multiply it.

The Lord brought to mind, accounts of people in the Bible, who took all they had, and gave it to the Lord. A little boy brought his lunch of five loaves and two fish to Jesus. The Lord then broke it and blessed it, and fed 5,000 people. After all the people had eaten, twelve baskets of scraps were picked up. (John 6:5-13).

The Wise men when they came to worship baby Jesus, brought what they had with them. The gifts they offered to the infant were gold, frankincense and myrrh. (Matthew 2:11).

Another worshiper, Mary anointed Jesus with costly perfume, prior to His crucifixion. (Matthew 26:6-13).

A good example of using what we have for the Lord is when Elijah asked a widow to feed him. The woman told the servant of God that she had no bread. She stated she had a handful of flour and a little oil. Elijah then commanded her to make him some bread. Her bowl of flour and the jar of oil did not run dry. (1 Kings 17:12-16). God multiplied her flour and oil because of her obedience.

Another widow had creditors who were going to take her sons to be bondsmen. The prophet Elisha asked her what he should do for her. She also told him that she didn't have anything in her house but a pot of oil.

Elisha told her to go borrow jars from all her neighbors. She was instructed to fill the jars with oil. The widow continued to pour oil out of her jar until all the vessels were filled. Then Elisha told her to sell the oil and pay all her bills and live on the rest of her profits. (2 Kings 4:2-7).

This passage really encouraged me. Both of the widows used what they had and it was blessed. God is telling us today, take what you have and He will use it.

## "I Am" Is With You

God used a strange dream to deliver a message to me. In my sleep trance, I woke up and heard a strange noise in a bedroom across the hall. I ask my husband who it was, and he said it was the cleaning lady. I said, "I have to see this. We've never had a cleaning lady before."

I went to the other sleep area. It had been made into a hospital room. That was strange, so I checked the rest of the house. As I entered each area, I found it was a hospital unit. When I stepped into the utility room, I saw doctors and nurses standing around. I knew it was a room where Electric Shock Treatments were given. The doctors told me to go in there. I knew what they had in mind. I wasn't crazy, sick, or depressed. So I told the doctors, I needed to go to the bathroom. They told me I couldn't walk. I told them I could walk and did it every day. We argued for a while and finally they told me to go ahead and go to the toilet. As I proceeded down the hall, the doctors and nurses surrounded me, and we all walked together.

Along the way the carpet became tiles with drains in it. There were coins scattered all over the floor. I began picking up coins and gave one to each doctor and nurse. I could suddenly read their minds. They were thinking, wow, she's not sick, she is okay. Then I entered the bathroom and was met by a huge cloud. Out of the fog God's voice boomed. "I am with you always. I am with you no matter what happens." Then the dream ended.

After awakening, I reflected on the night vision and asked myself two key questions. Did this dream line up with the Bible and did I have peace? "And God said unto Moses, I AM, THAT I AM . . . I am has sent me unto you." Exodus 3:14. "I will never leave thee, nor forsake thee." Hebrews 13:5. The dream lined up with the Word of God, but I didn't have complete peace. So I sought the Lord about the meaning of the dream. He spoke into my spirit. He showed me, when I picked up the coins and handed them to the doctors and nurses, this was an act of giving treasures of wisdom to others. It healed me and blessed them. As I understood the symbolic meaning of the sleep vision, I had peace.

At the time of this dream, I didn't feel very peaceful. My son moved overseas, an uncle died and a family member had colon cancer. The Lord reassured me that no matter what happened, I would be okay. Whenever I remember this message, I know I'm going to be okay and I'm not crazy.

## What Is Heaven Like?

Another night illusion came about the time we moved back home. I wished I could tell my dad about it, but he had gone to heaven many years before.

The Lord blessed me with a special dream. In slumber, I could see my dad talking to others and I could feel God's presence nearby. I knew my Heavenly Father and my dad were both pleased with what I was doing. Finally, I got my dad's attention. I shook his shoulder and asked him a question. "Dad, what is heaven like?" He answered, "It takes till tomorrow to do roll call." As he began to talk, I could see down a long corridor. It had many rooms made of rose-colored stone. Light was shining as far as the eye could see. It was beautiful and gave me such a sense of peace. I knew my dad had found his work to do in paradise.

In another sleep trance, I found myself experiencing heaven. The flowers and scenery were all so beautiful. I had never seen colors like these before; they were indescribable. Everyone was happy and doing something. There were people of every race, creeds and from every era of time. No one was sick, crippled or obese! Everyone had their new bodies.

I was upset that I had to go and couldn't stay in heaven. But I soon got over it. I was very convinced, heaven is for real. I didn't want anyone to miss their eternal home.

## Good Example Deserved

God often gives dreams, to guide, motivate and keep us safe. In this night vision a female relative was preparing to quit her job. As she gathered up her things, she stated enjoying some of the people, but the teenagers didn't deserve her. I was listening and said, "Let's turn that around. Maybe they do deserve you. Do they deserve to have a good example set for them? Will they be better because of you?" Then the dream ended.

After waking up, God started speaking to me. He said none of us deserves anything, but that is what grace is for. *Grace is - GOD'S riches at Christ's expense.*

Because of God's grace we all get (not what we deserve) but we get the benefit of others good examples. What would we be like without God's grace? Who was I to question what I or others might deserve? God really humbled me through that sleep message.

## Visions from God's Messengers

Dreams and visions can instruct us to trust in God and not our own power. They are often similar. It's difficult for us to tell which it is. That was exactly the case with the Apostle Paul's manifestation when he was caught up into the third heaven. "And I know such a man, (whether in the body, or out of the body, I cannot tell: God knoweth;) How he was caught up into paradise, and heard unspeakable words which it is not lawful for a man to utter" (2 Corinthians 12:3-4).

Peter also had a trance-like illusion when he went to the roof top to pray. Peter saw heaven open and a great sheet came down to the earth. There were all manners of beasts on this sheet. And the Lord told Peter to arise, kill, and eat. Peter (a Jew) said no, because he'd never eaten anything unclean. The Spirit spoke to him again and said what God had cleansed is not to be called common or unclean (Acts 10).

About the same time Cornelius (a Gentile) also had a vision while praying. Cornelius was told to seek out Peter because God had heard his prayers (Acts 10).

Because of Peter's and Cornelius' trances, Peter was able to bring Jesus' salvation message to the Gentiles. He did not consider them unclean people.

In Paul's and Peter's visions, they weren't sure whether they were awake or sleeping. Sometimes we experience the same kinds of visitations from the Lord.

Saul had a daytime vision on his way to Damascus. Jesus appeared to him with a blinding light so he would know who Jesus was. Saul had a conversion experience. Jesus changed his name to Paul and gave him a ministry.

Ananias and Saul both had visions. The Lord showed Ananias to go minister to Saul so he could receive his sight. God had a work for him. See (Acts 9:4-17). This vision was very important because it brought conversion and instructions for Paul.

## Cascading Waterfall of People

Many daytime trances are given to help us become more effective in service for the Lord. "A Vision for Household Salvation," was told by Evangelist Phil Cameron on the Richard Roberts Live Show. The minister related he was preaching on household salvation but it hadn't clicked in his spirit yet.

He asks the Lord to show him what was missing. Jesus gave him a vision of a waterfall of people cascading off the edge of time into eternity. He saw men and women who would never laugh, feel peace or know rest again. These people were lost forever.

## Kick the Devil Out

After that vision, God took the evangelist into a beautiful field. He said, "This grassy plot, is your life. Whatever you sow in this meadow, you're going to reap." The preacher stated, all his family and friends were surrounding him, and he was joyful. Right in the middle of the field, he saw Satan sitting there. The enemy had a couple of his loved ones bound with chains. Then the evangelist's joy turned to anguish. He said, "Lord, the devil's in my field,' God said, 'It's your field. I've given you authority over it. Kick him out."[3]

This two-part vision was powerful. It is God's way of showing us that we need to take authority and kick the Devil out of our lives. It will lose the chains from our loved ones and friends so they don't cascade over the waterfall of time, into eternity lost forever. This picture was an assurance of household salvation. The evangelist got it into his spirit. This message was helpful for many people.

## Put Yourself, On the Cross

My sister experienced a vision but wasn't fully aware of what it was. She was unable to sleep. The Lord spoke to her, as she prayed. At times she felt like she was a tiny cell. She stated, heaven opened up and she felt the presence of the Lord. As she prayed for every family member, the Lord told her she needed to put herself on the cross for her family. My sister said, "I will put myself on the cross. But Lord, you are going to have to raise the cross"

That was a powerful vision. I had to ask myself, "Am I willing to put myself on the cross so others can know the Father?" Yes Lord, help me come to this point of surrender.

## Visions Instruct

Visions are an important way God ministers instructions to us. A fellow Christian conveyed a message to me. He received a picture while he was working on a backhoe. As he sat there digging up dirt, he saw a place for discarded people who needed housing. These folks would know the Lord and be freed from bondage. They would also learn two occupational trades. The recipients of this program would live a productive life. This project would be self supporting and have a far reaching impact upon many people. The man was told, "Don't despise small beginnings."

The man shared his vision, he had experienced four years prior to telling me. My mother and I also had a similar vision about the same time. His revelation was confirmation to us. There were also other people who had a similar visitation. The Lord was saying, He wanted me involved in a ministry, and it would require a degree in social work.

At the time I received the vision, I had just entered the School of Social Welfare. I didn't even realize why I was pursuing this field of study, except that I felt a call. It was a way I could eventually fulfill God's instructions of being a counselor.

A few years later I had another vision that added instructions for training people the world had discarded. In this picture, I saw the tent being stretched to allow for growth of the project.

I heard the Lord speak, "Stretch the tent." And I responded, "Which way?" The Lord replied, "Usually you stretch it in all directions." I responded with, "Then we are to stretch to the north, south, east and west." God spoke again, "Now what type of land mass do you have." And I replied, "It's in the shape of a cross." "Precisely, and it will be outlined with evergreen trees. This is so people can see it from the air as they fly over it," said the Lord.

Later as I contemplated sharing this vision with my mother, she shared the exact same illustration. Often Christ gives others the same ideas. It's His way of confirming the instructions he has given us.

## Be Still and Listen

Oswald Chambers tells us that whenever God gives a vision to us, He puts us in the shadow of His hand. Then it is our duty to be still and listen. When there is darkness from excess of light, then it is time to listen.[4] Genesis 15 illustrates the darkness. "And when the sun was going down, a deep sleep fell upon Abram, and, lo, a horror of great darkness fell upon him." (Genesis 15:12).

Abram had darkness with this vision. He never saw his seed, the Israelites, deliverance from Egypt. This image was given before Abram even had a son. Sometimes we have to linger a long time to see a promise fulfilled. If we wait on God, Chambers reminds us that He will make us in accordance with the vision. We are never to try to help Him fulfill His Word.[5] "For the vision is yet for an appointed time . . . though it tarry, wait for it; because it will surely come, it will not tarry" (Habakkuk 2:3).

Dreams and visions are vehicles God uses to communicate with us. They are ways He warns or instructs without frightening us. We must be sensitive to recognize His voice. Sleep messages from the Lord should leave us with a sense of peace, boldness and authority over a situation. It must also line up with the Word of God. "In a dream, in a vision of the night, when sleep falleth upon men . . . then He openeth the ears of men, and sealeth their instruction" (Job 33:15-16).

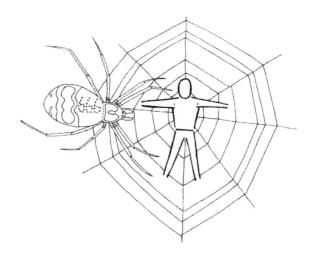

## CHAPTER 11

# Satan's Web of Deception

"No one calls for justice; no one pleads his case with integrity. They . . . speak
lies . . . They hatch the eggs of vipers and spin a spider's web . . ."
(Isaiah 59: 4-5 NIV).

"The thief (Satan) comes only to steal and kill and destroy . . ."
(John 10:10 NIV).

Many situations that require discerning decisions will come across our
paths. It's imperative we know the truth, which is God's Word. And we
must recognize our Father's voice. It is essential to be able to discern God's
call no matter how, when or where we hear it. If we don't know the truth,
we will be easily deceived.

## Master of Deception

Satan is the master of delusion. He began by tricking Eve in the
Garden of Eden. The serpent was a very subtle beast. He said to the

woman, has God said, you can't eat of every tree of the garden. Eve said, we may eat, but not of the fruit of the tree that is in the middle of the garden. If we eat of it, we will die. Then the serpent said to the woman, you won't die (Genesis 3:1-4).

Many other men and women of the Bible were also deceived. David was entrapped when he fell into adultery (2 Samuel 11:2-5). Abram ran ahead of God's schedule and took Sarai's handmaiden (Hagar) as his wife (Genesis 16:1-4).

The Israelites were duped when they grumbled and complained and made a golden calf. They worshiped the idol while Moses was on the mountain with God. They said to Aaron, ". . . Make us gods, which shall go before us: as for this Moses . . . we know not what is become of him" (Exodus 32:23).

Sampson was beguiled when he told Delilah the secret of his strength. He let her tie him up. When he fell asleep, she cut his hair. Then the Philistines attacked him and gouged out his eyes. He was forced to grind grain in the prison house (Judges 16:4-21). Even though all these people were deceived, they repented and returned to the Lord. He used them mightily.

Satan even tried to deceive Jesus, when He was in the wilderness forty days without food. The tempter came to Jesus and told Him that if He was the Son of God He could command the stones to become bread. "But he answered and said, 'It is written, Man shall not live by bread alone . . . Then saith Jesus unto him, 'Get thee hence, Satan: for it is written, Thou shalt worship the Lord thy God and Him only shalt thou serve.'" (Matthew 4: 4 & 10). Jesus resisted temptation three times. Then the devil left Him and the angels ministered unto Him.

## Be on Guard

If Satan tried to deceive Jesus, you can be sure he will try to dupe us. "Be self-controlled and alert. Your enemy the devil prowls around like a roaring lion looking for someone to devour." (I Peter 5:8 NIV). The Word tells us to be on guard. It is important to remember Satan can trip us easier in our strengths, than in our weaknesses. We tend to be more vigilant in weak areas than we are in our might. Avoid Satan's web of destruction and sin's tragedy. Learn the enemies' strategy.

## Imposter's Job Description

It is essential we know Satan's job description. He comes to steal, kill and destroy. The devil accomplishes his mission by deception, fear, temptation and accusations. He is an imposter who tries to imitate God's work and power. Some of the indications that Satan fabricates, is born out in scripture. He poses as many things. He is a light bearer. (Isaiah 14:12). He appears as an angel of light. (2 Corinthians 11:14). He was a disloyal angel and God cast him out of heaven. "And there was war in heaven . . . And the great dragon was cast out, that old serpent, called the Devil, . . . which deceiveth the whole world . . . for the accuser of our brethren is cast down, which accused them before our God day and night" (Revelation 12:9-10).

Because of the enemy's former position, he is still walking around, thinking he's something. He claims authority and tries to imitate God. Satan even tried to attend worship. "Again there was a day when the sons of God came to present themselves before the Lord, and Satan came also among them to present himself before the Lord" (Job 2:1).

The enemy poses in many roles and tries to fabricate things. He seeks to make us believe he has the ultimate power. The Devil cannot recreate salvation, life or love because he is an imposter. "For the (Devil), is a liar, and the father of it" (John 8:44. Lucifer seeks man's ruin.

## Tools of the Trade

Satan has many tools of deception he uses to try to destroy God's work and children. He blinds the unbeliever. (II Corinthians 4:3-4).

Satan slanders the saints and opposes God's people. "Then Satan answered the Lord, and said, doth Job fear God for nought? Hast not thou made a hedge about him? . . . But put forth thine hand now, and touch all that he hath, and he will curse thee to thy face" (Job 1:9-11).

Satan incites men to evil. "And supper being ended, the devil having now put into the heart of Judas Iscariot, Simon's son, to betray him (Jesus)" (John 13:2).

The imposter uses many tools to accomplish his mission. The Lord instructed me that Satan's best tools are deception, fear, selfishness, and pride. When the devil deludes us, he frightens us. Then we can't accomplish anything. Fear controls us from the very core of our being. Satan ties us in knots of panic by feeding us lies. He doesn't want us to achieve anything for God or others. An anonymous author states, "Satan has many tools, but a lie is the handle that fits them all."

The devil fabricates the truth. He tells us it isn't going to turn out right. We need to be afraid. When we are bound with fear, chaos could result if we let our minds spin out of control. We need to, "Bring into captivity every thought to the obedience of Christ" (2 Corinthians 10:5 b).

## Remember God's Faithfulness

I asked the Lord how to stay out of fear and handle problems. He instructed me to go to His Word, and remember His faithfulness to the Israelites as they made their exit from Egypt. Exodus 12 tells us how the Israelites prepared for the Passover. They ate the roasted lamb with unleavened bread in haste with their clothes on, and their staffs in their hands. They painted the door posts of their houses with lambs' blood. The death angel passed over their homes, and no first born children or animals died. Because the Israelites listened to God's instructions, they were saved from a terrible disaster.

We can be spared from devastation if we will prepare. Jesus in His parable of the ten virgins tells us the importance of being prepared for His return. Matthew 25:1-13, tells us five maidens were wise and took oil with them. The others were foolish and took no oil. They all slept until midnight when the cry went forth, "The bridegroom was coming." Then all the virgins arose and trimmed their lamps. The foolish ones begged the wise maidens to sell them some oil. But the astute ladies refused to sell their oil. The silly women went away to buy oil. When they got back, they were shut out of the marriage feast with the bridegroom.

We need to prepare as the Lord instructs, focus on God and trust Him. Then we will not be afraid of anything. The Word of God says "For God hath not given us the spirit of fear; but of power, and of love, and of a sound mind" (2 Timothy 1:7). "The fear of man bringeth a snare: but whoso putteth his trust in the Lord shall be safe" (Proverbs 29:25). When we are tied up with terror, we won't be able to express any power, or have a stable mind. Fear taken to extremes can make us mentally unstable. Panic snares us into Satan's web of duplicity.

There is a way out of deception. "There is no fear in love; but perfect love casteth out fear . . ." (1 John 4:18). Love counteracts terror.

## The Enemy's Snares and Traps

Selfishness is another big tool Satan uses to snare and trap us in falsehood. We are born self-centered creatures. We like to have our own way. One of the biggest fears is not being in control of our lives. If we don't get our way, we get discontent at times. We start to pout. "If Satan is allowed to drive a little wedge of complaint into the soul, all it was, or all its inner fortitude and strength ebbs away."[1]

The spirit of dissatisfaction shows a lack of faith in Christ, and a streak of selfish egotism. When we sow a murmuring spirit, we reap an overwhelmed spirit. The only way to get rid of a complaining spirit is to start praising. ". . . To give unto them beauty for ashes, the oil of joy for mourning, the garment of praise for the spirit of heaviness . . ." (Isaiah 61:3). We must exchange the spirit of weightiness for a garment of praise. If we are thankful, we will be less selfish and more grateful.

Selfishness is looking after our own interest and not the concerns of others. We are instructed in the Word, ". . . Let each, esteem others better than themselves. Look not every man on his own things, but every man also on the things of others" (Philippians 2:3-4).

Pride is another big tool Satan uses against us. We want to feel good about ourselves, and be in control of things. Self respect is a good thing. We need to have satisfaction in our work, families and in who we are. But taken to excess, pride bears ugly haughtiness. Egotism is an exalted opinion of oneself, an exaggerated self esteem, and arrogance. It makes us feel we are better than the next guy. We think we deserve more than others. Our worth is exalted. This is counter to the Word of God. "When pride cometh, then cometh shame: but with the lowly is wisdom" (Proverbs 11:2). "Pride goeth before destruction and a haughty spirit before a fall . . ." (Proverbs 16:18). God doesn't honor proud people but levels them and exalts humble people. If Satan can get us involved in pride, he can bring us down for the kill.

Satan's biggest tools of deception, fear, selfishness and pride, have an exact parallel to God's primary fruits of the spirit, "love, peace and joy." When the primary fruits are combined, they create all other fruits of the spirit. Love and joy creates kindness etc. The same thing is true of Satan's fruit or tools of selfishness, pride and fear. Fear is the opposite of love. Selfishness leaves us with no joy and pride leaves us with no peace.

A self consumed person is greedy and holds on to things tightly. Consequently, they aren't able to take hold of anything else. This reminds me of the fable of the greedy monkey who was caught in a trap in a jungle. He put his hand into a small opening of a hidden jar filled with peanuts. He grabbed what he could hold in his hand. To his surprise, when he tried to remove his hand from the jar, he was stuck. He wouldn't let go of the peanuts. The monkey was caught by the trappers and sent to captivity.

The gluttonous person is much like that and can't escape the trap or grasp anything else of value. Selfishness, pride and fear are important tools that Satan uses against us.

We can see that fear binds us up and we can't think logically. One of the most subtle forms of fear is frustration. It is a dread that we won't have our needs meet. It is a snare. It puts us into Satan's web of deception. Hence, we don't believe the truths about the Word of God, ourselves, or our situations.

Selfishness creates emotions of self-pity, envy and greed. But one of the most subtle forms of selfishness is discontent. It shows lack of faith in Christ, and an abundance of egotism. Disillusionment marked the Israelite's journey in the wilderness. It was a sin that kept them out of The Promised Land. The Bible tells us that discontent and murmuring are synonymous. Murmuring hinders our progress just as it did the Israelites. "Do all things without complaining or arguing" (Philippians 2:14 NIV).

Complaining reduces our value and negatively affects others. We can either depreciate or appreciate people and things. When we appreciate someone or something, it increases in value to us. Conversely, when we condemn others, they decrease in value to us. Depreciation hinders our progress but appreciation opens the way to stronger relationships and a closer walk with God.²

## Subtle Deception

Another crafty form of devaluing is to elevate ourselves above others and look down on them. Discontentment, murmuring and depreciation are subtle. We must kick them out of our lives. They lead to discouragement. These are all forms of self-centeredness and arrogance. Satan is so cunning and feeds us a lie, "We don't have what we need." That builds and eventually traps a person.

206

When selfishness and pride are combined they birth distress. Pride contains stubbornness and un-forgiveness and often leads to anger, bitterness, quarrels and self-destruction. "Only by pride cometh contention: but with the well advised is wisdom" (Proverbs 13:10). "Let all bitterness, and wrath . . . be put away from you . . ." (Ephesians 4:31). Anger, fighting, and bitterness combined with malice can lead to murder.

The combination of pride, selfishness and fear make many of Satan's fruits of his spirit. His tools produce evil works and catch us in a web of delusion that destroys our lives.

An anonymous author states, "One of the weapons Satan utilizes is to get unscrupulous people in key places to deny the saving power of the gospel." So we need to be on guard against the father of lies and be ready to oppose him with the truth.

Discouragement is another subtle tool of Satan's. A fable states that the Devil held a sale and offered the tools of his trade. Discouragement was priced higher than all other items. When Satan was asked why it was priced higher than any other device, he stated, "No one knows it belongs to me. So it opens doors that are tightly bolted against other tools."[3]

This emotion comes from our selfishness and faulty belief that we are better than others and shouldn't have to go through hard times. We doubt that God knows what is best for us. Discouragement is a sin of unbelief in God's care for us. It's so subtle and something that all of us have experienced. That's why it is so valuable to Satan.

## Imbalance Causes Falls

Another cunning instrument Satan uses is imbalances. If he can get us out of equilibrium, on any point in our lives, then he can deceive us.

A good example of this is the balancing acts some children try to perform. As a child I entertained myself by walking on a four inch wide board, attached to the top of our cattle watering tanks. Sometimes I was successful and would balance the whole way. Other times I fell into the cow tank full of water, and smelly moss. Sometimes the tumble gouged my legs on the barbed wire surrounding the tank. Other times I fell on the ground. Without poise I was more likely to get hurt.

Swimming is another activity that requires balance. If there is no rhythm while swimming, water easily gets into your mouth. It could sink you. Imbalances are a subtle way Satan pulls us down.

I've seen this happen many times in people and churches. When people obsess on one thing, they get weak and are more open to deception.

Another one of the enemy's instruments is death. If he can render us lifeless, we won't be here to do the Lord's work. That's just another way the devil is fulfilling scripture about, his self. Jesus says that, "Satan has come to steal, kill and destroy, but I have come to give life more abundantly" (John 10:10). Jesus came to give abundant life.

All of the devices Satan uses are designed to trap us in his web of deception. Once in that net, we are immobile. We're defenseless and ready for the kill. We must be on guard, so we don't get caught.

The devil catches us in his web of deceit, by giving us a half truth. Satan baits his hook with just enough accuracy so we'll swallow it. That's why we need to know the Word of God well. If we aren't reading the Bible and praying, we won't be able to discern the voice of the Father from the voice of Satan. The Word and prayer are two most important ways God speaks. The enemy can't recreate it. But he will try to pervert or deceive us anyway he can.

Nature gives us many examples of what happens to animals that are caught in spider webs or vegetation. Some plants are very beautiful, with a sweet aroma and they entice insects. It isn't long before the bug is trapped. This is Satan's plan for our lives. He wants to trap and kill us.

The enemy is like that plant, he gives us a half truth. Satan also tempts and condemns. We need to be aware that the devil will use any tactics to trick us. "Let no man deceive you by any means . . ." (2 Thessalonians 2:3a). We aren't to be beguiled as Eve was in the Garden of Eden, or as Sampson was with Delilah.

Remember, Satan will use any person, thing or situation he can to delude us. His job is to pervert the truth. I like what one of my son's said, "Satan is a sterile creature. He hates us making children in God's image. Abortion is a devise to destroy God's creation."

The enemy can't create like our Father has. He can't give salvation or reproduce love. But he tries to destroy or corrupt all God has given and ordained.

# Father of Lies

"...He (Satan) was a murderer from the beginning, and abode not in the truth . . . because there is no truth in him . . . for he is a liar. . ." (John 8:44b).

The devil is the father of lies, and is unable to create any good thing. He quotes God's Word inaccurately. That's why it is so important to know the Word, so we can spot a half truth from the enemy.

Satan tries to speak to us in many ways but God is the only true communicator. Prayer has great power and it's God's way of talking with us. Often the enemy puts hindrances in our path so we won't pray. He knows if we are praying, we will be successful. Therefore, he deludes us into believing that prayer is not effective.

Satan tries to keep us from climbing higher with the Lord. Pastor Dale Kurtz likens Satan's tactics to greasing the pole of a bird feeder to keep the squirrels from climbing to the feathered friend's food. The devil uses our natural instincts of selfishness, pride, fear, complacency and self-sufficiency, to grease the pole. When these traits are operating in our lives, it makes us slide down the spiritual pole after we begin to climb.

There is a way to keep the oil off the pole. We can take the Apostle Peter's advice. Submit to one another. Humble ourselves before Almighty God. *Cast* all our cares on the Lord. Discipline ourselves and be watchful (1 Peter 5:5-8). If we follow this counsel, we will live more productive lives.

As we walk further with the Lord, we know His Word better. We become stronger and more disciplined in our prayer life. Then Satan's deceptive attacks become more cunning and tailor made for us.

# Cunning Temptations

One such subtle temptation from the enemy seemed designed for me. I had ministered to my sister, a teaching from the Lord. She and I prayed and felt the blessings of Jesus.

After leaving her house, I went to a Bluegrass festival where I met my husband. Later that evening we would see a Bluegrass Entertainer - Ricky Skaggs perform. As I hurried down the path to the entrance of the festival, a man rolled down the window of his car and asked, "Do you want a free pass?" I was stunned, and answered, "I guess so." He gave me his ticket, which he had used for a short time. He recapped his story of cancer and pain. He had just taken medication to kill the ache. He needed to go home and rest.

At first this seemed innocent. I wasn't sure whether this was a blessing for being obedient with my sister; or was it a temptation. The next thought, which I spoke out, was "Are you sure, it's okay to do this." That should have been enough of a red flag, but it wasn't. I took the pass, not wanting to offend the stranger. He was sick and had lost his wife several months ago.

This scenario was familiar to me as a hospice social worker. I visited with the man for a few minutes. Then I had presence of mind enough to be about the Lord's business. I ask him if he had Jesus in his heart. He said he wasn't sure. So I told him God's plan of redemption. He was receptive. He let me pray with him about his illness and upcoming treatment. I scribbled down the man's telephone number so I could follow up on his cancer prognosis.

Then I went into the festival grounds on the pass. I immediately told my husband what I had done. He didn't say much, but the Lord quickly convicted me that what I did was wrong. Immediately, I went to the ticket booth. There I explained my actions and purchased a pass. The ticket taker questioned me on whether I really wanted to purchase entrance to the fair. I confirmed I did. She said, "It's refreshing to see integrity."

The next day, I checked in with the man who gave me the pass. I explained, conviction hit me and I bought another ticket. He understood and thanked me for praying with him.

Jesus showed me once again, through this incident, just how subtle Satan is. He instructed me on His mercy and forgiveness. The devil meant this temptation for a fall. But God knew He could trust me to do His work. The Lord knew I would repent and exhibit integrity. I learned trust and grace anew through this situation. How could I fall to a temptation and my Maker still use me for good?

This was hard to understand until I remembered what author, minister, Joyce Meyer says, "Every new level brings a new devil." She stressed, as we grow spiritually, Satan has to devise a more subtle temptation to trick us.

It is so crucial for us to understand what we are hearing, and whose speaking. It wasn't God telling me to take the pass. He permitted me to have the temptation. He gave me free will to make choices about whom I listen to.

There are many voices we hear. Often these utterances are wolves disguised in sheep's clothing. We need to be on guard whenever Jesus Christ or His teachings are put down.

It's imperative to be discerning and know when it's God and when it's not.

## Missing the Mark

Another experience of missing The Lord's voice was at an interview. A dairy company was going out of business. They needed workers to help with their auction. It would be good part time work. I attended an interview per the Lord's instructions. There were seven men and myself, applying for six positions. The supervisor explained about the job. He said, he would have to cut two people. The first utterance I heard was, "See how far you can get - just hang in there. Take a chance, trust me." But immediately there was another voice. It said, "You probably don't need this job as much as the guys sitting here. You should be unselfish and let someone else have it." That sounds good. I didn't listen to the first voice which asked me to trust. I listened to the second message that sounded humble. I realized this job would be a good opportunity to bring honor to the Lord. But, I'd already said to the interviewer, "I'll volunteer to be cut. After the supervisor had finished his selections, he spoke with me. He said, "I wish you hadn't done that. I was going to select you. I needed someone with maturity. None of them had that quality. I wanted you for the job."

As the supervisor said that, I realized I had listened to the wrong voice. God was telling me to trust Him. After all if The Lord hadn't wanted me, I shouldn't have been out there interviewing. The devil was so subtle. He used a tactic of unselfishness to get me off track.

Satan wasn't thinking about my best or anyone else's. He wanted to short circuit God's plan. The enemy wanted to catch me in the web of deception. He didn't want me blessed or where The Lord wanted me.

## Which Voice Will You Listen To

This experience humbled me. It showed the need to be very discerning of the voice's we hear. One of the best ways we can stay out of deception is to line everything up with the Word of God.

Another incident of listening to the wrong message was mentioned earlier. It was a trip in a snow storm, to take a final math test. In that incident, the first inner voice I heard said, "Wait till morning, it will be safer and you can see better in the light than in the darkness with a storm." The second argument said, "If you don't go you're letting fear control you." Again I didn't listen to the first voice which was God's, but I obeyed the second voice, Satan's.

The devil was saying if you don't go you're afraid. And fear is of the enemy. He gave me a half truth. Fear is of the enemy. But for me to stay home wasn't fear; it was common sense. Satan is so clever. The closer we grow to the Lord, the more subtle Satan has to be to trick us.

God reminded me that in both instances, His voice was the first one I heard. The second one was an argument with the first utterance. Remember The Lord said, "Wait till morning, it's safer in the light." This lines up with the word of God. ". . . Walk while ye have the light, lest darkness come upon you; for he that walketh in darkness knoweth not whither he goeth" (John 12:35).

The second utterance made me feel guilty and fearful. This was a scare tactic. God doesn't use fear, but Satan does.

The Lord communicates clearly His messages to us. He expects us to be sensitive to listen and quickly obey for our protection and blessing. God isn't playing games like Satan.

Be speedy to discern who is talking to you. If we do this, we won't be caught in Satan's web of deception, and ready for his kill.

## The Devil is Like a Lion

When we are in that trap, we are much like the deer, being stalked by the lion. Often the lion waits until it is almost dark to attack. Satan is the same. The lion waits until the antelope is isolated before attacking it. Our enemy does that too. He pounces on us when we are alone or in a low spot. The lion calls in all the other big cats after he has pounced on the deer. Satan calls in all his demons to help him devour us.

The Lord instructs us how to keep from being devoured by our enemy. "Be self controlled and alert. Your enemy the devil prowls around like a roaring lion looking for someone to devour. Resist him; stand firm in your faith . . ." (1 Peter 5:8, NAS). We must also, "Put on the full armor of God"

(Ephesians 6:11 NAS). "Listen, O my people, to my instruction; incline your ears to the words of my mouth" (Psalms 78:1, NAS).

This is God's answer to keep us out of deception. Cunning from Satan weakens us and makes us compromise. And it leaves us ignorant. "My people are destroyed for lack of knowledge . . . (Hosea 4:6a). Delusion really is ignorance.

## Window of Control

In another incident, I was deceived by what a woman said in a lecture. She stated, when a person dies they have a window of control. I believed it for a long time. It certainly looked like people were waiting till favorite loved ones were with them, before they passed away.

A Christian man whose spouse was dying, pointed out, this philosophy didn't line up with the Word of God. The Bible states, "And your eyes saw my unformed body. All the days ordained for me were written in your book before one of them came to be" (Psalm 139:16 NIV).

An explanation of why some people appear to have some control in the dying process is, God knows and grants the desires of their hearts. "Delight thyself in the Lord and he shall give you the desires of your heart" (Psalm 37:4).

Satan is very subtle. He tells us half truths and what our flesh wants to hear. The enemy's delusions can show up anyplace. Whatever we fill our minds with, needs to match the Word of God.

## Red Flags

One book was helpful in keeping me out of deception. The author gives several red flags that alert us to cults. This belief usually puts a ritual or leader on equal footing with Jesus Christ. Cults usually attempt to instill fear into their followers. They usually exalt a person who is trying to gain power, money or manipulate people. The final mark of this deception is the unwillingness of the leader to let the people grow up. Sometimes the followers lose the ability to make independent rational decisions. This doesn't follow God's pattern.[4] "Jesus saith unto him, I am the way, the truth and the life; no man cometh unto the Father but by me," (John 14:6).

We can only come to the Father through truth. That is why it is so important to align everything with the Word of God.

There wasn't peace, nor did the dream line up with the Bible, when a relative was raised from the dead. I lived with that nightmare for six years.

One day I met with my pastor. The Lord showed him the dream wasn't from God.

He showed me through God's Word this dream wasn't according to the Word or will of God. "...Sirs, what must I do to be saved? And they said, Believe on the Lord Jesus Christ, and thou shalt be saved, and thy house," (Acts 16:30- 31). It's not a miracle happening, but believing in Jesus and repenting of our sins that rescues us. The pastor also instructed me, death isn't a tool of God's but an instrument of Satan's.

The story Jesus told about the rich man and Lazarus shows us death isn't God's work. The prosperous man and Lazarus died. The well to do man went to hell and Lazarus was in the bosom of Abraham. The rich man asks Father Abraham to send Lazarus to warn his brothers. "He said unto him, if they hear not Moses and the prophets, neither will they be persuaded, though one rose from the dead" (Luke 16: 31).

In my dream, someone had been raised from the dead and this miracle caused many people to believe and be saved. That didn't line up with the passage of scripture in Luke. God never uses Satan's tools to accomplish His work or purposes.

## Deception Conquered

My pastor prayed, and bound the spirit of death from the dream. I felt a heavy weight lift and peace flooded me.

The pastor stated, I would likely experience some depression, because I wouldn't experience a mighty miracle. He knew I had been set up for deception by Satan. To help me through this spiritual fight, the pastor had his wife cover me in prayer for two weeks.

This man of God was right. I went through a period of depression. I really appreciated the minister and his wife's obedience in praying for me. I had no more problems with that dream. Total peace was mine.

After conquering deception and fighting that spiritual battle for a couple weeks, I began to plead with God. "Lord, please don't ever let me be deceived again, even in the smallest ways!" I know He heard my prayer. God has given me wisdom and the desire never to be tricked again. I've tried to stay out of delusion by asking, "Does this line up with the Word of God?" If it doesn't measure up with the Bible, and there isn't peace, it's not from The Lord.

## Authority Not Ability

God's Word tells us we have authority over Satan and his deception. "Behold, I give unto you authority to tread on serpents and scorpions, and over all the power (ability) of the enemy" (Luke 10:19, NAS). Rev. Larry Allen gave a powerful example to explain this verse. "A policeman stands in the middle of the street. He has the authority to stop a truck, but he doesn't have the ability. The driver of the truck has the ability to run over the policeman, but he doesn't have the authority."[5]

Satan may have ability but he doesn't have authority over us. We are The Lord's children. It's time to take authority and say, "Halt, devil, in the Name of Jesus. You may have ability, but you have no authority over my life." Use God's Word, His name and His blood as your authority. Satan won't have the ability to overpower you.

The devil looks for every opportunity to trip us. One minister used this metaphor. Satan comes to our front door with deception. If we don't let him in, he will return. But the next time He comes, he will try to enter by the back door. If he gets in the rear entrance, he will steal from us. He loots because there is something valuable - your life. The devil will try to steal everything he can. He must be forced to obey God's law.[6]

Use your authority (the Bible), call Satan's bluff. He's a declawed and toothless lion. Our enemy will try to gum us and bruise us, but he can't kill us unless we let him. If we let the devil harass us, we are being deluded.

## Flee Deception

Here are some practical things that will help us stay out of falsehood. We can test our conduct by God's Word. "Whether therefore ye eat, or drink, or whatsoever ye do, do all to the glory of God" (1 Corinthians 10:31). If what we do brings glory to God, we will stay out of Satan's delusions.

Another way to skirt deception is, remember we don't have to impress others. God's approval matters most. Beware of posing as a profound person. Remember, Jesus became a baby.

"Take no one serious but God. The first person we may find we have to leave alone as the greatest fraud, we have ever known is our self.[7] We can't even trust ourselves at times, but we can always trust The Lord.

Knowing what things are not from Our Maker is another way to avoid the web of deception. A minister relates four things that are not from God. These things are fear, worry, discouragement and confusion.[8]

Another pastor added more advice. God isn't the author of fear, discouragement, cares of this world, and run away ideas [9] If Satan can put these thoughts in our minds, he can get us off balance and we won't have peace. Then we are trapped, oppressed, and snared in Satan's web of deception.

Author Thomas Guthrie gives us a note of warning, "If you find yourself loving any pleasure better than your prayers, any book better than the Bible, any person better than Christ, or any indulgence better than the hope of heaven - take alarm!"[10]

Satan doesn't have the right to harass us with deception. He has no authority over us. The only place he has a right to be is under our feet.

When we recognize, Satan is trying to con us, we can immediately take action, and cut ourselves free from the net. We do this by taking dominion over it, going to God in prayer, and praising Him. Victory and deception both begin in our mind. We can choose triumph instead of fraud.

## Fog of Duplicity

Satan's webs create a fog like we experience early of a morning. It's a form of depression or oppression that binds us, and limits our vision. But when the sun comes out, it burns off the cloudy mist quickly. It's the same with the Son of God. He ignites the fog for us. If we turn to Jesus, and line everything up with His word, we will not be caught in the enemy's trap. Remember "The thief (Satan) comes to steal, kill and destroy." (John 10:10).

Stay out of the web of deception. It is possible, if we know the Word of God and listen to His voice with a discerning ear. "Listen, listen to me, and eat what is good . . . Give ear and come to me; hear me, that your soul may live . . . "(Isaiah 55:2b-3a, NIV).

# CHAPTER 12

# *Obedience*

"And being found in appearance as a man, he humbled himself and became
obedient unto death, even death on a cross"
(Philippians 2:8 NIV).

Jesus was always obedient to His Father. "Jesus said unto them, 'My meat
is to do the will of Him that sent me, and to finish His work'" (John 4:34).

Obedience means we respond comfortably in action, and conform to
a guiding principle. Compliance implies we are following someone else's
directive and not our own.

The Word of God tells us that Jesus followed God's directives. "And he
(Jesus) . . . prayed, saying, O my Father, if it be possible, let this cup pass
from me: nevertheless not as I will, but as thou wilt" (Matthew 26:39).
Jesus approached the cross in the Garden of Gethsemane, with pleading
and submission.

## Example of Obedience

Our Lord is the best example of obedience. God's directive was that Jesus would go to the cross. This was His primary purpose for coming to earth. The Lord wrestled, to the point, of sweating great drops of blood as He petitioned His Father. Jesus struggled with His own will.

He understood the necessity of not only taking on our sins, but actually becoming sin for us. Christ knew God, could not look on sin. Consequently He would be forsaken. Jesus cringed at how He would get through the awful blackness of being forsaken by His Eternal Father.

One account of our Lord in the Garden of Gethsemane, helped me understand some of the emotional and spiritual magnitude of suffering. Jesus, as Son of Man, wondered if He could survive being forsaken by His Father as He died on the cross.

Jesus was obedient because of His great love for you and me. He desired to fulfill God's plan to restore us to Himself.

Jesus had peace about His decision to hang on the wooden tree. He conformed to what He needed to do.

## Agony of the Cross

The cross was a place of torment. An excerpt from Dan Baumann's book, *"Dare to Believe,"* tells about the agony of crucifixion. It was one of the most painful ways of public death in the first century. Victims were placed on a wooden cross. The nails were driven into the hands and feet of the victims. Then the structure was lifted up and jarred into the ground. That sometimes would tear the flesh of the person being sentenced to death.[1]

Seeing someone crucified must have been a horrible sight. The soldiers had a difficult time getting through this ordeal. They obviously felt compassion on those being crucified because they had strong drink (sour wine -vinegar mixed with myrrh) available for those being tortured. "And they gave him to drink wine mingled with myrrh; but he received it not" (Mark 15:23). Later when Jesus cried out the soldiers again tried to lessen His suffering by giving Him strong drink. "And at the ninth hour Jesus cried with a loud voice, saying . . . My God, My God, why hast thou forsaken me? . . . And one ran and filled a sponge full of vinegar, and put it on a reed and gave him to drink . . ." (Mark 15:34, 36).

By dying on the cross, Jesus was submissive to His father's will. None of us have learned obedience to the point of death, and we never will. We aren't sinless like Christ. Jesus' loyalty benefited all of us. But it cost Him, His earthly life.

## Blessings or Curses

We reaped many blessings because Jesus was obedient. His compliance with God's directive gave us the ability to have forgiveness and eternal life. Christ's submission exalted Him above all others. "That at the name of Jesus every knee should bow . . . and that every tongue should confess that Jesus Christ is Lord, to the glory of God the Father" (Philippians 2:10-11).

We can choose to obey or disobey. God has given us the choice to have blessings or a curse. We will see the rewards if we are obedient to the Lord and His commands. (Deuteronomy 11:26-28). If we choose to comply, we are blessed. Our daily lives need to reflect, Christ like submission.

## Choose to Obey

We really can't talk about obedience without first dealing with disobedience. What would have happened if Christ had not obeyed His father, when He asked Him to go to the cross and redeem His People? If Jesus hadn't complied, we would not have the hope and assurance of salvation. I shudder to think what we would be like.

What Christ did for us is awesome! When we hear the Lord's voice, it can constrain us to follow His directives.

Elizabeth Elliott (an author, speaker) defines obedience well. "If I choose when I will obey and when I won't; I'm not obeying at all. Unless I'm obedient all the time, I'm not obedient."[2]

There are many times, I've been disobedient. Sometimes I don't hear or I'm unsure of what I've heard. Other times, I procrastinate about being compliant. Sometimes, I'm only half way obedient. Anything that isn't total obedience is disobedience. "Stop listening to instruction, my son, and you will stray from the words of knowledge" (Proverbs 19:27 NIV).

Disobedience is to neglect or refuse to comply with directives; to transgress, violate, or defy someone. To defy means to challenge the power of someone, to resist boldly or openly. God's Word tells us that He hates rebellion. "For rebellion is as the sin of witchcraft, and stubbornness is as iniquity and idolatry . . ." (1 Samuel 15: 23).

Our Heavenly Father wants us to be obedient out of our love for him. "The love of Christ, constrains us . . ." (2 Corinthians 5:14). The Lord wants us to desire to heed His voice out of love for Him. God wants to give us His best. Obedience really is the measure of our love for God. Our Maker can't bless us unless we obey. "But if you be willing and obedient, ye shall eat the good of the land . . ." (Isaiah 1:19-20).

Our compliance can often be the answer to ours or other's prayers. God's work can't be accomplished without our obedience. The Lord is trying to protect us by asking us to follow His commands. Part of that process is discipline or self control.

Remember the story of the missionary's sons' who were playing in a tree in the jungle. Their father saw danger and called to his boys. They immediately followed their father's orders to jump from the tree and run. This quick action saved their lives. This is a beautiful example of children obeying their earthly father.

Our obedience to God needs to be unquestioning like that. Even though we know the importance of complying, we are not always responsive.

## Reasons for Disobedience

There are several reasons we are often rebellious. Most often, we want to please the Lord. Jesus told His disciples that the spirit was willing but the flesh was weak.

There are three main reasons we don't obey. Prejudice is one reason for disobedience. This was evident in the biblical story of Jonah. The Lord asked this Hebrew man to go to Nineveh (a Gentile city). He was to preach to the people in that wicked place. But Jonah fled from God and the assignment, and headed for Tarshish. (Jonah 1: 2 & 3). Jonah had prejudice against the gentiles. He didn't want to be merciful to them. That was his number one road block to obedience.

We often find some bias in our own lives. Sometimes its racism, other times its culture or social class. Each one of us faces some issues of discrimination in our daily lives. The key is to recognize our prejudices. Work to overcome them so we won't be disobedient when God asks us to minister to others.

The second reason for disobedience is concern about our reputation. Jonah was worried about how others saw him. He was a Hebrew, commanded by God to preach a harsh message to the Gentiles.

How many times have we thought we'd look stupid, or someone else would talk bad about us? Often we are more concerned with our reputation than obeying God. That was exactly what Jonah thought. He didn't have a corner on that market. We often wonder what people might think of us before we do something.

The third reason for disobedience is expecting God to change his mind, or being angry when he shows mercy to others. That was very evident in the situation with Jonah. He ran from His Maker. He wanted God to choose someone else to deliver the message to Nineveh. Jonah was angry when The Lord was merciful to that city.[3]

The Lord reasoned with his rebellious servant. God used a gourd that Jonah had pity on, to help him understand the need to spare thousands of people in the city of Nineveh. (Jonah 4:10-11).

This helped Jonah realize that following God's directive was important and He was right to be merciful. Most of us are a lot like Jonah. We have our times of obedience and disobedience. Jonah's rebellion netted him three days in a whale's belly. But after He returned to His Maker in humility, he saw the city of Nineveh repent.

Moses made a mistake similar to Jonah. Moses expected God to change His mind. He argued with the Lord and told Him he had a speech problem and couldn't lead the Israelites out of Egypt. God asked Moses who made his mouth. Then the Lord assured His servant He would help him lead His people out of bondage. He gave Aaron to Moses as his spokesman. (Exodus 4:14-15).

Moses wasn't completely obedient. He wasn't able to trust God to work through him. The Lord still used Moses and Aaron as a team to accomplish a great deliverance for the Israelites.

Most of us are like Moses and Jonah; we feel very inadequate to do the job. We wish Our Maker would find someone else to do it. We give Him excuses why He can't use us. We are so imperfect. The Lord knows what He can do through us if we will just let Him. The following poem expresses it well.

### "God Can Use You"
...If we are magically in love with Him,
If we hunger for Him more than our next breath,
He'll use us, in spite of whom we are,
Where we've been; or what we look like!

In our own fleshly abilities, we can't do what Our Heavenly Father God asks us to do. But with His help, we can do all He instructs.

Fear is another hindrance to obedience. We dread the possibility of getting hurt. We're anxious things won't turn out like we want them to. We're often afraid of failure.

Instead of being fearful, we need to be obedient and leave the results with the Lord. God doesn't choose us for our abilities, he chooses us for our availability. Our Master wants willing compliance. Then he can equip us for the task. He is the giver of all gifts. He can empower us to do His work. We can do all things through Christ who gives us strength. (Philippians 4: 13).

## Cost of Rebellion

Rebellion or disobedience has a high price tag. Uzziah's life shows us the cost of rebellion. He became king at sixteen years old. As long as he sought the Lord, God prospered him. But when he became proud, he rebelled and acted corruptly. The king entered the temple and burned incense on the altar. The priests told him to get out of the altar area but the king got angry. While he was enraged the leprosy broke out on his forehead. He remained a leper the rest of his life, and he was banished from the house of the Lord. (2 Chronicles 26:5, 16, 19 - 21).

Uzziah's rebellion resulted from pride and caused him to be cut off from the Lord. This is the highest price we can pay for disobedience.

Often transgressions cause us to miss many blessings for ourselves and others. The Israelites were very obstinate. They wandered 40 years in the desert. Most of them were not permitted to enter the Promised Land. A researcher stated; "It shouldn't have taken the Israelites 40 years. They could have made their trek through the desert in much less time." Disobedience costs them time.

Many people in Biblical times violated God's law and paid a price. Jonahs' rebellion, netted him a three-day excursion in a whale's belly. Abraham also disobeyed when he tried to hurry God's plan along. Abraham had a child (Ishmael) by Sarah's hand maid. Ishmael and all his seed ended up being a wild breed of people. Abraham was eventually obedient and God blessed him and all generations of people down through the ages.

## Obedience Seems Hard

If we repent of our disobedient, The Lord can still use and bless us. Obedience many times does seem hard. This poem expresses it well:

> "Obeying God at first seems hard
> Until we come to see that all he asks,
> Us to do is for our good.
> It makes life full and free."[4]

The cost of obedience is nothing compared to what we lose when we're disobedient. One of the fallouts of resistance is a gap in our relationship with our Lord and maker.

What does it take to produce obedience in us? Most of us have obeyed at times to avoid punishment. The Lord convicted me of this. I used to comply with speed limits so I wouldn't get a speeding ticket. That shouldn't be the motivating force for me to obey. My obedience must come out of love for the Lord, not law.

The law of road rules doesn't make us obey. Laws are lifeless words in a statute book, and they don't restrain us. They will stop us only if there is power to back it up, such as a police officer. It takes a force stronger than the fear of getting caught to make us obedient. That power comes from a personal relationship with Jesus.[5] "He that hath my commandments, and keepeth them, he it is that loveth me . . ." (John 14:21).

One of the Lord's commands is for us to obey those in authority over us. We are to be subject to the governing authorities. There is no authority except from God (Romans 13:1-2).

The law tells us what God expects us to do. That drives us to our knees to ask for mercy.

We know we are inadequate and need His help to obey Him. This call to worship expresses our need to be filled with God's love and power.

"Call to Worship"
"Come and talk with me, O my people'!"

The Lord wants us to come to Him with our inadequacies and disobedience, so He can fill us with loyalty. The essential ingredients that produce obedience are love and trust. We trust people whom we love. If we trust someone, we are more likely to comply. We will obey our Heavenly Father if we have a relationship with Him and trust Him.

## Children are Trusting

Children are a good example of how to trust. One day a grandpa asked his preschool grandson if he wanted to go for a ride in the pickup with him. The little boy climbed in eager to go. The mother asks her son, "Where are you going with grandpa?" The little boy answered, "Not know." Promptly the mother asks, "What are you going to do with grandpa?" Again the little boy said, "Not know." Even though the little boy didn't know where he was going or what he was doing, he trusted his grandpa. We need this child's confidence in our Heavenly Father.

Children are so trusting. They often sleep in their parents arms. This shows real confidence. We need to learn to trust in the Lord's arms like a child.

God wants us to be childlike in our confidence of Him and His Word. Trust is a firm belief, confidence in honesty and reliability. To trust is to have a belief in the justice of another person or thing, a faith or reliance on something. It's an anticipation or hope, a confident expectation. Trust is something given to another person. It involves a promise. We can't rely on God without trusting His Word. We are told many times in the Word to "Trust in the Lord and do good . . ." (Psalms 37:3).

## Trust and Obey

God wants us to put our complete confidence in Him. He wants a committed life. Our Father desires we trust Him to know what is best for us. All God asks of us is that we believe Him.

The benefits of trusting will make us more obedient. Conversely, we can't have obedience without confidence. Trust and obedience go together. "Blessed is the man that trusteth in the Lord, and whose hope the Lord is. For he shall be as a tree planted by the waters . . ." (Jeremiah 17:7-8). If we trust, we will bear much fruit even in difficult times.

The song "Trust and Obey," reminds us of this. "Trust and obey for there is no other way to be happy in Jesus, but to trust and obey."

God considers obedience much better than any other sacrifice we could make in our lives. (1 Samuel 15:22). Our desire to please God is the best motive for obedience.

"Do I comply because I understand or because I trust?" After hearing the question posed, I had to ask myself what prompts me to obey. Usually I want to understand the situation before I respond.

I'm like the man Evangelist, Dr. Tony Evans told about in one of his messages. "A man was walking near a cliff and fell off. The only thing he could grab onto was a single tree branch jutting out from the cliff. The man caught hold of the branch. Then he hollered, 'Help, is there anyone up there.' A voice answered, 'Yes, I am.' The fallen man said, "Who is that." The voice answered, 'God.' The man said, 'will you help me?' God said, 'Do you completely trust me?' 'Yes, I completely trust you, God,' the man said. 'Then turn loose of the tree branch,' God said. 'No, do you think I'm crazy,' said the man. Then the man hollered, 'Is there anyone else up there?"[6]

I tend to be like that man. If I can't understand how a situation will work out, or it defies logic, then I'm more inclined to trust my own intellect than God. This isn't trust. And I ask myself, am I hanging onto something when God has said to let go?

## What Are You Hanging Onto

This is a searching question. The Lord used the following story to make me think about what I'm holding onto. The cheerful girl with bouncy golden curls was almost five. Waiting with her mother at the checkout stand, she saw them; a circle of glistening white pearls in a pink foil box. "Oh please, Mommy. Can I have them? Please, Mommy, please!"

Quickly the mother checked the back of the little foil box and then looked back into the pleading blue eyes of her little girl's upturned face.

"It cost a dollar ninety-five. That's almost two dollars. If you really want them, I'll think of some extra chores for you and in no time you can save enough money to buy them for yourself. Your birthday's only a week away. You might get another crisp dollar bill from grandma."

As soon as Jenny got home, she emptied her penny bank and counted out seventeen pennies. After dinner, she did more than her share of chores. She went to the neighbor and asked her if she could pick dandelions for ten cents. On her birthday, grandma did give her another new dollar bill and at last she had enough money to buy the necklace.

Jenny loved her pearls. They made her feel grown up. She wore them everywhere, even to bed. The only time she took them off was when she went swimming or had a bubble bath. Mother said, if they got wet, they might turn her neck green.

Jenny had a loving daddy and every night when she was ready for bed, he would stop whatever he was doing and come upstairs to read her a story. One night when he finished the story, he asked Jenny, "Do you love me?" "Oh yes, Daddy. You know that I love you." "Then give me your pearls." "Oh, Daddy, not my pearls. But you can have Princess, the white horse from my collection. She is the one with the pink tail. Remember, Daddy?" The one you gave me. She's my favorite." "That's okay, Honey. Daddy loves you. Good night." And he brushed her cheek with a kiss.

About a week later, after the story time, Jenny's daddy asked again, "Do you love me?" "Daddy, you know I love you." "Then give me your pearls." "Oh, Daddy, I don't want to give you my pearls. But you can have my baby doll. The brand-new one I got for my birthday. She is so beautiful and you can have the yellow blanket that matches her sleeper." "That's okay. Sleep well. God bless you, little one. Daddy loves you." And as always, he brushed her cheek with a gentle kiss.

A few nights later when her daddy came in, Jenny was sitting on her bed with her legs crossed Indian-style. As he came close, he noticed her chin was trembling and one silent tear rolled down her cheek. "What is it, Jenny? What's the matter?" Jenny didn't say anything but lifted her little hand up to her daddy. And when she opened it, there was her little pearl necklace. With a little quiver, she finally said, "Here, Daddy. It's for you." With tears gathering in his own eyes, Jenny's kind daddy reached out with one hand to take the dime-store necklace. With his other hand he reached into his pocket, and pulled out a blue velvet case with a strand of genuine pearls and gave them to Jenny. He had them all the time. He was just waiting for her to give up the dime-store stuff so he could give her a genuine treasure. This is so like our heavenly Father.

Like Jenny, I often hold onto the dime-store stuff and offer God something else. He wants to give me the real thing. He wants me to rely on Him. Trusting means, I do it even when I don't understand. "Trust in the Lord with all thine heart; and lean not unto thine own understanding. In all thy ways acknowledge Him and he shall direct thy paths" (Proverbs 3:5-6).

## Trusting Defies Logic

To trust God, we must believe His Word is true. "Jesus answered and said unto them, 'This is the work of God, that ye believe on Him whom He hath sent'" (John 6:29). Believing that God sent His son is our part. Faith is a gift. It is an most important work God wants from us. Once we believe, we will be able to trust and obey.

There are many Bible characters or saints that give us good examples of trusting beyond logic, and obeying. God tested Abraham beyond anything we could ever imagine. He asked Abraham to take his son Isaac, his only son, and sacrifice him as a burnt offering. Abraham had Isaac carry the wood for the offering. After they had journeyed a few days, Isaac asked where the lamb was for the celebration. His dad replied, God will provide the lamb for the sacrifice. Then Abraham bound Isaac on the altar and raised the knife to slay him. Isaac must have been very trusting, at this point. Suddenly, an angel of the Lord called to Abraham and told him not to harm the lad. There was a ram caught in the thorn bushes. He sacrificed the ram that day instead of his son. (Genesis 22:1-12).

Abraham depended on God when everything defied logic. He didn't understand, but he obeyed. Abraham trusted God's promises to make him a great nation. That's the kind of obedience God wants from His servants.

Whomever we obey, we become their servants. (Romans 6:16). So obedience to our Lord brings us righteousness and it tells who our master is. Our obedience gives us the treasure of being Our Maker's possession. (Exodus 19:5). God (unlike many of us) takes good care of His possessions. Isn't it great to know that another benefit of obedience is God's protection?

Joseph was another faithful servant. He was obedient to God and his master Potifer, even when his wife tried to seduce Joseph. (Genesis 39: 7-8). Joseph was later framed and suffered injustice, but his obedience had great rewards for him and many others during the famine in Egypt.

Daniel was another loyal servant. He prayed three times a day even after King Darius set a decree that no one should petition any God or man except him for thirty days. Daniel knew he must obediently worship the Lord in prayer. (Daniel 6:10). Yet, he was thrown into a lion's den. He survived, and the king decreed that all should worship the God of Daniel.

Daniel's friends, Shadrach, Meshach and Abednigo wouldn't bow to a golden image and worship it. The king had them bound with ropes and thrown into a fiery furnace. These three men weren't harmed by the fire. Their hair wasn't singed or their robes scorched. They didn't even have a smell of smoke on them when they came out of the fire. (Daniel 3: 26 & 27). These obedient servants' lives were spared because of their ability to trust and obey God.

The only things burned off the three men in that fiery furnace were the ropes that bound them. This would be helpful to remember when we are in the heat of the battle. When we obey, the only things that will be consumed are the ropes that bind us. When we obey, we are unbound and free.

## Just Obey

One Saturday evening I felt prompted to make a copy of a prophecy I had received earlier. The Lord's instructions were to take the prophecy to church. I wasn't sure why but I complied.

During the worship service, the worship leader kept saying the Holy Spirit wanted to do something more in our service. Finally, I obeyed the prompt. I slipped in beside the pastor and asked if I could read a prophecy. The pastor nodded yes, and said the timing was right. I read the prophecy. This message said, "Trust me, be obedient . . . Rest in me and the work I have for you will be accomplished . . . I am your only source of strength . . . I will free you from your bondage."

As I read the prophecy, I felt the power of the Holy Spirit. I could see others responding to His dynamite. An elder exhorted us and said the Holy

Spirit was like an ocean. We needed to let ourselves go with His power. Many people were set free from bondage in their lives.

My obedience, in sharing a prophecy, caused a chain reaction and others obeyed. As we all followed the Holy Spirits leading, we had freedom and rewards. Obedience always brings blessings.

Another reward awaited me after compliance to the Lord's voice. I was in the hospital awaiting surgery. My instructions were to pray aloud, on the operating table, before going under the anesthesia. I didn't understand the purpose. But I summoned the courage to be obedient, and prayed before succumbing to the anesthesia.

The doctor described the surgical procedure as a text book operation. Everything went according to his plan. I healed quickly and went home from the hospital sooner than expected. When we obey it brings blessings and rewards.

It was an act of obedience, when I packed the whole families' suitcases in preparation for a trip to my dad's funeral. It didn't even look possible for us to go. We couldn't connect with a mode of transportation that would get us there before the funeral. My obedience in packing the suitcases, and trusting God was rewarded. My family and I all traveled via automobile. We arrived in time for the funeral.

Our obedience can bless us and build us up. It is also a way God works to confirm His direction to us. This was the case, when talking to a fellow Christian. I felt the urge to share what the Lord had shown me. This friend, related a vision he had four years before. It confirmed what God had planted in my heart as a ministry. I was so encouraged, because both of us had been compliant to speak the Lord's message. Each time we obey God, it becomes easier to recognize God's voice and direction.

Once we've experienced the goodness of Our Maker, we will always want to be more compliant. We'll realize God loves us and wants only the best for us.

## Obedience, an Issue of the Heart

Obedience requires a partnership with the Father. This relationship must be built on love and trust. "Thou shalt love the Lord thy God with all thy heart, and with all thy soul, and with all thy strength, and with all, thy mind . . ." (Luke 10:27). God wants all our love, not part of it. A great way to proclaim our love is by obedience. "If you love me, keep my commandments" (John 14:15).

Obedience is an issue of the heart. Do I love God enough to trust Him? Can I die to self - will and submit to God's plan? Obedience is a measure of my love for the Lord. When we love and trust our Savior, we know our compliance will bring blessings and protection for us.

We develop a relationship with the Father, by seeking the giver and not the gift. The way to seek our provider is through the Word, prayer and listening to His voice. We need to listen intently, no matter how the Lord speaks to us.

When you've heard from The Lord, always line it up with the Word of God. If it measures up, then obey it.

The Golden Rule for understanding spiritually isn't our intellect but our obedience. God's purpose is that I depend on Him and on His power now. If I can stay calm and steady in the middle of the turmoil, this is the end of the purpose of God. He is not working toward a particular finish. "It is the process, not the end which is glorifying to The Lord. . . . God's end is to enable me to see that He can walk on the chaos of my life just now. . . . If we realize that obedience is the end, then each moment as it comes is precious."[7]

## Speak Lord

When I hear God's voice, I want to be like Samuel and say, "Speak for thy servant heareth" (I Samuel 3:9). That is the action I want to take. Obedience releases God's power. "I will hear what God the Lord will say; for He will speak peace to His people . . ." (Psalm 85:8, NAS).

When we begin to listen and obey God's voice we will see miracles in our lives. Jesus preformed a mighty miracle when He raised Lazarus from the dead. But Jesus didn't take away the stone or Lazarus' grave clothes. "Jesus said, 'Take away the stone . . . Loose Him, and let him go'" (John 11:39 & 44). J. Boyd Nicholson wrote about this passage and reminded us that the Lord demanded something of those who longed for a miracle. The Lord raised Lazarus from the grave. Surely he could have moved the stone with a word. "Here is a great principle. The Lord will not do by a miracle what we are to do by obedience . . . Is there a stone Jesus wants you (me) to roll away? Is there some hard, unyielding attitude; someone you will not forgive, some step of obedience Jesus awaits? It is ours to obey. It is His to do the miracles."[8] We can expect awesome things to happen, only if we're being obedient to God.

## Urgency to Obey

The following true story illustrates the importance of obedience when we have an urgency to pray. A missionary on furlough told this story while visiting his home church. While serving at a small field hospital in Africa, every two weeks, he traveled by bicycle through the jungle to a nearby city for supplies. This was a journey of two days and required camping overnight at the halfway point. On one of these trips, he arrived in the city. He collected money from a bank, purchase medicine and supplies. He began his two-day journey back to the field hospital.

Upon arrival in the city, he observed two men fighting, one of whom had been seriously injured. He had treated him for his injuries and at the same time witnessed to him about the Lord Jesus Christ. He then traveled two days, camping overnight, and arrived home without incident.

Two weeks later he repeated his journey. Upon arriving in the city, I was approached by the young man I had treated. He told me he had known I carried money and medicines. He said, "Some friends and I followed you into the jungle, knowing you would camp overnight. We planned to kill you and take your money and drugs. But just as we were about to move into your camp, we saw that you were surrounded by twenty-six armed guards." The missionary laughed, and said he was all alone out in that jungle campsite. The young man pressed the point, however, and said, "No sir, I was not the only person to see the guards. My five friends also saw them, and we all counted them. It was because of those guards that we were afraid and left you alone."

At this point in the sermon, one of the men in the congregation jumped to his feet and interrupted the missionary and asked if he could tell him the exact day this happened. The missionary told the congregation the day, and the man who interrupted, told him this story.

On the night of your incident in Africa, it was morning here and I was preparing to go play golf. The urging of the Lord was so strong; I called men in this church to meet with me here in the sanctuary to pray for you. Would all of those men who met with me on that day stand up?' The men who had gathered to pray that day, stood up. The missionary wasn't concerned with whom they were, he was too busy counting how many men he saw. There were twenty-six!"

This story is an incredible example of how the Lord moves in mysterious ways to protect His servants. If the Lord prompts you to pray for someone, obey Him immediately. The only thing hurt by our prayers and obedience is the gates of hell. When we follow God's directives, we and others are protected and kept in the perfect will of God. By our obedience others will see Jesus manifests in us.

## Obedient Servant

Jesus was obedient to death on a cross for us. That sacrifice deserves compliance from us. Submission shows trust in Christ and that His work on the cross was enough. Our obedience truly is much better than any sacrifice we could offer to God. It is the key to victory and miracles.

Remember, no matter how disobedient you've been, or how many mistakes you've made; there is a way to turn it around. You can become an obedient servant who is grateful for what Jesus did on the cross. He sacrificed His very life so we could have a more abundant life.

One of the most reassuring passages in the Bible is: "The blood of Jesus Christ His son cleanses us from all sin . . . If we confess our sins, he is faithful and just to forgive us our sins and to cleanse us from all unrighteousness" (1 John 1:7& 9). It's like a red carpet of salvation that God provides for everyone.

# Three Page Book

This story ministered powerfully to me. An elderly Christian used to carry a small book with him. He often took it out of his pocket to show others. He called it his biography. It had only three pages, yet it contained the whole story of his life. The first page was black. That he said was his sin, his condition by nature. The second page was red. It represented the blood of Christ that was shed for his sins. The third and last page was white. The last page stood for his self. He had been washed in the blood and made whiter than snow. [9] We all have the first page of our biography, the sin stained one. The second and third pages are added when we receive Christ as our Savior. How many pages do you have in your spiritual biography?

Listen to the Lord's voice and when He says come unto me, I died for you. I was obedient to the cross so you could have an abundant life. Listen to Him. He wants you to have three pages in your spiritual biography. He wants you to have eternal life. If you don't have those three pages in your spiritual biography, you may pray this prayer.

Lord, Jesus, Thank you for being obedient to your Father's will and dying on the cross for my wrongs. I confess my sins and ask you to forgive me. Your Word says, "That if thou shalt confess with thy mouth the Lord Jesus, and shalt believe in thine heart that God hath raised him from the dead, thou shalt be saved" (Romans 10: 9-10). I confess with my mouth, and believe in my heart, that Jesus arose from the dead. I open the door of my heart to receive you as Lord and Savior. Take control of my life now. Make me the kind of person you want me to be. Thank you for forgiving my sins and giving me eternal life. Amen.

Now that you've prayed this prayer with a repentant heart, you are a child of God. You've taken the first step of obedience. Begin to listen to the Lord through His Word. Go to Him in prayer and develop a relationship with Jesus. Then attach yourself to a body of believers that teaches the Word of God.

# Obedience Worships God

Our obedience is one of the greatest ways to worship and show gratefulness to God. It requires that we trust God as our unfailing guide, even when we don't understand our trials. When God tells us to do something, He's going to provide whatever we need. I want to grow spiritually until I can say, "Lord, I'm delighted to obey you completely."

There is great wisdom in the Savior's leading. Jesus has been there before and knows what lies down the path He's asking us to travel.

### THE PARABLE OF TOMORROW
"Take my hand,' He whispered, 'I will be your strength. . .'
We walk together now and shall forever!"[10]

If we are obeying the Lord we will walk with him always. We don't ever have to worry about where He is leading.

"Learn to obey. It will lead you straight to God.
There is a very straight way to the heart of Jesus.
You will never, never go astray,
Never make a mistake, if you obey."

"Give ear and hear my voice, listen and hear my words"
(Isaiah 28:23).

# *About the Author*

Doris Arwine is a Licensed Clinical Social Worker / Therapist. She owns and operates a Christian Counseling business, "In His Image - Christian Counseling." She offers Individual, Marriage, Family and Play Therapy to a culturally-diverse population. The author has worked with hospice, foster care, and adoptions. She has presented workshops on a variety of topics. She has also written a children's book, *"4 Keys to Unlock a Sad Heart."*

Author lives with her husband, a retired United States Army veteran, in Southwest Kansas. She has two grown sons. One, a professor at University of Kansas, Lawrence, KS and the other son lives in Bali, Indonesia. The author and her family lived and traveled as a military family, extensively.

# *Note on Sources*

Adkins, Mike, "Not a Prancing Horse" and "Be at peace My Child," *Thank you for the Dove,* Mike Adkins Ministries, West Frankfort, IL, 62896, Used by Permission.

Edwards, Deanna, "Listen With Your Heart, Rock Canyon Music Publishers, 71 Canterbury Lane, Logan, UT 84321, Used by permission.

Fehlauer, Jim D., Fourteen Illustrations, Black and White, Used by permission.

Gaither, William J, and Gloria, Song, "I Am Loved," Hanna Street Music / BMI / All rights controlled by Gaither Copyright Management. Used by permission.

Gass, Bob, "The Word for You Today," Copyright, 2012, Used by permission.

Kauffman, David, "I'm Sorry," Words and Music by David Kauffman Copyright 1999,
GFTSMUSIC PUBLISHING COMPANY, INC., All rights reserved. Used by permission.

Machen, Chris and Diane, *"Time to Trust,"* Copyright: c 1994 Desert North Music (Admin. By Music Services) All Rights Reserved. ASCAP, Used by permission.

Marino, Paul, "The Only Scars in Heaven," Words and Music by: Paul Marino c 1995, Paul Marino Music/ASCAP. Used by permission

# *Endnotes*

## Chapter 1

1   De Haan, Richard W., "Light For Each Step." *Our Daily Bread*, July 27, 1994.

2   Gass, Bob, "Your Bible - Read it Every Day," "*The Word for You Today*," February 2011, pp 49 - 50.

3   Hickey, Marilyn, (Sermon), 1988.

4   Roberts, Richard, "Whose Battle Really." *Daily Blessings*, September 18, 1990.

5   Bosch, Henry G., "Carried By God," April 28, 1998, *Our Daily Bread*.

6   Grounds, Vernon C., "It's Always Needed." *Our Daily Bread*, May 20, 1994

7   Chambers, Oswalt, *My Utmost For His Highest*, Westwood, N.J., Barbour and Company Inc., 1963, 6/10.

8   Bosch, Henry G., "Look In the Book First," August 30, 1994 *Our Daily Bread*.

## Chapter 2

1   Savelle, Jerry Rev., "Righteousness, Right Standing With God," (Sermon) 1985.

2   Hunter, Frances, *Hot Line to Heaven*, Anderson, IN., Warner Press, 1976, p 82.

3   Chambers, Oswalt, *My Utmost For His Highest*, Westwood, N.J., Barbour and Company Inc., 1963, 6/26.

4   *The Kneeling Christian*, Grand Rapids, MI., Zondervan Publishing House, 1971, p 53.

5   Chambers, Oswalt, *My Utmost For His Highest*, Westwood, N.J., Barbour and Company Inc., 1963, 3/30.

6   Poole, Curt Rev, "The Mechanics of Intercession," (Sermon) 1986.

7   Chambers, Oswalt, *My Utmost For His Highest*, Westwood, N.J., Barbour and Company Inc., 1963, 8/28,9/16, 10/17.

8    Hess, "Because You Prayed For me Today," *Our Daily Bread*, March - April, 1997.

9    Van Gorder, Our Daily Bread, 1992.

10   Bunce, Darold Rev., "A Changing Prayer," (Sermon), 1998.

11   Jakes, T.D. "Anointing Fall On Me," Pg 72-74.

12   Lea, Larry, *Your Guide to Successful Prayer*, Lake Mary, FL., Creation House, Strang Communications Company, 1987, pp. 7 - 9.

13   Sheridan, Nathan, sermon, "Bold Prayers," 2011.

14   Miller, Betty, "A Cake Recipe," (Sermon), 1980.

15   Chambers, Oswalt, *My Utmost For His Highest*, Westwood, N.J., Barbour and Company Inc., 1963, 10/11,10/17,5/26.


**Chapter 3**

1    Egner, David C., "Soil Preparation," June 5, 1997, *Our Daily Bread*.

2    Bosch, Henry G., "The Witness of a Watermelon," June 1, 1991, *Our Daily Bread*.

3    Butler, Charles Rev., "Root of Bitterness." (Sermon) 1990.

4    Roberts, Evelyn, "We grow in the valley," *Daily Blessings*, August 2, 1989.

5    Bosch, Henry G., "Be a Pine Tree," January 13, 1989, *Our Daily Bread*.

6    De Haan, Dennis J., "Leaning Christians," October 26, 1988, *Our Daily Bread*.

7    Bosch, Henry G., "Pressed Close to God," January 19, 1994, *Our Daily Bread*.

8    Egner, David C., "Adding Growth Rings," January 17, 1992, *Our Daily Bread*.

9    Bosch, Henry G., "Build Again,"   November 5, 1988, *Our Daily Bread*.

10   Roberts, Oral, "Move Up Higher," February 20, 1984, *Daily Blessings*.

11   Butler, Charles Rev., "Danger of Lodging In the Wilderness," (Sermon) 1990.

12   Ibid.

13   Ibid.

14   Roberts, Oral, "New Purposes," July 19, 1988, *Daily Blessings*.

15   Egner, David C., "Lesson of the Osprey" August 27, 1988, *Our Daily Bread*.

16  Van Gorder, Paul R., "Flight School," *Our Daily Bread,* June 2, 1988.

17  De Haan, Dennis J. "Heavy Tasks," (Poem) 1990, *Our Daily Bread.*

18  Bosch, Henry G., "Holy Blue," April 21, 1997, *Our Daily Bread.*

19  De Haan, Martin R. II, "Even Animals Come Home," June 6, 1991, *Our Daily Bread.*

20  Roberts, Oral, "New Channels," February 20, 1984, *Daily Blessings.*

21  De Haan, Dennis J., "What Moves You?" June 18, 1990, *Our Daily Bread.*

22  Branon J. David, "Parents 10 Commandments," April 27, 1990, *Our Daily Bread.*

### Chapter 4

1  Smith, Joseph, "Potters Parable," Passion Play Site, Eureka Springs, AK.

2  Yoder, Joanie E., "Limp Gloves," *Our Daily Bread,* February 2, 1996.

3  Meyer, Joyce, "Believer or Achiever," (Sermon), 1987.

4  De Haan, Dennis J., "Pulling Power" *Our Daily Bread, July 31, 1994.*

5  Oliver, Ruth L. "Putting On the Christian Armor," (Message) 1990.

6  Fowler, Lisa, "The Lamp," (Bible Study Message) 1986.

7  Van Gorder, Paul R., *Our Daily Bread,* 1992.

8  Lugt, Herbert Vander, "The Salt of Gratitude," *Our Daily Bread,* November 28, 1991.

9  Van Gorder, Paul R., "Faith and Safety," *Our Daily Bread,* July 18, 1988.

10  Oliver, Ruth L., "Steps to Revival," (Message) 1990.

### Chapter 5

1  Chambers, Oswalt, *My Utmost For His Highest,* Westwood, N.J., Barbour and Company Inc.,1963, 7/28.

2  De Haan, Martin R. II, "Gator Aid," *Our Daily Bread,* July 3, 1997.

3  Chambers, Oswalt, *My Utmost For His Highest,* Westwood, N.J., Barbour and Company Inc., 1963, 2/14.

4  Chambers, Oswalt, *My Utmost For His Highest,* Westwood, N.J., Barbour and Company Inc., 1963, 7/4.

5  Elliott, Elizabeth, "Gateway to Joy," KLJC Radio Broadcast, Kansas City, MO., 1997.

6  Chambers, Oswalt, *My Utmost For His Highest,* Westwood, N.J., Barbour and Company Inc., 1963, 9/30.

7   Roberts, Oral, "When You're Criticized," Daily Blessings, May 30, 1989.

## Chapter 6
1   Van Gorder, Paul R., "Something to Leave Behind," *Our Daily Bread*, May 31, 1988.
2   Bunce, Darold Rev., "Take Me In," (Sermon), 1997.
3   Chambers, Oswalt, *My Utmost For His Highest*, Westwood, N.J., Barbour and Company Inc., 1963, 5/11.
4   Jeremiah, Dr., "Encouraging the Write Way," KLJC Radio Broadcast, Kansas City, MO., 1997.
5   De Haan, Richard W., "How to Cancel Criticism." February 13, 1988, *Our Daily Bread*.
6   Roberts, Lindsay, "Four Don'ts That Result in Good," *Daily Blessings*, March 15 - 18, 1991.
7   De Haan, Richard W., "Burying The Hatchet," June 18, 1994, *Our Daily Bread*.

## Chapter 7
1   Osbeck, Kenneth W., *Amazing Grace,* "God Moves in Mysterious Ways," Grand Rapids, MI., Kregel Publications, 1990.
2   Carswell, Eddie; Mason, Babbie (Words and Music), Sung by Clawson, Cynthia, "Trust His Heart," *Words Will Never Do,* Irving, TX., Word Inc, 1990.
3   Paris, Twila, "Do I Trust You," *The Warrior is a Child,* Nashville, TN., Benson Music Group, Inc., 1995.
4   Marino, Paul; Reesner, Phil; & Linn, Kurt, "The Only Scars in Heaven," *River Faithful,* New Hope, MN., River Ministries, 1995.
5   Gaither, William J. and Gloria, "I Am Loved," The Best of the Gaither's Live, Nashville, TN., Benson Music Group, Inc., 1992.
6   Osbeck, Kenneth W., *Amazing Grace,* "It Is Well With My Soul," Grand Rapids, MI., Kregel Publications, 1990.
7   Osbeck, Kenneth W., *Amazing Grace,* "Amazing Grace," Grand Rapids, MI., Kregel Publications, 1990.
8   Edwards, Deanne, *Listen With Your Heart,* Studio City, CA., Rock Canyon Music, 1985.

9   Adkins, Mike, "Not a Prancing Horse," *Thank You For the Dove.*

10  Tucker, Tanya, "Strong Enough to Bend," Hollywood, CA., Capitol Records, Inc., 1988.

11  Kauffman, David, "I'm Sorry."

12  Hyde, Gay, "Edelweiss," *Joined to the Vine,* Bexhill-on-Sea, East Sussex, England, Evangelical, Communications, 1980.

13  Willow Creek Singers, "Audience of One," *A Place to Call Home,* Nashville, TN., Willow Creek Music, Word Inc., 1995.

14  Hyde, Gay, "He's Doing Something Far More Wonderful," *Joined to the Vine,* Bexhill-on- Sea, East Sussex, England, Evangelical Communications, 1980.

15  Brooks-Welch, Myra, "Touch of The Master's Hand." Gospel Messenger, 1921.

16  Adkins, Mike, "Be At Peace My Child," *Thank You For the Dove.*

17  Boltz, Ray, "Shepherd Boy," *Moments For the Heart,* Nashville, TN., Ray Boltz Music, 1992.

18  Harris, Larnell / McHugh, Phil, "I Miss My Time With You," From a Servant's Heart, Nashville, TN., Benson Music Group, Inc., 1993.

19  Sapp, David, *Step Out (Into the Water),* Modesto, CA., David Sapp Ministries, 1984.

20  Machen, Chris and Diane, *"Time to Trust,"* Grand Rapids, MI., Discovery House Publishers, 1995.

21  Hyde, Gay, "Joined to The Vine," *Joined to the Vine,* Bexhill-on-Sea, East Sussex, England, Evangelical Communications, 1980.

22  Hyde, Gay, "You're Going in His Name," *Joined to the Vine,* Bexhill-on-Sea, East Sussex, England, Evangelical Communications, 1980.


## Chapter 8

1   Dyer, Dick Rev., "Abiding in God's Leadership," (Sermons) 1982.

2   Barton, Page Dr., "Success or Failure," (Sermon) 1989.

3   Baldwin, Robert Rev., "Seven Deadly Sins," (Sermon) 1989.

4   Barton, Page Dr., "Crisis or Opportunity," (Sermon) 1989.

5   Landry, Sharyn, "How to Resist the Devil," (Sermon) 1985.

6   Mudd, George, "Four Kinds of Walls," (Sermon) 1984.

7   Bunce, Darold Rev., "How to Escape Depression," (Sermon) 1995.

8   Thompson, Daniel Rev., "Two Battles We Fight," (Sermon) 1992.

9   Thompson, Daniel Rev., "When Do We Get to do what's In the Book," (Sermon) 1992.

10  Thompson, Daniel Rev., "Resurrection," (Sermon) 1992.

11  Bunce, Darold Rev., "Moving the Target," (Sermon) 1993.

12  Brown, Beth, (1971) *"Your Words Are Your Magic Power"*, New York, N.Y., Essandess Special Edition, pp. 17, 35, 38, 46 & 47.

13  Galloway, Dale E., 1975, *12 "Ways to Develop a Positive Attitude"*, Wheaton, IL., Tyndale House Publishers Inc., pp. 31 - 40.

14  Sheldon, Charles M., 1960, *"In His Steps"*, Westwood, N.J., Pyramid Publications, pp. 14 - 16.

15  Frodsham, Stanley Howard, 1948, *"Smith Wigglesworth, Apostle of Faith,"* Springfield, MO., Gospel Publishing House, pp. 36, 109 - 111.

16  An Unknown Christian, 1971, *"The Kneeling Christian,"* Grand Rapids, MI., Zondervan Publishing House, pp. 14, 15, 17, 35, 106, 119 - 125.

17  Partow, Donna, *"Becoming a Vessel God Can Use,"* 1996.

## Chapter 9

1   Roberts, Oral, "Most High Protection," *Daily Blessings,* November 2, 1988.

## Chapter 10

1   Shaw, Gwen, 1978, *"The Power of the Precious Blood,"* Jasper, Ark., End - timeHandmaidens, Inc., pp. 1 - 3.

2   Powers, Margaret Fishback, 1993, *Footprints,* Toronto, Canada, Harper Collins Publishers, pp. 38 - 45.

3   Roberts, Richard, "A Vision for Household Salvation," *Daily Blessings,* November 21, 1988.

4   Chambers, Oswalt, *My Utmost for His Highest,* Westwood, H.J. Barbour and Company Inc., 1963. 1/19.

5   Chambers, Oswalt, *My Utmost for His Highest,* Westwood, H.J. Barbour and Company Inc., 1963. 5/2, 7/6.

## Chapter 11

1   Bosch, Henry G., "Stop Pouting - Start Praising," January 30, 1985, *Our Daily Bread.*

2   Roberts, Oral, "Increasing Our Value," October 21, 1987, *Daily Blessings.*

3   Roberts, Oral, "Bringing Out the Best," March 24, 1989, *Daily Blessings.*

4   Robertson, Pat, 1984, *Answers to 200 of Life's Most Probing Questions,* Virginia Beach, VA., Christian Broadcasting Network, Inc., pp. 97- 98.

5   Allen, Larry Rev., Devotional, *Daily Blessings.*

6   Bunce, Darold Rev., "Dumb Criminal," (Sermon) 1997.

7   Chambers, Oswalt, *My Utmost For His Highest,* Westwood, N.J., Barbour and Company Inc., 1963, 1/22.

8   Duell, Dave, "Authority Comes Through Revelation," (Sermon) 1986.

9   Poole, Curt Rev., "Four Things That Are Not of God," (Sermon) 1985.

10  DeHaan, Richard W., 1998, *Our Daily Bread.*


## Chapter 12

1   De Haan, Richard W., "The Agony of the Cross," *Our Daily Bread,* April 1, 1988.

2   Elliott, Elizabeth, "Gateway to Joy," KLJC Radio Broadcast, Kansas City, MO., 1990.

3   Roberts, Richard, "Reasons For Disobedience," *Daily Blessings,* August 9, 1990.

4   De Haan, Dennis J., "Obedience Seems Hard," (Poem), April 7, 1990, *Our Daily Bread.*

5   De Haan, Dennis J. "Lifeless Law," March 12, 1990, *Our Daily Bread.*

6   Evans, Tony Dr., "The Urban Alternative," KLJC Radio Broadcast, Kansas City, MO., 1996.

7   Chambers, Oswalt, *My Utmost For His Highest,* Westwood, N.J., Barbour and Company Inc., 1963,7/28.

8   Bosch, Henry G., "What Jesus Won't Do," October 10, 1987, *Our Daily Bread.*

9   Bosch, Henry G., "The Three Page Book," August 1, 1990, *Our Daily Bread.*

10  Zwall, Ruth Gibbs, "Our Unfailing Guide, *the Parable of Tomorrow,*" (Poem), June 18, 1991, *Our Daily Bread.*

CPSIA information can be obtained at www.ICGtesting.com
Printed in the USA
LVOW06s0028060614

388783LV00002B/2/P